PROGRAMMING WITH ADA

An Introduction
by Means of Graduated Examples

PRENTICE-HALL SOFTWARE SERIES

Brian W. Kernighan, advisor

PROGRAMMING WITH ADA

An Introduction
by Means of Graduated Examples

PETER WEGNER

Department of Computer Science
Brown University

Prentice-Hall, Inc., Englewood Cliffs, New Jersey 07632

Library of Congress Cataloging in Publication Data

Wegner, Peter.
  Programming with Ada.

  (Prentice-Hall software series)
  Includes index.
  1. Ada (Computer program language)
I. Title. II. Series.
QA76.73.A35W46   1980   001.6'424   79-24152
ISBN 0-13-730697-0

To Ada
May she inspire a new generation of programmers

© 1980 by Prentice-Hall, Inc., Englewood Cliffs, N.J. 07632

Printed in the United States of America

10 9 8 7 6 5 4 3

Prentice-Hall International, Inc., London
Prentice-Hall of Australia Pty. Limited, Sydney
Prentice-Hall of Canada, Ltd., Toronto
Prentice-Hall of India Private Limited, New Delhi
Prentice-Hall of Japan, Inc., Tokyo
Prentice-Hall of Southeast Asia Pte. Ltd., Singapore
Whitehall Books Limited, Wellington, New Zealand

CONTENTS

PREFACE

Ada is a programming language for numerical applications, systems programming applications, and applications with real-time and concurrent execution requirements. It was named after Ada Augusta, Countess of Lovelace, who was a leading computer pioneer of the nineteenth century, a colleague of Charles Babbage, and the daughter of Lord Byron. It was designed by a Paris-based design team led by Jean Ichbiah which has included Bernd Krieg-Bruckner, Brian A. Wichman, Henry F. Ledgard, Jean Claude Heliard, Jean-Raymond Abrial, John G. P. Barnes, and Olivier Roubine.

The language was developed at the initiative of the U.S. Department of Defense (DOD). The purpose of this initiative was to develop a programming language suited to the application programming needs of the Army, the Navy and the Air Force. The process of language development was started in 1975 with the formation of the DOD Higher-Order Language Working Group (HOLWG), whose charter was to establish a single high-level language appropriate to DOD embedded computer systems.

The first step was to develop a set of requirements for a common programming language with input from the three services, industry and universities. This task was ably coordinated by David Fisher and resulted in the sequence of requirements called Strawman (1975), Woodenman (1975), Tinman (1976), Ironman (SIGPLAN Notices, December 1978) and Steelman (1979). The idea of starting from a set of requirements in developing a programming language was a novel one, and it was not obvious how the requirements should be stated. The final (Steelman) version contains about one hundred requirements which constrain the language to have language constructs with specified characteristics in areas such as data types, control structures, modules, tasks and exceptions. Certain global requirements on "readability", "no excessive generality", "simplicity" and "verifiability" were also included.

The next step was to determine whether any existing language met the requirements and, if not, to recommend a procedure for the design and development of a language that would do so. After an intensive study of twenty-six existing languages it was concluded early in 1977 that no existing language came close to meeting the (Tinman) requirements and that a new language should be competitively designed. It was recommended that one of the three languages Pascal, Algol 68 or PL/I should be used as a starting point in the design of the new language.

A language design procurement embodying these recommendations was issued in May 1977, and sixteen language design proposals were received of which four were funded for a six-month preliminary design phase (August 1977 - February 1978). The four winning designs were submitted by CII-Honeywell-Bull, Intermetrics, SRI International and SofTech. They were called Green, Red, Yellow and Blue to preserve their anonymity for purposes of evaluation.

All four design groups proposed Pascal as a starting point. This fact, as well as the fact that the designs had to meet the requirements, considerably constrained the language designers. It relieved them from having to make certain global decisions and even some low-level decisions, thereby considerably reducing the scope and timescale of the project and making it possible to produce a preliminary design within six months. However, these constraints still left considerable room for variation, and the preliminary designs produced by the four design teams were surprisingly different.

The four preliminary designs were completed on schedule on February 15, 1978 and evaluated during the period February-March 1978 by approximately eighty different evaluators from universities, industry and government. As a result of these evaluations two of the four languages were chosen for one year of further development to a complete design (April 1978 - March 1979). The two languages were Green (CII-Honeywell-Bull) and Red (Intermetrics).

The completed designs were delivered on schedule on March 15, 1979 and subjected to intensive analysis by over fifty analysis teams. Their findings were evaluated at a four-day meeting in Washington at the end of April. At a meeting of the HOLWG on May 2, the Green language was chosen as the winner and renamed Ada in honor of Ada Lovelace. The reference manual and rationale for Ada were published as the June 1979 issue of SIGPLAN Notices and are widely available.

In the choice of the Green language over the Red language, the following factors appeared to be the most important:

    1. Green was perceived as a lower-risk language, both because its constructs were perceived to be more

state-of-the-art and more implementable, and because
its design had been stable over several months, while
the Red design had been evolving until the last minute.
2. Green had an integrated approach to specification and
    separate compilation of program units which allowed
    effective checking of interfaces by the compiler, as
    well as language-level support of programming method-
    ology. Red had not adequately addressed the question
    of language-level support for building large systems
    consisting of many interdependent modules.

Since May 1979 Ada has been undergoing an extensive technical test and evaluation phase with applications being programmed at over 100 application sites. The results of these application programming activities will be evaluated at a four-day
meeting in October 1979 and will result in language change
recommendations to the designers. A revised and, it is hoped,
final version of the language which takes these suggestions into
account is scheduled to be delivered by April 1980.

A test translator which performs complete syntactic checking of the language and executes a substantial subset has been
available since August 15 1979. There are several implementation
efforts currently under way and it is expected that additional
test translators will be available by the end of 1979. Procure-
ments for a production compiler have been issued. The earliest
projected date for availability of a production compiler is the
summer of 1981.

The purpose of this book is to present an introduction to
Ada for programmers with at least one year's experience in a
higher-level language such as Fortran. The degree to which a
language is understood and accepted depends not only on its
technical quality but also on the quality of expository materials.
The aim of this book is to provide a readable and relatively pain-
less introduction to the language quite early in its development
so that the process of acceptance can be accelerated.

The method of presentation - by means of examples which
vary from relatively trivial illustrations of programming language principles to nontrivial developments of "real" programs -
has not, to the author's knowledge, been tried before on this
scale. The author has for a number of years wanted to write a
programming language introduction along these lines, and Ada has
provided a worthy excuse.

The book is incomplete in a number of respects. It is a
book about a language which is still a moving target. It does
not consider certain "advanced" features of the language such as
representation specifications. It is not intended to replace
the reference manual but merely to supplement it.

The author plans to develop in the summer of 1980 an updated
version of this book which reflects the language changes to be
introduced as a result of language evaluation. However, it is

felt that meanwhile the present volume may serve a useful purpose
for the many programmers who are interested in Ada now. Although
the current edition of this book is thus likely to have a short
life (unless it becomes a collector's item), it could well play
an important educational role in this interim period in paving
the way for the more rapid acceptance of Ada.

The book has five chapters. The first is an in-depth overview of Ada sufficient to enable programmers to read and understand most Ada programs. The material in this chapter falls
naturally into three parts. Sections 1.1 to 1.6 develop the
"classical" features of the language which are already present
in languages like Pascal. Sections 1.7 to 1.12 present "novel"
language features which facilitate modularity and concurrent
programming. Sections 1.13-1.18 describe program structure and
compilation issues necessary to understanding how large programs
fit together. This chapter may be regarded as a top-down introduction which allows the reader to view the forest before examining individual trees.

The remaining chapters consist of a more detailed bottom-up
presentation at a level of detail sufficient for writing programs
in the language. There is inevitably some duplication between
the material in Chapter 1 and the more detailed presentation of
the same concepts in later chapters. Wherever possible, the
second pass over a given topic treats the material from a different perspective, so that there is pedagogic reinforcement.

Chapter 2 considers expressions, statements, control structures, simple declarations, procedures and functions. These
language features are present in earlier languages like Pascal,
but Ada has attempted to learn from mistakes in earlier languages,
and its integration of statements, control structures and subprograms is well-engineered. A sequence of programming examples
for computing prime numbers serves to illustrate how control
structure mechanisms such as while loops, exit statements, go to
statements and flags should be used.

Chapter 3 is concerned with data description. The Ada
facilities for defining numeric types, enumeration types, array
types, record types and access types are described. Ada mechanisms for type definition are Pascal-like, but avoid some of the
problems of Pascal in areas such as variant records and facilitate
checking by the compiler for consistency of types. Here again
Ada presents a well-engineered synthesis which builds on the
experience of previous languages.

Chapter 4 treats program structure and modularity. The
central concept here is the package which allows the user to
package logically related collections of resources, and facili-
tates the definition of common data pools, collections of related subprograms and abstract data types. Several examples of
packages are given, including complex numbers, key management,
symbol table management and list processing. The very rich
facilities in Ada for name space management and separate

compilation are then analyzed. This chapter describes the mechanisms available in Ada for building large programs out of modular components. The availability of these features was one of the reasons for choosing Ada over its competitors.

Chapter 5 is concerned with concurrent programming. After an introductory discussion of concepts such as shared variables and message passing, examples are developed which illustrate initiation, execution, synchronization and communication among tasks. The Ada facilities for task families, generic tasks and semaphores are described. Several different solutions for mailboxes and the reader-writer problem are developed in order to illustrate different ways of using the multitasking primitives. Optimization of certain kinds of tasks (server tasks) by distribution of executable code among callers of the task is discussed in order to provide further insights into the mechanisms of multitasking.

Tasks in Ada are concurrently executable modules which are more like packages than subprograms. Each task can provide a set of resources to other tasks by means of a task specification that is separate from the implementation. The process of building large programs from modular components which are concurrently executable is supported in Ada by means of language mechanisms which are similar to those for sequential programming.

The author would like to thank the many individuals who have read the manuscript and offered suggestions. In particular, the author is grateful to Jean Ichbiah who has taken a personal interest in the development of this manuscript, patiently corrected errors in examples, and offered numerous other suggestions. Brian Kernighan was extremely helpful in reviewing the manuscript on behalf of Prentice-Hall. Donald Knuth and Robert Sedgewick helped to improve some of the algorithms. Steven Reiss helped to improve Chapters 1 through 4. Thomas Doeppner contributed many ideas to Chapter 5. Mark Davis and Steven Feiner proofread the manuscript very carefully and helped to remove errors of both form and substance. Students in my programming languages course (CS 273) participated in reviewing and debugging the manuscript. Katrina Avery was responsible for typing, formatting and some copyediting, and helped to shorten considerably the production time for the book. Last but not least, the author would like to thank the instructors at the Ada workshop in Monterey (Jean Ichbiah, John Barnes, Robert Firth and John Goodenough) for valuable insights into how the language should be presented, as well as permission to use some of their examples.

Peter Wegner
Brown University
September 1979

1

AN OVERVIEW OF ADA

1.1 A Simple Ada Program

Chapter 1 presents an overview of Ada as a whole so that the reader can view the forest before examining individual trees. The principal concepts and features are illustrated by means of graduated examples at a level of detail that should be sufficient to read and understand most Ada programs. A more detailed presentation sufficient for writing programs in the language is given in later chapters.

Our first example is a procedure called SIMPLE_ADD which reads two numbers, computes their sum, and prints the result. Each line includes a comment using the Ada notation for comments ("--" followed by the text of the comment).

Example 1.1. A very simple program

```
procedure SIMPLE_ADD is    -- a procedure called SIMPLE_ADD
   X,Y,Z: INTEGER;          -- which has three declared variables X,Y,Z
begin                       -- and a sequence of statements which consists of
   GET(X);                  -- a GET statement which reads a value into X
   GET(Y);                  -- a GET statement which reads a value into Y
   Z := X+Y;                -- an assignment statement which assigns a value to Z
   PUT(Z);                  -- a PUT statement which prints the value of Z
end SIMPLE_ADD;             -- and which is terminated by the keyword end
                            -- followed optionally by the procedure name
```

The first line specifies that this program is a procedure called SIMPLE_ADD. The second line declares the three "identifiers" X, Y, Z to be integer variables. These two lines together constitute the declarative part of the procedure and are followed by a sequence of executable statements enclosed by the keywords begin..end. The statement sequence contains two input statements which read data from an input medium into X and Y, an assignment statement which computes the sum of X and Y, and an output statement which outputs the result.

The structure of this program is as follows:

Example 1.2. Program structure

```
procedure name is           ] declarative part
   declarations of variables ]  (describes data)
begin                        ] statement part
   statements that may use the variables ]  (describes computation)
end;                         ]
```

This program structure is a prototype for the structure of all programs in the language. Every program contains a declarative part which names and describes variables and other program entities, and a sequence of statements which specify computations using the entities introduced in the declarative part. Section 1.2 below further explores constructs that occur in the statement part of an Ada program, while section 1.3 further explores constructs that may occur in the declarative part.

Names introduced by the programmer in a declarative part are called identifiers. Each declaration introduces one or more identifiers and specifies a set of attributes for each identifier. The declaration for X, Y, Z specifies the attributes of X, Y, Z in terms of the data type INTEGER. The attributes in this case include the set of values which may be taken by the variables X, Y, Z and the operations applicable to X, Y, Z.

Ada is a strongly typed language in the sense that every identifier used in a program must be defined by a declaration. The declaration imposes restrictions on the way in which an identifier may be used, which may be checked at compile time. Such checks allow many programming errors to be caught earlier than would otherwise be possible.

In describing computations performed by programs it is convenient to use the terminology that declarations are elaborated, statements are executed and expressions are evaluated. Thus the procedure SIMPLE_ADD is performed by first elaborating the declarations for X, Y, Z and then executing the four statements of the procedure body. Execution of the third statement "Z := X+Y;" involves evaluation of the expression X+Y and assignment of the resulting value to Z.

1.2 Programming Examples

Programs generally contain control structures which control the order of execution of statements of a program. The two most important kinds of control statements in Ada are conditional statements (which select among alternative actions) and loop statements (which specify controlled repetition of an action).

Conditional statements are illustrated by the following if statement for computing the absolute value of X.

Example 1.3. Simple if statement

```
if X < 0 then             -- if X is less than zero then
   X := -X;               -- replace X by -X
end if;                   -- otherwise do nothing
```


Loop statements are illustrated by the following for statement, which sums the first ten elements of the vector V̄.

Example 1.4. Simple loop statement

```
SUM := 0;                 -- initialize variable SUM to zero
for I in 1..10 loop       -- loop for successive values of I
   SUM := SUM + V(I);     -- add Ith element of vector V to SUM
end loop;                 -- end of loop
```


The following program fragment for computing the maximum of the first ten elements of V contains an if statement nested in a for statement.

Example 1.5. Loop with embedded if statement

```
MAX := V(1);              -- initialize MAX to first element of V
for I in 2..10 loop       -- loop for successive values of I
   if V(I) > MAX then     -- if new V(I) > maximum so far
      MAX := V(I);        -- V(I) becomes new provisional maximum
   end if;                -- end of if statement
end loop;                 -- end of loop
```


Nesting of statements within other statements is typical of the structure of Ada programs. The nested structure of the above program fragment is as follows:

Example 1.6. Nested control structures

```
assignment statement
for statement (special kind of loop statement)
   if statement nested in the for statement
      assignment statement nested in the if statement
   end of nested if statement
end of for statement
```


This program fragment performs a well-defined function (the function of computing the maximum of a vector of values). The facility of computing the maximum of a vector can be provided in a modular fashion to an arbitrary number of users by embedding the code for computing the maximum in a function definition.

Example 1.7. Function definition for computing the maximum

```
function MAX_TEN(V: VECTOR) return INTEGER is  -- a function called MAX_TEN
                                 -- which has parameter V of type VECTOR and returns
                                 -- an INTEGER result
   MAX: INTEGER;                 -- it has a local variable MAX
begin                            -- and a sequence of statements
   MAX := V(1);                  -- which assigns V(1) to MAX
   for I in 2..10 loop           -- and then loops
      if V(I) > MAX then         -- and tests if V(I) > MAX
         MAX := V(I);            -- if so, V(I) is maximum so far
      end if;                    -- if V(I) <= MAX take no action
   end loop;                     -- end of loop
   return MAX;                   -- when loop is completed, return with value MAX
end  MAX_TEN;                    -- end of MAX_TEN function definition
```

The above function provides a computational resource to the
user (for computing the maximum of a ten-element vector). The
following statement computes the sum of the maxima of a ten-
element vector A and a ten-element vector B and assigns the result
to the variable Y.

Example 1.8. Function call

```
Y := MAX_TEN(A) + MAX_TEN(B);
```

Calls of a function like MAX_TEN may appear in an expression
on the right-hand side of an assignment statement anywhere that a
constant or variable may appear.

The function MAX_TEN above illustrates the basic idea of
defining a computational resource and subsequently using it. But
MAX_TEN has the following imperfections:

   1. The restriction that vectors have precisely ten elements
      is unrealistic. A resource for computing the maximum of
      a vector should work for vectors of any "reasonable" size.
   2. It is sometimes necessary to know not only the value of
      the maximum element but also its location (index) within
      the vector, so that further operations on the maximum
      element can be performed.

The following function MAX_INDEX computes the index of the
maximum element for vectors of arbitrary length. It has a parameter V of the type VECTOR which is assumed to have been previously
defined by the programmer as a one-dimensional array of integers
(see section 1.3). It makes use of the "attribute enquiries"
V'FIRST and V'LAST which yield as their values the indices of the
first and last elements of the vector V. It also makes use of the
Ada facility for initializing declarations.

4

Example 1.9. Function definition for computing the maximum index

```
function MAX_INDEX(V: VECTOR) return INTEGER is  -- a function MAX_INDEX with
   MAX: INTEGER := V(V'FIRST); -- local variable MAX initialized to V(V'FIRST)
   INDEX: INTEGER := V'FIRST;  -- local variable INDEX initialized to V'FIRST
begin                         -- and a body which iterates
   for I in V'FIRST..V'LAST loop   -- over elements of the vector
     if V(I) > MAX then       -- tests if V(I) > MAX
       MAX := V(I);           -- if so sets MAX to V(I)
       INDEX := I;            -- and remembers value of INDEX
     end if;                  -- if V(I) <= MAX takes no action
   end loop;                  -- ends the loop
   return INDEX;              -- and returns with index of maximum element
end MAX_INDEX;
```

The call "MAX_INDEX(A)" returns the index of the maximum element. Thus the maximum element of A is given by "A(MAX_INDEX(A))". The difference of the maxima of two vectors A, B (possibly of different lengths) may be computed as follows:

Example 1.10. Call of MAX INDEX function

```
DIFF := A(MAX_INDEX(A)) - B(MAX_INDEX(B));
```

The usefulness of returning the index of the maximum element rather than its value is illustrated by the following program fragment for interchanging the values of the first element and maximum element of a vector.

Example 1.11. Use of MAX INDEX

```
K := MAX_INDEX(A);
TEMP := A(K);
A(K) := A(1);
A(1) := TEMP;
```

This mechanism can be used as a basis for sorting by finding successive maxima of subvectors, as illustrated for the following vector with the five elements 3, 1, 7, 6, 4.

Example 1.12. Example of sorting by successive maxima

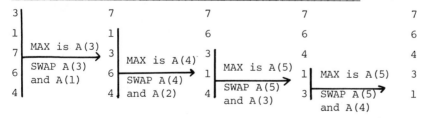

5

In order to perform sorting by successive maxima using the MAX_INDEX subprogram we must permit parameters that are sub-arrays (slices) of contiguous elements of the array being sorted. Ada permits slices (subarrays) of contiguous elements of an array to be specified by the notation A(I..J), which denotes the sub-array consisting of the contiguous array elements A(I) through A(J).

In the next example the call "MAX_INDEX(A(I..N))" yields the index of the maximum element of the slice A(I..N). It is assumed that the vector A to be sorted has A'FIRST = 1.

Example 1.13. Sorting by successive maxima

```
N := A'LAST;                    -- assign array size to N
for I in 1..N loop              -- and iterate
  K := MAX_INDEX(A(I..N));      -- find MAX_INDEX of slice A(I..N)
  TEMP := A(K);                 -- interchange maximum element A(K)
  A(K) := A(I);                 -- with first element A(I)
  A(I) := TEMP;                 -- of the slice A(I..N)
end loop;                       -- and repeat for next value of I
```

Sorting is a well-defined task that may conveniently be specified by a procedure. Procedures, like functions, are defined by a definition which specifies the task to be performed, and may subsequently be called by a procedure call. Unlike functions, procedures do not return a result but instead perform their task by modifying values of variables whose names are known to users of the procedure. The following procedure SORT has a parameter of the type VECTOR whose value is modified (sorted) as a result of executing the procedure.

Example 1.14. Sort procedure

```
procedure SORT(A: in out VECTOR) is
  N: constant INTEGER := A'LAST;
  K, TEMP: INTEGER;
begin
  for I in 1..N loop
    K := MAX_INDEX(A(I..N));
    TEMP := A(K);
    A(K) := A(I);
    A(I) := TEMP;
  end loop;
end SORT;
```

The SORT program makes use of two language features we have not previously encountered:

  1. Constant declaration. The local identifier N is initial-ized each time the procedure is entered to a constant (the length of the vector A) and is therefore introduced

by a constant declaration. The constant N may have different values for different invocations of the SORT procedure but is constant during any given invocation.
2. Input-output parameters. The vector parameter A of the SORT procedure is both accessed and modified during execution of the SORT procedure and therefore must be specified by the binding mode in out. This contrasts with the parameter V of the function MAX_INDEX which was used purely for input and never modified. Input parameters in Ada need not have their mode explicitly specified so that "V: VECTOR" is a sufficient parameter specification for V although "V: in VECTOR", which explicitly specifies that V is an input parameter, is more complete. However, for input-output parameters the binding mode in out must be explicitly specified.

The SORT procedure may be called by a procedure call statement as follows.

Example 1.15. Call of SORT procedure

SORT(INT_VECT);

Note that a call of the SORT procedure affects the environment by changing the order of the elements of its vector parameter, while the MAX_INDEX function cannot affect its environment by changing values of its parameters, but affects its environment only by the result which it returns. It is true in general that functions have only input parameters and can affect their environment only by returning a result, while procedures do not return a result and must affect their environment by modifying parameter values.

The SORT procedure may be used without any knowledge about how sorting is implemented. If the SORT procedure is replaced by a functionally equivalent procedure which performs sorting in an entirely different way, it will not affect the user.

Sorting is in fact one of the most intensively studied problems in the literature, and there are literally hundreds of essentially different ways of sorting a vector. Sorting by successive maxima was chosen for purposes of illustration because it is one of the simplest to explain and because it allows us to illustrate some interesting features of Ada.

1.3 Type and Object Declarations

Now that we have seen some examples of Ada programs, we shall examine in greater detail the Ada facilities for data description. The key notion for data description is the notion of a data type. A data type determines a set of values which may be taken by identifiers declared to be of the data type, and a set of operations applicable to objects of the data type.

7

Ada supports the <u>predefined</u> data types INTEGER, FLOAT, BOOLEAN and CHARACTER. However, the power of Ada lies in the programmer's ability to define <u>programmer-defined data types</u> tailored to particular applications by means of <u>type definitions</u>.

One reason for defining a new type is simply to prevent mixing of operations on logically distinct kinds of objects. For example, if we want to count apples and oranges, but avoid mixing apples and oranges, we can introduce the two programmer-defined integer types APPLES and ORANGES, as in the following example.

<u>Example 1.16.</u> Type compatibility and type conversion

```
procedure DERIVED_TYPES is        -- a procedure
   type APPLES is new INTEGER;    -- which defines a new type APPLES
   type ORANGES is new INTEGER;   -- and a new type ORANGES
   A: APPLES;                     -- an object of the type APPLES
   B: ORANGES;                    -- an object of type ORANGES
   I: INTEGER;                    -- and an object of type INTEGER
begin
   A := 0;      -- integer literal assigned to object of type APPLES
   B := 0;      -- and to object of type ORANGES
   A := A+A;    -- apples can be added to each other
   I := A+B;    -- but apples cannot be added to oranges (illegal statement)
   I := INTEGER(A) + INTEGER(B);    -- unless forcibly converted to integers
end DERIVED_TYPES;
```

The types APPLES and ORANGES in the above example are called <u>derived types</u> because they are derived from an existing type INTEGER. Derived types inherit literals from their defining type. Thus the statement "A := 0;" which assigns the literal "0" to a variable of the type APPLES, is legal. They also inherit operations from their defining type. Thus the expression "A + A" which applies the "+" operator to variables of the type APPLES is legal. So is "A + 1". However, the addition operator requires its two operands to be of the same type (so that "A + B" and "A + I" are illegal). The assignment operator requires the expressions on the right-hand side to have the same type as the name on the left-hand side (so that "I := A;" is illegal). However, explicit conversion is possible between a derived type and its defining type (INTEGER(A) is of type INTEGER while APPLES(I) would be of type APPLES). Thus "I := INTEGER(A) + INTEGER(B);" is legal since both operands of the addition operator are of type INTEGER, the sum is of type INTEGER, and the type of the value on the left-hand side is compatible with the type of the variable on the right-hand side.

The declaration of the derived type APPLES automatically extends the meaning of the addition operator + so that it can be used to add not only integers but also apples. Extending the meaning of an operator to operands of a new type is referred to as <u>overloading</u> the operator. Ada permits operators to be overloaded both implicitly by defining a new type derived from a type for which that operator is meaningful, and explicitly by a

8

function definition (see section 1.8).

The "+" operator is already overloaded because addition is
defined for both fixed- and floating-point operands (fixed- and
floating-point addition are in fact implemented by different
machine-language instructions on most computers). The type declarations for APPLES and ORANGES overload the "+" operator with
additional programmer-defined meanings. The meaning of any particular occurrence of the operator "+" depends on the types of
its operands. Since the types of the operands of any operator
are always known at compile time, the compiler can always determine which of the several meanings of + is intended and can compile code which reflects the desired meaning.

The predefined data type INTEGER has an implicit (implementation-defined) range of values. Explicit control over the range
of values of integer variables may be accomplished by a type
definition with an explicit range constraint, as in the following
example.

Example 1.17. Programmer-defined integer type

```
procedure FIBONACCI is   -- a procedure for computing Fibonacci numbers
   type SHORT_INT is range -32768..32767; -- with a type SHORT_INT
   J: SHORT_INT := 0;       -- two variables of the type SHORT_INT
   K: SHORT_INT := 1;       -- initialized for generating Fibonacci numbers
begin                       -- and a statement sequence
   while K < 10000 loop     -- which tests if last Fibonacci number < 10000
      PUT(K);               -- outputs the current Fibonacci number
      K := J+K;             -- sets K to the next Fibonacci number
      J := K-J;             -- sets J to previous value of K
   end loop;                -- and repeats this process
end FIBONACCI;
```

This example declares a programmer-defined type SHORT_INT
and two initialized objects J, K of the type SHORT_INT. The
programmer-defined type has an explicitly defined range which
ensures that the program will be portable among implementations.
Moreover, the range may be implemented in a 16-bit word, ensuring both time and space efficiency on computers whose hardware
supports implementation of 16-bit integers.

There is a fundamental distinction between the type declaration of SHORT_INT which creates a new type from which an arbitrary number of instances can be created by subsequent declarations, and the object declaration of J, K which creates objects
of the data type that can be used in subsequent computations.

The data types INTEGER and SHORT_INT are referred to as
scalar types because objects of the type have no components.
Another important class of scalar types is enumeration types.
Enumeration types have finite value sets which may be explicitly
enumerated, as in the following example.

Example 1.18. Enumeration types

```
procedure ENUMERATION_TYPES is
   type COLOR is (RED,GREEN,YELLOW,BLUE);   -- COLOR has four possible values
   ADA: COLOR;                              -- ADA is object of type COLOR
begin
   ADA := GREEN;            -- value GREEN of type COLOR is assigned to ADA
end ENUMERATION_TYPES;
```

Enumeration types are very useful for defining finite sets
of everyday objects such as colors, weekdays (MON, TUE,..),
directions (N, E, S, W), digits (0, 1, 2,..), computer op codes
(ADD, MULT,..), etc. Ada supports iteration over enumeration
types and the use of enumeration types as index sets for arrays.

Scalar types have no components and may be contrasted with
structured types such as arrays whose components are selectable
by indexing. The next example declares a programmer-defined
array type VECTOR, two objects V, W of the type VECTOR, and
illustrates assignment to vector components and complete vectors.

Example 1.19. Array data types

```
procedure ARRAY_TYPES is      -- a procedure called ARRAY_TYPES
   type VECTOR is array(1..5) of INTEGER;   -- with type declaration for VECTOR
   V,W: VECTOR;               -- and object declarations for V, W
begin                         -- and a sequence of statements
   V(5) := 8;                 -- which assigns to element of vector
   W := (2,4,6,8,10);         -- assigns an aggregate to a complete vector
   V := W;                    -- assigns value of vector W to vector V
end ARRAY_TYPES;              -- and then is terminated
```

The type declaration for VECTOR defines a template from
which an arbitrary number of vector objects can be created by
object declarations. Array objects have components (elements)
which may be individually accessed by indexing (V(5), W(I)),
which may be initialized to array aggregates (W := (2,4,6,8,10);)
or which may be assigned values of compatible array variables
(V := W;). Thus array data structures may be viewed as abstract
entities which have aggregate values as well as individual values.

The bounds of an array type definition may be left unspecified by using a type definition (INDEX) rather than a range
specification (1..5) to specify the index type of the array.
Array types whose bounds are unspecified must have their bounds
specified at object declaration time.

Example 1.20. Vectors with unspecified bounds

```
type INDEX is range 1..1000;          -- type INDEX is used to define
type VECTOR is array(INDEX) of INTEGER; -- arraytype VECTOR with unspecified bounds
U, V: VECTOR(1..20);                  -- 20-element vector objects
W: VECTOR(1..10);                     -- 10-element vector object
```

The type VECTOR above has unspecified bounds and allows vector objects of any size between 1 and 1000 to be created. In general, the bounds may be any subrange of the range determined by the index type of the type definition.

Array types with unspecified bounds are particularly important in subprograms with array parameters such as the SORT procedure and MAX_INDEX function discussed in the previous section. The parameter VECTOR in these subprograms must have unspecified bounds to allow calls for vectors of different sizes. Another example of a subprogram requiring vector parameters of unspecified bounds is the following vector multiplication (inner product) function.

Example 1.21. Vector multiplication

```
function VECMULT(X,Y: VECTOR) return INTEGER is  -- vector multiplication function
   RESULT: INTEGER := 0;              -- which initializes result to zero
begin                                 -- and has a statement sequence
   assert X'FIRST = Y'FIRST;          -- with two assert statements
   assert X'LAST = Y'LAST;            -- that check compatibility of vectors
   for I in X'FIRST..X'LAST loop      -- which iterates over vector elements
      RESULT := RESULT+X(I)*Y(I);     -- accumulates inner product
   end loop;                          -- repeats for successive vector elements
   return RESULT;                     -- and returns value of inner product
end VECMULT;
```

The VECMULT function, like the SORT and MAX_INDEX subprograms of the previous section, make use of attribute enquiries to determine the bounds of actual vector parameters. The attribute enquiries X'FIRST, X'LAST yield the index of the first and last components and are used to control iteration.

This example illustrates the use of assert statements. An assert statement is conceptually executed in line during execution, although its truth may sometimes be verified at compile time by an optimizing compiler. If the condition determined by the assert statement is true, the computation may continue. If it is false, then an error action is executed.

Array types have components which must all be of the same type and which may be accessed by indices. Ada supports a second important class of programmer-defined data structures called records whose components may be of different type and are accessed by a selector name qualified by the name of the record.

Example 1.22. Record data types

```
procedure RECORD_TYPES is
   type COMPLEX is            -- the programmer-defined type COMPLEX is
      record                  -- a record with
         RE: INTEGER;         -- a component named RE of type INTEGER
         IM: INTEGER;         -- and a component IM of type INTEGER
      end record;             -- end of record type definition
   C,C1: COMPLEX;             -- two objects C, C1 of the type COMPLEX
begin
   C.RE := 2;                 -- assign to RE component of C
   C.IM := C.RE+1;            -- assign to IM component of C
   C1 := (0,0);               -- assign aggregate to complete record C1
   C1 := C;                   -- assign value of C to complete record C1
   C := (C.RE*C1.RE-C.IM*C1.IM,C.RE*C1.IM+C.IM*C1.RE); -- product C*C1
end RECORD_TYPES;
```

Records, like arrays, may be manipulated not only by access-ing individual record components (such as C.RE) but also by the assignment of record aggregates to record variables (C1 := (0,0);) and by direct assignment between compatible record variables (C1 := C;).

The record COMPLEX in the previous example has two components of type INTEGER. Ada permits record types to have components of undetermined size and/or type. The following record type has a dynamic array component whose size is determined by the value of a second component whose value is a constant determined at the time of creation of instances of the record.

Example 1.23. Record types of varying size

```
type BUFFER is
   record
      SIZE: constant INTEGER range 1..N;  -- discriminant component
      BLOCK: array(1..SIZE) of INTEGER;   -- array whose size depends on
   end record;                            -- discriminant
```

Record types having components of varying size or type are called variant records. Such records must contain an explicit constant component in which the size is explicitly specified at record allocation time. The constant component is called a discriminant because it discriminates among records of different sizes.

Ada permits variant records with components whose type and component name vary for different objects of the type. The following type PERSON has a second component whose type and com-ponent name depend on whether the person is male or female.

Example 1.24. Components of varying type

```
type PERSON is
  record
    SEX: constant (M,F);   -- discriminant component (deferred constant)
    case SEX of     -- component whose name and type depend on discriminant
      when M => BEARDED: BOOLEAN;
      when F => CHILDREN: INTEGER range 0..100;
    end case;
  end record;
```

The record PERSON has a discriminant SEX which is an enumeration type and may take one of the two values M or F. The discriminant is said to be a deferred constant because assignment of a value is deferred from type declaration time to the time that values are assigned to record variables. Assignment to a discriminant is possible only when assigning a value to the complete record.

The discriminant components of a record are in a sense redundant because the information they contain is already present in the components which they discriminate. However, a discriminant makes explicit the structure variation of a record in a form in which it can be used to check the validity and security of operations on a record.

From another point of view, a discriminant of a variant record may be viewed as a parameter whose value is supplied at object creation time rather than type definition time. Ada allows discriminants of variant records to be specified by a parametric notation.

Example 1.25. Parametrized types

```
B: BUFFER(N);
P: PERSON(M);
```

Records of varying size, such as BUFFER, may have "dynamic" parameters whose values are determined at the time the declaration is elaborated. Records of varying type require the parameter to be statically determined, so that type compatibility can be checked at compile time.

1.4   Program Structure

Now that statements and data declarations have been introduced, we are ready to discuss the overall structure of Ada programs.

In describing how an Ada program is constructed from its constituents, we can identify the following levels of program structure:

Characters, which are the lowest-level atomic constituents
  of a program;
Lexical units, which are the atomic units of meaning
  (semantic units);
Expressions, which specify a computation that computes a
  "value";
Assignment statements, which assign the value computed by
  an expression to a variable;
Control structures, which control the sequence in which
  assignment statements and other statements of the program
  are executed;
Declarations, which define the attributes of identifiers
  used in the statements of a program;
Program units, which associate declarations defining the
  attributes of identifiers with statements which use them;
Compilation units, which are the units of structure for
  program development and separate compilation.

A compilation unit may be a subprogram or a module. Subprograms are either procedures or functions, while modules are
either packages or tasks, as illustrated in figure 1.1.

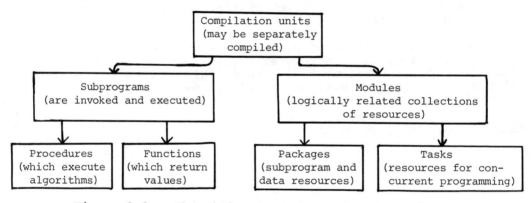

Figure 1.1. Classification of compilation units.

Procedures and functions are "traditional" programming language constructs taken from earlier higher-level languages like
Fortran and Pascal. Packages and tasks are novel language constructs which reflect recent advances in language design.

Packages support the modular specification of logically
related collections of computational resources. For example, a
matrix package provides a logically related collection of computational resources for performing computations on matrices, while
an input-output package provides a logically related collection
of computational resources for performing input-output. Tasks
are the modular units for concurrent programming. They support
communication among concurrently executing tasks by a novel
mechanism called the rendezvous mechanism which requires synchronization between a called task and a calling task whenever messages
between tasks are communicated.

14

Subprograms and modules may be compilation units (they may be separately compiled) as well as program units (they associate identifier declarations with statements which use them). In fact, every compilation unit is automatically a program unit. However, not every program unit is a compilation unit. In particular, subprograms and modules defined in a declarative part of an enclosing compilation unit are not compilation units. The nesting of subprogram definitions in enclosing compilation units is illustrated in the next section.

1.5 Subprograms

Subprograms were introduced informally in section 1.2. In this and the next section we consider in greater detail the nested declaration of subprograms and the nature of subprogram parameters.

Subprograms are defined by a subprogram declaration which specifies the subprogram name, formal parameters, local declarations and statement sequence. They are invoked by a subprogram call which specifies the name and actual parameters to be used in place of the formal parameters for the given instance of invocation. Function declarations, which return a result, specify in addition the type of the result that will be returned by the function.

The following function F has an integer input parameter and a local variable called LOCAL, and returns an integer result.

Example 1.26. Function declarations

```
function F(N: INTEGER) return INTEGER is   -- F has integer parameter and result
   LOCAL: INTEGER;         -- and local variable of type INTEGER
begin                      -- and two statements which
   LOCAL := N**2+N+1;      -- use local variable for intermediate result
   return LOCAL;           -- return value of type integer
end F;
```

The first line of this function declaration specifies its name, its formal parameter, and the type of its result, and constitutes the complete user interface specification. The second line specifies an internal local variable (inaccessible to the user of F). The two statements make use of the local variable and parameter, and compute the function $F(N) = N^2 + N + 1$.

This function may be called by a function call which has the same syntactic status as a variable appearing on the right-hand side of an assignment statement.

Example 1.27. Function calls

```
I := F(3)            -- the value 13 is assigned to I
J := F(3)+F(4);      -- the value 34 (13 + 21) is assigned to J
```

Function declarations and calls can be put together into a
single program in which both the integer variables I, J and the
function F are declared in the declarative part of an enclosing
procedure.

Example 1.28. Nested function declaration

```
procedure FUNCTIONS is
   I,J: INTEGER;
   function F(N: INTEGER) return INTEGER;          ⎤ n          ⎤
     LOCAL: INTEGER;                               ⎟ e          ⎟ declarative part
   begin                                           ⎟ s          ⎬ of procedure
     LOCAL := N**2+N+1;                            ⎟ t          ⎟
     return LOCAL;                                 ⎟ e          ⎟
   end;                                            ⎦ d          ⎦
begin                                                f
   I := F(3);         -- value is 13                u          ⎤
   J := F(3)+F(4);    -- value is 34                n          ⎬ statements of
end FUNCTIONS;                                      c          ⎦ procedure
                                                    t
                                                    i
                                                    o
                                                    n
                                                    F
```

This example illustrates the nesting of subprogram declarations in the declarative part of other subprograms that is typical of the structure of Ada programs. The procedure FUNCTIONS
has the declarations for the integers I, J and the procedure F
nested in its declarative part. The function F in turn has the
parameter N and the integer variable LOCAL declared in its
declarative part. The function F could in turn have a function
nested in its declarative part so that nesting of subprogram
declarations in the declarative part of textually enclosing subprogram declarations is possible to an arbitrary level.

1.6   Subroutine Parameters

The parameters of a subprogram definition are said to be
formal parameters since they are "dummy" identifiers (bound
variables) which can be replaced by other non-conflicting identifiers without changing the meaning of the subprogram. For
example, the parameter N of F in the example above can be
replaced by M or X (but not by LOCAL) in its three occurrences
within F without changing the meaning of F.

The parameters which occur in a subprogram call are called
actual parameters because they determine the values actually used
in executing a given call of the subprogram. When a subroutine
is called, actual parameters of the call are "substituted" for
formal parameters of the definition in a manner constrained by
the binding mode of each parameter.

The binding mode of a formal parameter determines whether
corresponding actual parameters are read-only, write-only or
read-write. These three binding modes are respectively called
in, out and in out.

When no binding mode is specified the default binding mode

16

is in. Thus the parameter N of the function F above has the default binding mode in.

Functions may have only in parameters because they are allowed to affect their environment only by the result they return. Procedures generally have at least one parameter with the binding mode out or in out by means of which they produce effects in their environment of call.*

The use of in out parameters is illustrated by the following procedure for swapping (exchanging) the values of its two integer parameters.

Example 1.29. In out procedure parameters

```
procedure SWAP(X,Y: in out INTEGER) is     -- SWAP has two in out parameters
   LOCAL: INTEGER:          -- and a local variable
begin                       -- and three statements
   LOCAL := X;              -- which use LOCAL for intermediate storage
   X := Y;                  -- while interchanging X and Y
   Y := LOCAL;
end;
```

The parameters X,Y above have the binding mode in out because the procedure both uses the parameter values (X, Y occur on the right-hand side of an assignment statement) and changes the parameter values (X, Y occur on the left-hand side of an assignment statement).

In parameters behave (within the procedure body) like local constants whose value is provided by the corresponding actual parameter at the point of call. The actual parameter can be a literal, a variable, or an expression. Thus the function F defined in example 1.8 can be called with the calls F(3), F(I), F(I+J), etc.

Actual parameters of the out and in out modes must be variables. Out parameters act as local variables whose value is assigned to the corresponding actual parameter as a result of execution of the subprogram. In out parameters act as local variables whose value is initialized from the actual parameter at the time of call and assigned to the actual parameter as a result of execution.

A call "SWAP(A,B);" of the procedure SWAP would cause the parameters X, Y of the procedure declaration to act as local variables initialized to the values of A, B at the time of call.

---

*Procedures can also affect their environments through non-local variables and by output statements which are effectively assignments to nonlocal storage in an output medium. However, procedure parameters are the preferred mechanism for controlled and flexible transfer of information between the calling and called environments, and good programming practice dictates that nonlocal variables be used with caution.

The final values of X, Y resulting from execution of the procedures would be assigned to A, B as a result of execution of the
procedure.

Use of the SWAP procedure may be illustrated by the following SORT procedure. It is assumed that the procedure SWAP, the
function MAX_INDEX and the data type VECTOR are defined in a declarative environment that is textually accessible to the SORT
procedure.

Example 1.30. Sort procedure

```
procedure SORT(A: in out VECTOR) is   -- a sort procedure
  K: INTEGER;                          -- with a local variable K
begin                                  -- and a statement sequence
  for I in 1..A'LENGTH loop            -- which finds the maximum of
    K := MAX_INDEX(A(I..A'LENGTH));    -- successive subarrays of A
    SWAP (A(I),A(K));         -- and swaps first and max elements of subarray
  end loop;                  -- in order to sort the vector A
end SORT;
```

The above sorting routine can be used only for sorting integers. In many applications it is convenient to define subprograms for tasks such as swapping and sorting not just for a
single type such as integers but for a wide variety of types.
This can be done in Ada by means of generic subprograms.

1.7. Generic Subprograms

Subprograms may have formal parameters which are variables
of any defined data type, but cannot have formal parameters whose
"values" are procedures or type definitions. Generic clauses
provide a translation-time facility for parametrization of subprograms which allows both types and subprograms to appear as
"generic" subprogram parameters. The generic SWAP procedure
below illustrates the use of generic clauses in defining computational operations, such as swapping of two variables, which
have a common pattern for a wide variety of types.

Example 1.31. Generic swap procedure

```
generic (type T)                 -- a generic clause with type parameter T
procedure SWAP(X,Y: in out T) is -- which becomes generic parameter of SWAP
  TEMP: T := constant X;  -- TEMP has type T, is initialized to X
begin            -- the three statements swap two objects of type T
  X := Y;        -- using the local object TEMP of type T
  Y := TEMP;     -- the required code may differ for different types T
end SWAP;
```

Generic procedures cannot be directly called. They may be
viewed as macro definitions which must be called with particular
values of generic parameters, and "expanded" at compile time,

before they can be executed. The compile-time process of calling
and "expanding" generic procedures is called <u>instantiation</u>. The
resulting procedures are called <u>instances</u> of the parent generic
procedure. The following example illustrates instantiation of
the generic SWAP procedure. Two instances of SWAP called
SWAP_INT and SWAP_VECT, which may respectively be used to swap
integer and vector objects, are created.

<u>Example 1.32. Instantiation of generic procedures</u>

<u>procedure</u> SWAP_INT <u>is</u> <u>new</u> SWAP(INTEGER);
<u>procedure</u> SWAP_VECT <u>is</u> <u>new</u> SWAP(VECTOR);

The SWAP procedure for vectors above will have very different code from the procedure for integers. Instantiation of
generic procedures in general may generate different code for
different instances, and may be viewed as a compile-time rather
than execution-time process. Generic procedures may be viewed
as macro definitions, and generic instantiations may be viewed
as macro calls which cause code to be generated.

The relation between translation-time instantiation with
specific values of generic parameters (by execution of a <u>new</u>
command) and run-time instantiation with specific actual <u>para-</u>
meters (by execution of a procedure call) is illustrated in
figure 1.2.

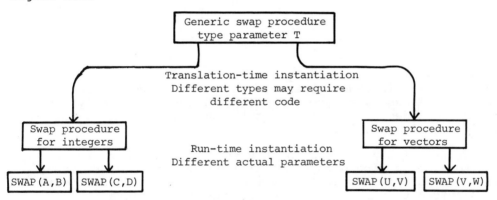

Figure 1.2.   Relation between generic instantiation
                 and procedure calling.

Generic parameters may include subprogram parameters as
well as type parameters. Type and subprogram parameters must
have their values statically determined at compile time because
they may affect the code generated by the compiler when the
generic subprogram is instantiated at compile time.

1.8   Packages

Packages are a mechanism for providing a collection of logically related computational resources. The package DATA below provides the user with two integer objects, a data type VECTOR and two vector objects.

Example 1.33.   Data packages

```
package DATA is
   I,J: INTEGER;
   type VECTOR is array (1..100) of INTEGER;
   V,W: VECTOR;
end;
```

Packages are specified in the declarative part of a program unit. Components of the package DATA may be referred to by means of qualified names such as DATA.I, DATA.V(K). Components of a package may be made directly accessible and referred to by unqualified names by means of a use clause.

Example 1.34.   The use clause

```
procedure USE_DATA is
   use DATA;
begin
   I := 5;
   V(K) := 3;
end USE_DATA;
```

A use clause can occur only as the first statement in a declarative part (in order to ensure uniform name conventions throughout the associated program unit). There can be only one use clause in a declarative part but the use clause can contain names of several packages.

Packages which provide data objects and data types are similar to named common data pools of languages such as Fortran, but are more powerful because data types as well as data objects may be provided to the user. However, the computational resources provided by a package may in general include not only data resources but also program resources. The following specification for a rational number package includes a record type which allows rational numbers (represented by integer pairs) to be created, an operation "=" which tests equality of rational numbers and two operations "+", "*" for addition and multiplication of rational numbers.

Example 1.35. Specification of a rational number package

```
package RATIONAL_NUMBERS is
  type RATIONAL is
    record
      NUMERATOR: INTEGER;
      DENOMINATOR: INTEGER range 1..INTEGER'LAST;
    end record;
  function "=" (X,Y: RATIONAL) return BOOLEAN;
  function "+" (X,Y: RATIONAL) return RATIONAL;
  function "*" (X,Y: RATIONAL) return RATIONAL;
end;
```

This specification is not complete, because it gives only the form and not the semantics of the "=", "+" and "*" operations. However, it provides the user with complete information concerning the form of user access to resources provided by the package, and provides the compiler with sufficient information to compile function calls, perform type checking, and allocate storage for object declarations in the environment of the user.

The program resources provided by the rational number packages are implemented in a package body whose details are hidden from the user. The package body for the rational numbers package given below includes a hidden procedure SAME_DENOMINATOR (invisible to users of the package) which reduces the arguments X and Y of the "=" and "+" operations to the same denominator so that (3,4) and (6,8) are equal, and (3,2)+(1,4) becomes (7,4).

Example 1.36. Body of rational numbers package

```
package body RATIONAL_NUMBERS is
  procedure SAME_DENOMINATOR (X,Y: in out RATIONAL) is
  begin
    -- reduces X and Y to the same denominator
  end;
  function "=" (X,Y: RATIONAL) return BOOLEAN is
    U,V: RATIONAL;
  begin
    U := X;
    V := Y;
    SAME_DENOMINATOR (U,V);
    return (U.NUMERATOR = V.NUMERATOR);
  end "=";
  function "+" (X,Y: RATIONAL) return RATIONAL is    ... end "+";
  function "*" (X,Y: RATIONAL) return RATIONAL is    ... end "*";
end RATIONAL_NUMBERS;
```

The example below illustrates the creation of objects of the type RATIONAL in a user environment, and the use of rational number equality, addition, multiplication and assignment.

Example 1.37. Use of rational numbers package

```
procedure USE_RATIONALS is    -- rational number package must be visible
   use RATIONAL_NUMBERS;      -- allow unqualified use of +, *, =
   X,Y,Z: RATIONAL := (1,1);  -- declare three initialized RATIONAL objects
begin
   X := (3,4);                -- rational number assignment
   Y := (6,8);                -- equality was defined so that (6,8) = (3,4)
   if X = Y then              -- rational number equality testing
      Z := X*X;               -- rational number multiplication and assignment
   else
      Z := X+Y;               -- rational number addition and assignment
   end if;
end;
```

In the statement "Z := X+Y;" above, + is interpreted as rational number addition because the operands X, Y are rational numbers, and := is interpreted as rational number assignment. When a new type such as RATIONAL is introduced, assignment and equality are automatically defined for objects of the type, but all other operations (such as +, *) must be explicitly defined. In the rational number package equality is redefined so that (3,4) and (6,8) are equal. The explicitly-defined meaning of equality supersedes the automatically-defined meaning.*

The rational number example illustrates that packages may contain type declarations, and that objects of the type may be created and manipulated using the operations for that type defined within the module.

1.9 Abstract Data Types

The rational number package provides a resource for creating objects of the type RATIONAL and for addition and multiplication of rational numbers. However, the user can also manipulate the components of objects of the type RATIONAL in a manner that is totally unrelated to the fact that they are rational numbers.

---

*If equality had not been defined within the package, then X=Y for rational number operands X, Y would be TRUE for identical integer pairs but FALSE for X = (3,4) and Y = (6,8). Every definition of equality automatically causes the complementary operator /= to be defined. However, the other relational operators, such as <, are not defined for new types and would have to be explicitly defined, just as + and *.

Example 1.38.   Direct operations on type components

```
procedure COMPONENTS is
  use RATIONAL_NUMBERS;
  X,Y,Z: RATIONAL := (1,2);
begin
  X.NUMERATOR := X.NUMERATOR+5;      -- X becomes (6,2)
  X.NUMERATOR := Y.DENOMINATOR;      -- X becomes (2,2)
end;
```

These operations treat rational numbers as records with two
components rather than as abstract objects subject to rational
number operations. Ada has a mechanism for hiding the record
representation of rational numbers so that it is accessible only
within the rational number package.

Example 1.39.   Private data types

```
package RATIONAL_NUMBERS is
  type RATIONAL is private;               -- hides representation of objects
  function "=" (X,Y: RATIONAL) return BOOLEAN;
  function "+" (X,Y: RATIONAL) return RATIONAL;
  function "*" (X,Y: RATIONAL) return RATIONAL;
  function "/" (X,Y: INTEGER) return RATIONAL;
private
  type RATIONAL is
    record
      NUMERATOR: INTEGER;
      DENOMINATOR: INTEGER range 1..INTEGER'LAST;
    end record;
end;
```

The above specification for rational numbers hides the representation of objects of the type RATIONAL, so that components
become inaccessible and can be manipulated only by rational number
operations defined within the package. Hiding of the representation makes it impossible to directly represent rational constants
as ordered pairs of integers. That is, "X := (3,4);" becomes
illegal, because the user can no longer assume that (3,4) is a
literal of the type RATIONAL.

This difficulty can be overcome by introducing a function
for creation of rational numbers from integer pairs into the
package body.

Example 1.40.   Create function for private data type

```
function "/" (X,Y: INTEGER) return RATIONAL is
begin
  return (X,Y);
end "/";
```

If "/" is introduced into the package body (where the representation of RATIONAL) is known) and the function specification (first line above) is introduced into the specification part of the package, then "/" can be used to convert integer pairs into rationals without the user being aware of the representation of rationals.

Example 1.41. Use of the create function

```
X := 3/4;                    -- create rational number, assign to X
```

The resulting package treats rational numbers as a true abstract data type. That is, rational numbers can be created from integer pairs, assigned to variables, tested for equality, added and multiplied, but the security of rational numbers cannot be violated by modifying their components.

The operator "/" which is defined above for integer arguments and a rational result is an overloading of the predefined operator "/" for integer (and floating-point) arguments and results. This example illustrates that Ada permits overloading of operators which have the same argument types but different result types. When the compiler encounters a statement "X := 3/4;" then "/" is interpreted as integer division if X is an integer type and as the creation function for rational numbers when X has the type RATIONAL. Since the type of every variable and literal is known at compile time, the overloaded operator "/" can always be disambiguated at compile time and the proper machine-language code can be compiled. The rational number package might well include still a further overloading of "/" to represent division of two rational numbers. This operator would have rational operands and produce a rational result.

In order to be truly useful a mechanism is required for printing rational numbers and possibly for converting rational numbers back into integer pairs. Such functions could be added to the rational number package in a straightforward manner.

Abstract data types will be further illustrated by a package for realizing stacks with PUSH and POP operations and a hidden representation for the stack structure. Since assignment to stack variables as well as equality testing of stacks is inappropriate, it is desirable to suppress the automatic creation of assignment and equality testing for the stack data type. This is accomplished by the keyword restricted.

Example 1.42. Stack example

```
package ALL_ABOUT_STACKS is
   restricted type STACK is private;
   procedure PUSH (E: in ELEMENT; S: in out STACK);
   procedure POP (E: out ELEMENT; S: in out STACK);
private
   type STACK is
     record
       TOP: INTEGER range 0..1000 := 0;
       SPACE: array(1..1000) of ELEMENT;
     end record;
end;
```

The record in the above example contains an integer (stack pointer) and an array with space for 1000 stack objects of type ELEMENT. The operations PUSH and POP must be defined in the package body (not given here) in terms of operations on the array.

The implementation of stacks by arrays is hidden from the user. It could be changed to an implementation of stacks by lists without affecting users. However, such a change in the representation of stacks would affect the data structures created in user modules by elaboration of object declarations for the type stack. It is for this reason that the "private part" of a module is considered to be part of the package specification rather than part of the package body.

Ada distinguishes between the logical interface of a package - determined by the visible part of the module, and the physical interface - which consists of the complete specification part and includes both the visible and the private part. The logical part includes everything the user needs to know in order to use the module, while the physical part includes additional information needed by the compiler to support use of the module. The private part is considered to be part of the physical interface because the compiler must know this information to allocate storage for objects of the private types created in the user environment.

1.10 Tasks

Tasks are the program units for concurrent programming. The task facilities of Ada will be illustrated by considering a "mailbox" task which accepts messages from a number of "sender" tasks S1, S2, ..., SM and can transmit messages to a number of receiving tasks R1, R2, ..., RN, as illustrated in figure 1.3.

We shall consider the specification and implementation of the mailbox task and the mechanisms required in sending and receiving tasks to communicate with the mailbox task. In our first example it is assumed that the mailbox task can handle only a single message at a time which must be transmitted to a receiving task before a second message can be accepted. A

25

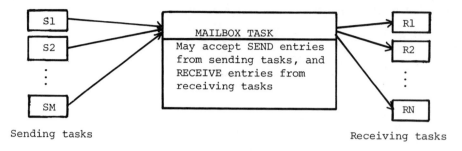

| S1 | | R1 |
| S2 | MAILBOX TASK | R2 |

Sending tasks   Receiving tasks

Figure 1.3. Mailbox with multiple sending
and receiving tasks.

second example will consider the case when the mailbox has a
finite buffer of messages.

Tasks, likc packages, have a specification part which specifies the resources made available to the user by a task, and a
body which defines the implementation of the resources. The
resources which can be provided to the user by a task include
entry resources which allow other tasks to communicate with the
given task. The following specification for a MAILBOX task has
an entry called SEND which allows other tasks to send mail to the
task and an entry called RECEIVE which allows other tasks to
receive mail from the task.

Example 1.43. Specification for a MAILBOX task

```
task MAILBOX is
   entry SEND(INMAIL: in MESSAGE);      -- entry for sending mail to task
   entry RECEIVE(OUTMAIL: out MESSAGE); -- entry for receiving mail from task
end;
```

The entries of a task may be called from other tasks by
entry calls which are syntactically just like procedure calls.
However, entry calls require synchronization between the calling
and called tasks before they can be executed. An entry call
in a calling task can be executed only if there is an accept
statement in the called task that is ready to accept it.

The mechanism for synchronizing an entry call in a calling
task and an accept statement in a called task will be illustrated
by considering the task body of the MAILBOX task.

26

Example 1.44. A task body

```
task body MAILBOX is
   BUFFER: MESSAGE;              -- local buffer, can store single message
begin
   loop
      accept SEND(INMAIL: in MESSAGE) do  -- accept SEND call from other task
         BUFFER := INMAIL;                -- store message from sending task
      end;
      accept RECEIVE(OUTMAIL: out MESSAGE) do  -- accept RECEIVE call
         OUTMAIL := BUFFER;            -- transmit message to receiving task
      end;
   end loop;
end MAILBOX;
```

The MAILBOX task has a buffer in which messages may be stored when SEND entries are accepted from sending tasks and which serves as the message source when RECEIVE entries are accepted from receiving tasks. Since messages must be sent to the mailbox before they are transmitted and there is room for only one message in the mailbox, SEND and RECEIVE entries must be accepted in strictly alternating order.

The task may be initiated by the command "initiate MAILBOX;". This will cause the MAILBOX task to start executing in parallel with other tasks. The local variable BUFFER will be created and the task will then go into an infinite loop which alternately accepts SEND and RECEIVE entries from other tasks.

The structure of a program which defines and initiates the MAILBOX task and a number of sending and receiving tasks might be as follows.

Example 1.45. Task initiation

```
procedure TASK_EXAMPLE is
   specification of S1,S2..SM
   specification of R1, R2..RN
   specification of MAILBOX task
begin
   initiate S1, S2..SM;
   initiate R1,R2..RN;
   initiate MAILBOX;
end;
```

The specification of tasks must be defined in a declarative part textually accessible at the point at which they are initiated. The bodies of the tasks may be separately compiled.

Tasks declared within a program unit must be completed before that program unit may be exited. Thus if the procedure TASK_EXAMPLE is called, exit from the procedure must wait until all M+N+1 tasks declared and initiated within the procedure have terminated their execution.

27

We shall now examine more closely the mechanism for communication between the MAILBOX task and the sending and receiving tasks.

Execution of a call from a sending task for the entry SEND in the MAILBOX task requires both that the calling task is waiting to execute the entry call and that the called task (MAILBOX task) is waiting to execute an <u>accept</u> statement for that entry call, as illustrated in figure 1.4.

entry call for entry SEND   <u>accept</u> SEND <u>do</u>..<u>end</u>

calling task   called task

Figure 1.4. Rendezvous between calling and called tasks.

If the entry call occurs before the called task is ready to accept it, then the calling task is forced to wait until control in the called task reaches the <u>accept</u> statement. If the <u>accept</u> statement is reached before the entry call occurs, then the call can be handled immediately but the called task will be waiting on its <u>accept</u> statement until the entry call arrives. Acceptance of the entry call requires synchronization between the calling and the called tasks. When the synchronization is achieved we say that a <u>rendezvous</u> occurs.   The rendezvous consists of executing statements between the <u>do</u> and <u>end</u> keywords following the <u>accept</u> statement. These statements may involve transfer of information between the calling and called tasks and require the calling task to be suspended while they are executed. When these statements have been executed we say that the rendezvous is complete and both tasks can proceed merrily on their way.

Thus a call of the SEND entry will result in a rendezvous during which the input mail transmitted from the calling task via the parameter INMAIL will be stored in a local buffer. A call of the RECEIVE entry results in a rendezvous during which the message in the buffer is transmitted to the calling program via the parameter OUTMAIL.

If entry calls for the entry SEND occur more rapidly than they can be accepted, they are placed in a queue and handled in a first-come-first-served order. In general, every entry of every task must have a queue to hold entry calls which have not yet been serviced.

The rendezvous mechanism is the basic Ada mechanism for synchronization between concurrently executing processes. It is a high-level structuring mechanism when compared to lower-level synchronization mechanisms such as semaphores. It imposes a discipline of communication between tasks that is akin to the discipline imposed by structured programming. It appears to be a natural mechanism for communication, although escape to a lower-level mechanism may sometimes be necessary, just as use of a goto statement is sometimes necessary in structured programming.

1.11 Selection Among Task Entries

The accept statement may be viewed as a mechanism which enables a task to wait for a predetermined event, indicated by the calling of an entry. However, in many parallel programming applications we cannot predict the order in which entries will occur, and wish to allow a task to choose its next action from among several entry calls.

Consider, for example, a mailbox whose buffer has a capacity of n messages with the property that a message can be written into the buffer provided it is not full and can be read from the buffer provided it is not empty.

In implementing such a mailbox we wish to execute SEND and RECEIVE entries in the order in which they arrive provided the buffer is not full when SEND is encountered and not empty when RECEIVE is encountered. The conditional execution of entries can be specified by conditional (guarded) accept statements as follows.

Example 1.46. Guarded accept statements

```
when NOT_FULL => accept SEND(..)..     -- SEND only when buffer is not full
when NOT_EMPTY => accept RECEIVE(..).. -- RECEIVE only when buffer not empty
```

We cannot predict the order in which SEND and RECEIVE entry calls for a buffered mailbox task will occur. If the language is to support execution of SEND and RECEIVE entries in the order of their occurrence, it needs a mechanism for choosing among alternative accept statements depending on the order in which entry calls occur. This mechanism is the select statement. Choice between accepting a SEND call (providing the buffer is not full) and accepting a RECEIVE call (provided the buffer is not empty) can be specified as follows.

Example 1.47. Selection among guarded accept statements

```
select
   when NOT_FULL => accept SEND(..)..
or
   when NOT_EMPTY => accept RECEIVE(..)..
end select;
```

A select statement is executed by first evaluating the when conditions (NOT_EMPTY and NOT_FULL) to determine the set of accept statements which are candidates for execution (called open accept statements). The set of open accept statements is then

29

checked to determine if there are waiting entry calls. If one or more open <u>accept</u> statements has a waiting entry call, then one of them is chosen nondeterministically* for execution. If no open <u>accept</u> statement has a waiting entry call, then execution is suspended until an entry call for one of the open <u>accept</u> statements occurs.

The buffered mailbox task below is essentially an infinite loop which repeatedly executes a <u>select</u> statement of the form given in the previous example. The local variables SIZE and COUNT respectively specify the buffer size and the number of elements in the buffer, while the local variables NEXTIN, NEXTOUT indicate the buffer index for the next SEND message and RECEIVE message.

Example 1.48. Buffered mailboxes

```
task body MAILBOX is
  SIZE: constant INTEGER := 20;              -- buffer size
  BUFFER: array(1..SIZE) of MESSAGE;
  NEXTIN, NEXTOUT: INTEGER range 1..SIZE := 1;
  COUNT: INTEGER range 0..SIZE := 0;         -- number of items in buffer
begin
  loop
    select
      when COUNT < SIZE =>      -- guard which checks that buffer is not full
        accept SEND(INMAIL: in MESSAGE) do  -- before accepting message
          BUFFER(NEXTIN) := INMAIL; -- critical section; must be executed
        end;                       -- before calling task resumes
        NEXTIN := NEXTIN mod SIZE + 1; -- statements outside critical section
        COUNT := COUNT+1;     -- may be executed concurrently with calling task
      or
      when COUNT > 0 =>          -- guard which checks that buffer is not empty
        accept RECEIVE(OUTMAIL: out MESSAGE) do  -- before transmitting message
          OUTMAIL := BUFFER(NEXTOUT);
        end;
        NEXTOUT := NEXTOUT mod SIZE + 1;  -- bookkeeping statements which record
        COUNT := COUNT - 1;       -- that message was transmitted
    end select;
  end loop;
end MAILBOX;
```

This task body illustrates that tasks are resources which may have locally declared identifiers (such as buffers and counters) required to implement the service provided by the task to its users. When the buffer is neither empty nor full, which is the usual case for a buffer of size 20, then both guarded <u>accept</u> statements will be open and SEND and RECEIVE calls may be accepted on a first-come-first-served basis.

_____

*The choice among entry calls of open accept statements is nondeterministic in the sense that user programs should not depend on particular scheduling assumptions. However, the choice need not be random. Any "fair" scheduling strategy, such as a "round-robin" strategy, can be used by the system to implement nondeterministic choice among entry calls of open <u>accept</u> statements.

30

The program text between <u>do</u> and <u>end</u> following an <u>accept</u>
statement is sometimes referred to as a <u>critical section</u>. A
calling task cannot resume execution until execution of the
critical section of the <u>accept</u> statement in the called task has
been completed, and such critical sections should therefore be
kept as short as possible. The present example illustrates that
the statements executed in the called task as a result of rendezvous may include both statements within the critical section
(which pass information between the calling and called task) and
statements outside the critical section which may be executed
concurrently with the calling task.

1.12 Generic Modules

Modules, like procedures, may be defined to be generic.
Generic modules may have formal parameters and may be instantiated with different actual parameter values for different
instances of the module.

A favorite example of generic modules is a stack package
with push and pop operations.* In the following example both the
stack size and the type of the stack elements are generic parameters.

Example 1.49. A generic package

```
generic (SIZE: INTEGER; type ELEMENT)
package STACK is
   procedure PUSH(IN_ELEM: in ELEMENT);
   procedure POP(OUT_ELEM: out ELEMENT);
   FULL, EMPTY: exception;
end STACK;
```

This generic definition is a template. Instances of stacks
each with a specific size and type may be created by instantiation.

Example 1.50. Instantiation of a generic package

```
package STACK1 is new STACK(100, INTEGER);
package STACK2 is new STACK(50, INTEGER);
package STACK3 is new STACK(75, CHARACTER);
package STACK4 is new STACK(W, RATIONAL);
```

———————
*A (pushdown) stack is a data structure in which elements can
be stored by "push" operations and retrieved by subsequent "pop"
operations. The pop operation retrieves the most recent element
pushed onto the stack, so that information is retrieved in a last-
in-first-out order. Nongeneric stack packages require elements to
be of a specific type (such as INTEGER) and have a fixed maximum
number of elements. The generic definition allows us to define
as many different stacks as we want, each with its own size and
element type.

31

The generic facility would be useful for creating multiple instances of a package (or task) even in the absence of parameters. The previous example illustrates not only the ability to vary stack attributes but also the ability to create multiple stacks which could all have the same attributes.

The ability to create multiple instances of a module is particularly important in the case of task modules. Many concurrent processing applications involve the modeling of situations where there are multiple instances of a given object, such as a ship, plane or radar monitor. In this case it is natural to create a prototype generic task for the class of object introduced by a declaration of the following form.

Example 1.51. Parameterless generic task module

```
generic task SHIP is
   specification of resources
   which constitute a ship
end SHIP;
```

Instantiations of this generic task may be defined by instantiation statements such as "task QE2 is new SHIP;".

Multiple instances of a task can be created either by instantiating a generic task as suggested above or by specifying a one-dimensional array of tasks of a given type called a task family. A one-dimensional array of ships could be specified as follows.

Example 1.52. Task families

```
task SHIP(1..1000) is
   specification of resources
   which constitute a ship
end SHIP;
```

The above specification allows the user to refer to individual tasks as SHIP(55) or SHIP(I).

A task family should be regarded, for purposes of optimizing storage space, as a potential rather than actual collection of tasks. Execution of an initiate statement for a given member of the family such as "initiate SHIP(55);" may be regarded as a command not only to initiate the task but also to create an instance of the task.

The generic mechanism for subprograms and modules is fundamentally the same, and provides a facility for both parametric variation of templates and for the creation of multiple instances of templates. However, the way in which the generic facility is used is likely to differ for modules and procedures.

Procedures already have a parameter facility. Moreover, a procedure call is effectively an instantiation of the procedure for specific values of actual parameters. Thus the generic facility for procedures duplicates many of the facilities already provided by procedures, and is useful primarily as providing more powerful parametrization (for types and subprograms) which may require the generation of different code for different instances.

Modules do not have parameters and there is no mechanism other than the generic mechanism for creating multiple instances. Thus there is much less duplication of already-existing facilities in the case of modules. The use of parameterless generic modules for creation of multiple instances of a prototype module is likely to be widespread in large systems.

1.13 Blocks

We have completed our review of the principal language features of Ada. In the remaining sections we shall consider issues of program structure and other details necessary to understand how large programs fit together. The reader may feel that the discussion in these sections is elementary and that they should logically precede the sections on packages, tasks and generics. However, this material was deliberately placed at the end of this language overview so as to provide a minimum of digression for the reader who wishes to proceed as quickly as possible to the "meat" of the language. The remaining sections of this overview may be skipped by the reader interested only in what is in the language. They are concerned with developing an understanding of the structure of the language rather than with introducing new features.

In the present section the notion of a block is introduced and the relation between blocks and other program units is considered. This leads into a discussion of separate compilation and of the (scope) rules which determine textual accessibility to declared identifiers.

There are three kinds of program units in Ada - subprograms, modules and blocks. Subprograms and modules have been discussed in some detail in earlier sections. They have <u>names</u>, and are either stand-alone compilation units with no <u>textual</u> environment or are specified in the declarative part of an enclosing program unit. In contrast, blocks are <u>anonymous</u> program units which have the syntactic status of a statement and must occur <u>in line</u> in the <u>statement part</u> of a program unit. The declarative <u>part</u> of a <u>block is</u> introduced by the keyword <u>declare</u> and the sequence of statements of a block are bracketed <u>by the</u> keywords <u>begin</u>..<u>end</u>.

Example 1.53. Syntax of blocks

```
[declare                        -- a block has an optional
   sequence of declarations]     -- declarative part
begin                            -- and a sequence of
   sequence of statements        -- statements bracketed by
end;                             -- the keywords begin..end
```

Blocks may be used to associate local nomenclature with a sequence of statements. There are also two other reasons for enclosing sequences of statements in a block which have nothing to do with nomenclature.

1. Blocks, just like other program units, cannot be exited until all tasks declared in the block have completed execution. Thus initiate statements for a logically related set of tasks might be placed within a block to ensure that the set of tasks is completed before code following the block is executed.

2. Exception handlers may be associated with blocks (and other program units) in a manner described in section 1.18.

Thus blocks are a unit of program structure not only for purposes of nomenclature but also for purposes of task completion and exception handling.

In order to illustrate the relation between blocks and other program units, we shall start by considering the following simple block for interchanging the values of X and Y.

Example 1.54. Blocks

```
declare                  -- declarative part of block
   LOCAL: INTEGER;        -- with local variable
begin                     -- and a sequence of statements
   LOCAL := X;            -- which uses LOCAL
   X := Y;                -- and nonlocal variables X and Y
   Y := LOCAL;            -- and interchanges X and Y
end;                      -- and is then exited
```

The above block uses both the local variable LOCAL and the nonlocal variables X, Y in its body. The nonlocal variables of a block must be declared in a textually enclosing declarative part, as in the following example.

Example 1.55. Block nested in a procedure body

```
procedure BLOCKS is               -- a procedure called BLOCKS
   X,Y: INTEGER;                  -- with local variables X, Y
begin                            -- and a sequence of statements
   X := 5;                       -- which initializes X
   Y := 7;                       -- and then initializes Y
   declare                       -- and then enters a nested block
      LOCAL: INTEGER;            -- with a local variable
   begin                         -- and a sequence of statements
      LOCAL := X;                -- which uses LOCAL
      X := Y;                    -- and nonlocal X, Y
      Y := LOCAL;                -- to interchange X, Y
   end;                          -- and is then exited
   -- do something useful
end BLOCKS;                       -- finally procedure is exited
```

The in-line occurrence of blocks with local nomenclature in a procedure body makes the body difficult to read, and it is likely that, for this and other reasons, they will not be used very frequently in procedures. The block for interchanging two variables can be rewritten as a procedure with formal parameters X, Y, as in the following example.

Example 1.56. Replacement of blocks by procedures

```
procedure NO_BLOCKS is                           -- a procedure called NO_BLOCKS
   I,J: INTEGER;                                 -- with local variables
   procedure SWAP(X,Y: in out INTEGER) is        -- and nested procedure declaration
      LOCAL: INTEGER;                            -- with a local variable
   begin                                         -- and a sequence of statements
      LOCAL := X;                                -- which uses LOCAL
      X := Y;                                    -- and parameters X, Y
      Y := LOCAL;                                -- to interchange X, Y
   end SWAP;                                     -- and is then exited
begin                                            -- the body of NO_BLOCKS
   I := 5;                                       -- initializes variables I,J of NO_BLOCKS
   J := 7;
   SWAP(I,J);                                    -- invokes procedure to interchange I,J
   -- do something useful
end;                                             -- and is eventually exited
```

The body of the procedure NO_BLOCKS may be read much more easily than that of the procedure BLOCKS. Moreover, the procedure SWAP may be called at more than one textual point of the body with different values of the parameters. Thus replacing the block by a procedure increases both the readability and the flexibility of the resulting program.

Replacement of an in-line block by a procedure call introduces additional overhead which may in certain critical situations be unacceptable. The overhead may be avoided by specifying a subprogram to be in-line.

35

Example 1.57. The pragma INLINE

pragma INLINE;

    Pragmas have no effect on the semantics of a program, but are used to convey information to the compiler. The pragma INLINE occurring in the declarative part of a subprogram definition suggests to the compiler that the subprogram body be expanded in line at all instances of call. The actual effect of the pragma INLINE depends on the kinds of optimization built into the compiler. Compilers may altogether ignore this pragma and still be considered correct.

1.14 Separate Compilation

    Readers may object that the body of the NO BLOCKS procedure has been made more readable at the expense of cluttering up the declarative part of the procedure. We can improve the readability of the procedure even further by declaring the SWAP procedure to be a separate compilation unit.

Example 1.58. Separately compiled procedure declaration

```
procedure SEPARATE_SWAP is
   I,J: INTEGER;
   procedure SWAP(X,Y: in out INTEGER) is separate;   -- SWAP is separately compiled
begin
   I := 5;
   J := 7;
   SWAP(I,J);
      -- do something useful
end;
```


    The text of procedures which are declared to be separate in the context of an enclosing program unit must be introduced by a restricted clause which specifies the program unit in which the procedure is textually embedded, followed by the keyword separate. Such procedure bodies may make use of identifiers declared in the textual environment of declaration (such as I, J above). They must be compiled after the program unit in which they are declared, and recompiled if the enclosing program unit is redeclared. Such procedures are dependent on a textual environment and must be carefully distinguished from stand-alone separately compiled program units not dependent on textual environment (which are discussed in sections 1.16 and 1.17).

Example 1.59. Separately compiled procedure implementation

```
restricted (SEPARATE_SWAP)
separate procedure SWAP(X,Y: in out INTEGER) is
   TEMP: INTEGER;
begin
   TEMP := X;
   X := Y;
   Y := TEMP;
end SWAP;
```

The is separate declaration provides complete information concerning the syntactic correctness of calls of the procedure and allows the compiler to check the correctness of such calls. Programs which use a separately specified procedure need not be aware of its implementation. Moreover, changes in implementation which do not affect its specification are guaranteed not to require changes in program units which use the procedure. The fact that changes in the implementation which do not affect the specification are localized greatly enhances the maintainability of large programs. The implementation of a procedure can be changed even after programs which use it are running without affecting other parts of the program. In this way program changes which take advantage of a new hardware configuration or of machine language optimizations can be introduced in a modular fashion.

1.15 Scope of Identifiers

The scope of an identifier is the region of text over which its declaration has an effect. The scope of an identifier declared in the declarative part of a given program unit extends from its point of declaration to the end of the program unit. The following example has a procedure called OUTER with two local integer variables, A, B and a nested procedure INNER with a re-declaration of B.

Example 1.60. Scope of identifiers

```
procedure OUTER is          -- a procedure called OUTER
   A: INTEGER := 0;          -- with an integer variable A
   B: INTEGER := A+1;        -- and an integer variable B
   procedure INNER is        -- and a nested procedure called INNER
      B: BOOLEAN;            -- with B redeclared as BOOLEAN
   begin                     -- INNER has a statement sequence
      A := 1;                -- which assigns an integer to A
      B := TRUE;             -- and assigns a BOOLEAN to the inner B
      OUTER.B := A+1;        -- and accesses the outer B by OUTER.B
   end;
begin                        -- OUTER has a statement sequence
   A := 2;                   -- which assigns an integer to A
   B := TRUE;                -- illegal assignment - can be caught by compiler
   B := A+1;                 -- and assigns to the outer B
end;
```

scope of A

scope of outer B

37

In this example B is declared to be an integer variable in
the outer procedure and a Boolean variable in the inner procedure. An unqualified reference to B in the inner procedure
refers to the **inner** declaration of B, so that "B := TRUE;" is a
valid statement of the inner procedure. However, the integer
variable B may be referred to in the inner block by the qualified
name OUTER.B so that the statement "OUTER.B := A+1;" is valid.
The scope of the inner declaration of B does not extend to the
sequence of statements of the outer procedure, so that the
statement "B := TRUE;" in the outer procedure is illegal.

This example also illustrates that the outer declaration of
B is in the scope of the outer A and can therefore use the value
of A to initialize the declaration of B. Interchange of the
declarations of A and B would be illegal because B would then no
longer be declared in the scope of A and could not then use the
value of A to initialize B.

1.16 Restricted Program Units

Program unit boundaries normally act like one-way membranes,
allowing identifiers declared in textually enclosing units to be
known within the program unit, but never allowing internally
declared identifiers to be known outside the program unit. Thus
a deeply nested program unit has access to several textually
enclosing layers of environment and this could in some instances
cause confusion.

Such free accessibility to the textually enclosing environment can be avoided by the <u>restricted</u> clause. The keyword
<u>restricted</u> immediately preceding the program unit causes the
textually enclosing environment to become inaccessible to the
program unit.

Example 1.61. No access to textually enclosing environment

```
restricted procedure P (parameters) is
   -- declarations and statements which cannot access
   -- any nonlocal identifiers declared in the
   -- textual environment of P
end P;
```

A restricted clause of a given program unit may in general
contain a <u>visibility list</u> of non-local program units accessible
within the restricted program unit. The rules which determine
the portion of the environment that becomes visible when a unit
is mentioned in a visibility list depend on the textual relation
between the restricted program unit and the program unit mentioned in the visibility list.

Figure 1.5 illustrates three possible textual relations
between accessible program units mentioned in a visibility list
and the restricted program unit P. That is, the accessible
program unit may textually enclose P (like P1), may be accessible

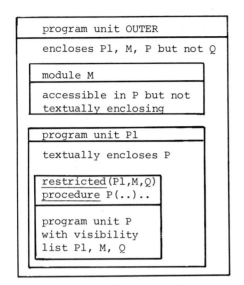

Figure 1.5.   Textual relations among program units.

but not textually enclosing (like M), or may be a stand-alone
separately compiled module (like Q).

   If P is textually nexted in Pl then occurrence of Pl in the
visibility list of P opens up accessibility of the textual environment as far out as Pl, but not beyond Pl. We can think of P as
being enclosed in a fog which allows everything to be seen as far
out as Pl but which is too thick for anything further out than Pl
to be visible.

   If M is an accessible but not textually enclosing module,
then occurrence of M in the visibility list of P provides access
to the computational resources of M but not to other identifiers
in the declarative environment of M.

   If Q is a stand-alone separately compiled module mentioned
in the visibility list of P, then P has access to the computational resources of Q.

   The first name in a visibility list may, but need not, be the
name of an enclosing program unit. The remaining names (if any)
must be names of modules that are outside the restricted unit and
outside the enclosing program unit (if the first parameter defines
one). Thus the units which are made visible by a visibility list
are essentially modules which define collections of resources
rather than individual resources.

   These rules are illustrated by the following example of a
restricted procedure P nested in a procedure Pl which is in turn
nested in a procedure OUTER containing a package M.

Example 1.62. Enclosing and non-enclosing program units

```
procedure OUTER is
   I: INTEGER;                              -- I is not accessible in P
   package M is                             -- M is accessible in P
      specification and body of M
   procedure P1 is                          -- P1 textually encloses P
      J: INTEGER;                           -- J is accessible in P
      restricted (P1,M)                     -- restricted clause for procedure P
      procedure P is                        -- P is restricted to P1, M
      begin
        J := 5;                             -- legal, we can "see" out as far as P1
        P1;                                 -- legal recursive call of P1
        I := 5;                             -- illegal; we can see M but not I
      end;
   statements of P1
statements of OUTER procedure
```

In this example the variable J declared in P1 is visible in P, but the variable I declared in OUTER but not in M is not visible in P.

1.17 Restricted Compilation Units and Libraries

Compilation units have no explicit textually enclosing environment, and it does not therefore make sense to impose visibility restrictions relating to the textual environment. However, there are implicit environments associated with compilation units whose visibility may be affected by restricted clauses.

1. The predefined environment which includes predefined types and other identifiers listed in the package STANDARD in appendix C of the language reference manual.
2. The "library" environment of compilation units which generally contain input-output packages, mathematical subroutine packages, and other standard library tools.
3. The set of stand-alone compilation units being defined by the user for the current application.

The visibility of identifiers of the predefined environment is not affected by restricted clauses. Identifiers such as INTEGER may be superseded by a redeclaration such as "type INTEGER is SHORT_INTEGER;". However, even in this case access to the original identifier is still possible by the qualified name STANDARD.INTEGER.

Library compilation units and user-defined compilation units may be made visible in a given user-defined compilation unit by mentioning them in the restricted clause of the compilation unit. Thus the input-output functions GET and PUT are in fact defined in a library package TEXT_IO, and compilation units using GET and PUT must include TEXT_IO in a restricted clause associated with the compilation unit.

Example 1.63. Communication among compilation units

```
restricted (TEXT_IO) -- the library package TEXT_IO is accessible in SIMPLE_ADD
procedure SIMPLE_ADD is
  use TEXT_IO;        -- its resources may be accessed without name qualification
  X,Y,Z: INTEGER;
begin
  GET(X);             -- GET and PUT are procedures declared in SIMPLE_ADD
  GET(Y);
  Z := X+Y;
  PUT(Z);
end;
```

Example 1.1 at the beginning of this chapter is, in fact, an incomplete program which would give rise to a compiler diagnostic indicating that GET and PUT are undefined. The above program is the complete version and could, with appropriate data, be executed.

User-defined compilation units have exactly the same status in the environment as library compilation units. The operating system for running Ada programs will generally contain a library file for each user which is updated whenever a compilation unit is compiled. Thus every compilation unit requires as input the text of the compilation unit and the library file and produces as output a compiled compilation unit and an updated library file (see figure 1.6).

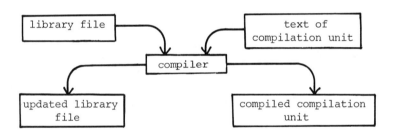

Figure 1.6. Effect of compiling a compilation unit.

Communication among compilation units of a user program requires mention of used compilation units in the visibility list of the restricted clause of the compilation unit in which they are used.

Mention of a compilation unit Cl in the restricted clause of a compilation unit C requires that the specification of Cl must already have been compiled at the time that C is compiled. The visibility dependencies determined by restricted clauses must determine a sequential (non-circular) hierarchy and must be compiled so that earlier program units of the hierarchy are compiled before later ones.

However, this dependency applies only to interface specifications of program units. Thus if Cl is a package, then the
specification of Cl must be compiled before any compilation units
which mention Cl in a restricted clause, but the package body of
Cl may be compiled and recompiled at any time without affecting
the compilation of compilation units which use Cl.

1.18 Exceptions

Exceptions provide a mechanism for the unusual termination
of program units. Normal termination of blocks and procedures
occurs by executing the last statement of the body, while normal
termination of functions is by executing a return statement.
Exceptions provide a dynamic mechanism for exit from program
units which bypasses the above normal termination mechanisms.

Exceptions may be defined by the user or predefined by the
system. Predefined exceptions may be illustrated by INDEX_ERROR
(when an index is outside the range specified by an array).
Since INDEX_ERROR is a predefined exception there is a system-
defined "default" action when an index error occurs. However,
this system-defined action may be superseded by user-defined
actions to handle index errors in specific parts of the program.

We shall illustrate below how exceptions may be declared,
raised and "handled" (by an exception handler). Declaration of
an exception is similar to declaration of a typed variable.

Example 1.64. Declaration of exceptions

```
OVERFLOW, UNDERFLOW: exception;      -- declare two exception identifiers
          SINGULAR:  exception;      -- and another one
```


Exceptions may be raised by use of the keyword raise.

Example 1.65. Raising of exceptions

```
if DETERMINANT = 0 then              -- raise SINGULAR
   raise SINGULAR;                   -- if DETERMINANT is zero
end if;
```


Exceptions which are raised are handled by exception handlers. Exception handlers may appear only after the statement
sequence of a subprogram, module or block after the keyword
exception. Each individual exception handler is introduced by
the keyword when, followed by the exception name, followed by
the sequence of statements which handle the exception.

42

Example 1.66. Handling of exceptions

```
exception                         -- exception handler for SINGULAR
  when SINGULAR =>                 -- must appear at the end of
    PUT ("MATRIX IS SINGULAR");    -- a block, subprogram or module
```

Raising of an exception has some of the properties of a parameterless procedure call, and an exception handler has some of the properties of a parameterless procedure specification. However, the mechanism for associating a handler with a raised exception differs from the corresponding mechanism for procedures.

When an exception is raised during execution of a subprogram, a handler is sought first local to the subprogram, then in the environment of call of the subprogram, and then in successive dynamically preceding program units. This dynamic criterion for determining the handler associated with a raised exception contrasts with the static scope criterion of associating a procedure with a procedure call.

The dynamic mechanism for associating handlers with raised exceptions is illustrated by the following procedure P which has a handler (the first handler) in the body of the main procedure P and a second handler in the body of the procedure R.

Example 1.66. Dynamic search for exception handlers

```
procedure P is
    SINGULAR: exception;              -- declare exception SINGULAR in P
    procedure Q is
    begin
      ...
      if DETERMINANT = 0 then         -- code in Q which raises
        raise SINGULAR;               -- the exception SINGULAR
      end if;
      ...
    end Q;
    procedure R is
    begin
      ...Q...                         -- call of Q within R
    exception                         -- if exception occurs during this call
      when SINGULAR =>                -- of Q then second handler is selected
        -- second handler for SINGULAR
    end R;
begin -- P
    ...R...Q...                       -- call of Q in main body of P
exception                             -- if exception occurs during this call
    when SINGULAR =>                  -- of Q then first handler is selected
      -- first handler for SINGULAR
end P;
```

If, in the above example, the exception SINGULAR is raised in the call of Q within R, a search is made first for a handler within Q and then for a handler within R, so that the second handler is selected. If SINGULAR is raised in a call of Q in the main body of P, then the first handler is selected.

The action when handling of an exception has been completed differs from the corresponding procedure action of returning to the environment of call. An exception is regarded as an error. The environments in which the exception occurs and the environment in which it is handled are always abandoned. The exception handler is a mechanism for unusual completion of the subprogram in which the exception is handled. Thus, in the above example, raising of the exception SINGULAR within Q (within R) would cause the exception handler to terminate Q, and would cause the exception handler for SINGULAR within R to be executed in place of the normal sequence of code for completing the execution of R. On completion of the exception handler, control would be returned to the program which called R.

The process of terminating a subprogram because a raised exception is not handled, and then reraising the exception in the calling program, is called propagating the exception. Thus an exception raised in a given subprogram is propagated backwards through the dynamic chain of calls until a subprogram which handles the exception is found. The exception is then executed in the environment of the handler, constitutes unusual completion of that subprogram, and results in return to the point of call of the subprogram in which the handler is defined.

In addition to user-defined exceptions, there are predefined exceptions whose handlers are defined by the system. Some predefined exceptions such as DIVIDE_ERROR or INDEX_ERROR are automatically raised by the system (when an attempt is made to divide by zero or to access a nonexistent array element). Other predefined exceptions, such as FAILURE (raising of failure of task T2 within task T1) must be explicitly raised by the user to activate the system implementation. A complete list of predefined exceptions is given in the language manual (section 11).

The detection of exceptions may be suppressed. For example, if a time-critical computation wishes to save the time of checking for index errors in a given program unit, this can be accomplished by including the following pragma in the declarative part of the program unit.

Example 1.67. Suppression of implicit exceptions

pragma SUPPRESS (INDEX_ERROR);

This pragma allows the compiler to omit run-time checks for index errors in compiling the program unit but does not require the compiler to do so. Both the pragma SUPPRESS and the previously-discussed pragma INLINE are suggestions to the compiler to perform certain kinds of optimization, but may be ignored by the compiler. The pragma SUPPRESS should be used with caution, both because it can lead to uncontrolled program

44

behavior when the suppressed exception occurs and is not properly
handled, and because programs with suppressed exceptions may
behave differently for different compilers.

2

BASIC LANGUAGE FEATURES

2.1   Introduction

Now that we have an overview of Ada as a whole, we are ready for a more detailed examination of its individual features. The present chapter will consider the expressions, statements, control structures and subprograms of Ada. Chapter 3 will examine data description facilities. Chapter 4 will consider packages, and Chapter 5 will deal with tasks.

We shall start by briefly considering "low-level" program constituents such as the character set and the lexical units of Ada, then consider expressions, statements and control structures, and finally discuss "high-level" program constituents (functions and procedures).

2.2   Character Set and Lexical Units

The basic Ada character set consists of 55 characters including the 26 letters, the 10 decimal digits, the space character, and the following special characters:

" # & ' ( ) * + , - . / : ; < = > _ |

There is also an extended character set which includes the above characters and, in addition, the lower-case letters and the following special characters:

! $ % ? @ [\ ] ^ ` { } ~

The basic character set is guaranteed to be available at every Ada installation. The extended character set provides greater expressive power but is not guaranteed to be available. Standard transliteration rules are defined for representing the extended character set in terms of the basic character set.

The lowest-level program constructs with linguistic meaning are called lexical units. The lexical units of Ada include identifiers (such as ALPHA, A), numbers (such as 365, 3.65, 3.65E2), strings (such as "I AM A STRING"), delimiters (such as ;, >=), and reserved words (such as for, task, and begin).

Identifiers must start with a letter and may contain letters, digits and the underscore character (as in I_53_52_6). Numbers may be integers (which contain no decimal point) or approximate numbers (which contain a decimal point and/or the exponent symbol E). Numbers may contain underscore characters for clarity (as in 1_000_000_000). Character strings appear in quotes. Delimiters include single characters such as + or double characters such as := (assignment).

Reserved words may not be used as identifiers in Ada programs, so that they need not be marked in any special way when writing programs. However, for the sake of clarity, reserved words are always underscored in the present text. The sixty-two reserved words of Ada are listed in Table 1 below.

abort	digits	initiate	pragma	type
accept	do	is	private	
access			procedure	use
all	else	loop		
and	elsif		raise	when
array	end	mod	range	while
assert	entry		record	
at	exception	new	renames	xor
	exit	not	restricted	
begin		null	return	
body	for		reverse	
	function	of		
case		or	select	
constant	generic	others	separate	
	goto	out	subtype	
declare				
delay	if	package	task	
delta	in	packing	then	

Table 1. List of reserved words.

Spaces cannot appear within lexical units but may appear freely with no effect on meaning between lexical units. At least one space must appear between lexical units such as identifiers and numbers where absence of a space would cause an ambiguity. However, spaces need not occur between lexical units when this causes no ambiguity (as in 3+4*5).

Comments start with a double minus sign (hyphen) and are terminated by the end of the line. They have no effect on the meaning of a program.

Example 2.1. Comments

```
-- comments can appear on any line
-- following all lexical units of the line
-- they can also appear as stand-alone
-- comments taking up the whole line
```

Note that the above comment uses lower-case letters (for readability) and is written in the extended character set rather than the basic character set. We shall mostly use the basic character set but will not hesitate to use the extended character set where this improves readability.

Pragmas are used to convey information to the compiler. They are like comments in that they generally have no effect on the computation performed by a program. But a pragma can have considerable effect on the information supplied to the user as a result of compiling or executing a program.

Example 2.2. A pragma which provides extra information

```
pragma LIST(ON);    -- provide the user with a listing of the program
```

Some pragmas, such as that above, specify a definite oblig-atory action on the part of the compiler. Other pragmas, such as the ones in the next example, are suggestions to the compiler which may or may not be implemented.

Example 2.3. Pragmas which perform optimization

```
pragma INLINE;            -- compile calls of subprogram in line
pragma OPTIMIZE(SPACE);   -- implement so that space utilization is small
```

Both of these pragmas suggest optimizations which do not change the functional effect of a program, and whose actual effect will depend heavily on the sophistication of the compiler.

The following pragmas perform compile-time actions which may affect the functional effect of a program.

Example 2.4. Pragmas which change functional effect

```
pragma INCLUDE("name");  -- substitute the text file named in the pragma at
                         -- the program point where this pragma occurs
pragma SUPPRESS(exception names);  -- run-time checks for the named exceptions
                         -- may (but need not) be suppressed in the program
                         -- unit where this pragma occurs
```

A more complete specification of pragmas available in the language is given in Appendix B of the language reference manual.

2.3 Simple Expressions and Assignment Statements

The lexical units which can occur in expressions include literals, variables, operators and delimiters. For example, the expression "2*(I+3)" contains the literals 2, 3, the variable I, the operators *, + and the delimiters (,).

Evaluation of an expression yields a value which can be assigned to a variable by an assignment statement.

Example 2.5. Assignment statements

```
I := 3;        -- assign the literal 3 to the variable I
J := 2*(I+3);  -- evaluate 2*(I+3) and assign the result to J
K := J*I**2;   -- if I=3 and J=12 then J*I**2 = 12*9 = 96
```

Every literal, variable and expression in Ada has an associated type which can be determined at compile time. All expressions in the above example have an integer type and the variables to which expressions are assigned likewise have an integer type. The following example embeds the above statements in a procedure which explicitly indicates that the variables I, J, K are integers.

Example 2.6. Statements with declarations

```
procedure INTEGERS is   -- a procedure called INTEGERS
   I,J,K: INTEGER;      -- with three declared integer variables
begin                   -- and a sequence of statements
   I := 3;              -- which assigns values to the variables
   J := I+1;
   K := J*I**2;
end INTEGERS;
```

Floating-point literals may be distinguished from integers by the fact that they contain a decimal point and/or the symbol E.

Example 2.7. Floating-point literals

```
3.65        -- a floating-point literal
3.65E2      -- a floating-point literal with value 365.0
1E-2        -- a floating-point literal with value .01
```

The following procedure illustrates the declaration and use of floating-point variables.

Example 2.8. Floating-point variables

```
procedure FLOATING is          -- a procedure called FLOATING
   X,Y,Z: FLOAT;               -- with three declared floating-point variables
begin                          -- and a sequence of statements
   X := 3.65;                  -- which assigns values to the variables
   Y := X+1E-2;                -- value of Y becomes 3.66
   Z := X*Y**2;                -- you work out value of Z
end FLOATING;
```

Operators such as + and * require both operands to be of the same type, so that an expression with an integer and floating-point operand, such as "1+3.5", is illegal. An assignment statement similarly requires the expression on the right-hand side to have the same type as the variable on the left-hand side.

Example 2.9. Mixed integer and floating types

```
procedure MIXED_TYPES is    -- a procedure which illustrates mixed types
   I,J: INTEGER;            -- with declarations of integer variables
   X,Y: FLOAT;              -- and floating-point variables
begin
   I := 3.5; -- illegal assignment of floating value to integer variable
   X := I+1; -- illegal assignment of integer expression to floating variable
   X := X+1; -- illegal mixed expression
   X := X+FLOAT(1);         -- legal conversion of integer to FLOAT
   X := FLOAT(I+J);         -- legal conversion of expression to FLOAT
   I := INTEGER(3.65);      -- conversion causes truncation; I gets value 3
end MIXED_TYPES;
```

This example illustrates that the type names INTEGER and FLOAT may be used as conversion functions which respectively convert values to the type INTEGER and FLOAT.

Numeric operands in Ada may be operated on not only by arithmetic operators which take arguments of a given numeric type and produce a value of the same type, but also by relational operators (such as "<") which take arguments of an arithmetic type and produce a value TRUE or FALSE.

Example 2.10. Relational expressions

```
3<4        -- a relational expression with value TRUE
4.5<3.5    -- a relational expression with value FALSE
3<4.5      -- illegal, cannot use integer and floating-point operands
X<Y        -- TRUE if X,Y are of same type and if value of X is less than
           -- value of Y
```

The literals TRUE, FALSE are literals of the type BOOLEAN and may be values of Boolean variables, The logical operators and, or, xor (exclusive or) and not have Boolean operands and produce Boolean results.

Example 2.11. Boolean expressions

```
TRUE, FALSE        -- the two Boolean literals
A := TRUE;         -- assignment to a Boolean variable
B := X<Y;          -- Boolean value of X<Y is assigned to B
C := A and B;      -- TRUE if both A and B are true
```

The operators which can occur in arithmetic and Boolean expressions have six levels of precedence, as illustrated in Table 2.

```
exponentiation operator:   **            -- highest precedence
multiplying operators:     * / mod
unary operators:           + - not
adding operators:          + -
relational operators:      = /= < <= > >=
logical operators:         and or xor -- lowest precedence
```

Table 2. Arithmetic, Boolean and relational operators.

These six levels of precedence reflect the usual conventions in writing mathematical expressions, but there are some slightly unusual implications when mixing arithmetic and Boolean expressions.

Example 2.12. Mixed arithmetic and Boolean expressions

```
X+1 > Y                -- means (X+1) > Y
X+1 > Y or X = 0       -- means ((X+1) > Y) or (X = 0)
X > Y or not(X = 0)    -- precedence of not over = causes anomaly
```

In the last example, leaving out the parentheses would be illegal since not X = 0 would be interpreted as (not X) = 0.

The only remaining unexplained operator in Table 2 is the mod operator which takes integer operands and returns as its value the remainder of dividing the first operand by the second operand. Thus 20 mod 7 has the value 6 and 14 mod 7 has the value 0.

2.4 Conditional Statements (If and Case Statements)

Assignment statements are the primary low-level mechanism for performing computations. The performance of a computational task generally requires the execution of a sequence of assignment statements. The order of execution and number of statements executed are controlled by control structures.

Conditional statements allow dynamic choice at execution time between alternative courses of action. For example, the following if statement, which assigns the maximum of X and Y to the variable Z, will give rise to a dynamic choice between execution of two alternative assignment statements, depending on the values of X and Y.

Example 2.13. If statement with two branches

```
if X < Y then            -- if the condition X < Y is true
   Z := Y;               -- then set Z to Y
else                     -- otherwise
   Z := X;               -- set Z to X
end if;                  -- explicit termination of if statement
```

The above if statement has two branches which may be referred to as a then clause and an else clause. If statements may also contain elsif clauses, as in the following example.

Example 2.14. Multiple-branch conditional statement

```
if X < 0 then            -- if this condition is true
   Y := -1;              -- then do this action
elsif X = 0 then         -- else if this condition is true
   Y := 0;               -- then do this action
else                     -- in all remaining cases
   Y := 1;               -- do this action
end if;                  -- terminate if statement
```

In general an if statement may contain a sequence of statements in each branch and may contain an arbitrary number of elsif statements, each with a condition that determines when its sequence of statements is executed. The general form of the if statement is follows:*

Example 2.15. Syntax of if statement

```
if condition then        -- an if statement has if part with a condition
   sequence of statements -- and then clause consisting of statement sequence
{elsif condition then    -- and an arbitrary (possibly zero) number of
   sequence of statements} -- elsif clauses
[else                    -- and an optional else clause
   sequence of statements] -- with an associated statement sequence
end if;                  -- and an explicit termination delimiter
```

An if statement must always have a then clause. It may have no elsif or else clauses, in which case truth of its then

---

*Following the conventions of the reference manual, we enclose constructs which can occur an arbitrary (possibly zero) number of times (such as elsif clauses) by curly brackets and enclose optional constructs (such as else clauses) by square brackets. We will not in general specify the syntax of language constructs, but include syntactic specifications in a few cases where this is judged to be especially helpful.

condition causes these statements to be skipped. Each elsif
clause determines a further set of statements which may condi-
tionally be executed. The else clause, if present, specifies
what is to be done in cases not covered by the sequence of
conditions in earlier clauses.

The case statement, like the if statement, has a set of
branches whose execution is triggered by associated conditions.
However, for case statements the conditions have a special form.
Moreover, it is guaranteed that only one of the conditions can
be true, so that the order in which conditions are specified and
tested can be changed without changing the meaning of the program.

The following case statement has a control variable Y and
three branches. The first branch is executed when Y has a value
of -1. The second branch is executed when Y has a value of 0 or
1. The third branch is executed for any other value of Y.

Example 2.16. Case statement with control variable

```
case Y of                              -- Y is a control variable
  when -1 => NEGATIVE_ACTION;          -- action when Y is -1
  when 0|1 => NON_NEGATIVE_ACTION;     -- action when Y is 0 or 1
  when others => ERROR_ACTION;         -- action for other values of Y
end case;
```

The expressions following the keyword when are called choice
expressions and specify value sets which must be statically deter-
minable at compile time. The value sets associated with each when
must be disjoint, and should between them include all possible
values of the control variable. The others alternative is
similar to the else alternative for if statements in that it is
a catch-all category which includes all potential values of the
control variable not mentioned in when alternatives.

2.5   Iteration Statements (For and While Statements)

Conditional statements are concerned with selection among
alternative component statements. In contrast, iteration statements are concerned with specifying patterns of repetition of
component statements.

The basic iteration construct in Ada is the loop statement.
Loop statements in their simplest form specify unconditional
repetitive execution of the loop body.

Example 2.17. Unconditional loop statement

```
loop                     -- beginning of a loop
  X := X+1;              -- with a loop body consisting of two statements
  exit when X = 1000;   -- including an exit statement (see section 2.6)
end loop;               -- end of loop
```

53

In the above example, exit from the loop is determined by a condition within the loop. Alternatively, loop statements may be qualified by a condition which specifies a pattern of repetition and the circumstances under which the loop will terminate. For statements and while statements represent two alternative mechanisms for associating a pattern of repetition with a loop statement.

The for statement specifies a pattern of repetition in terms of a sequence of values of a control variable, as in the following example for computing the sum of the first N integers.

Example 2.18. Simple for statement

```
SUM := 0;             -- initialize loop
for I in 1..10 loop   -- with control variable I taking values 1..10
   SUM := SUM+I;       -- and loop body which adds I to SUM
end loop;             -- and then repeats
```

The control variable is often used as an index of an array, as in the following example which sums the first ten elements of the array A.

Example 2.19. Iteration over arrays

```
SUM := 0;
for I in 1..10 loop
   SUM := SUM+A(I);
end loop;
```

The control variable of a for loop is accessible only within the loop. Thus in the following loop, which searches for an element with value V in the array A, the index value for which A(I) matches V must be assigned to a nonlocal variable K before exit from the loop.

Example 2.20. Search loop with exit

```
K := 0;                 -- value of K if no match is found
for I in 1..N loop      -- loop for successive values of control variable I
   if A(I) = V then     -- if A(I) matches V
      K := I;            -- then set K to matching index
      exit;             -- and exit
   end if;              -- if A(I) ≠ V then do nothing
end loop;               -- and repeat for next value of I
```

The set of values taken by the control variable (specified between the keywords in and loop) can be any ordered set having a minimum element, maximum element and a successor function which specifies a unique successor for all elements other than the maximum. Such a set is called a discrete range. The set 1..N is clearly a discrete range (it has a minimum, maximum and successor function). The set N..1 is another example of a discrete

54

range and can be specified as "reverse 1..N". The following for
loop computes N factorial by multiplying factors in the order
N*(N-1)*(N-2)...*2*1.

Example 2.21. Reverse for loop computation

```
FACT := 1;
for I in reverse 1..N loop
  FACT := I * FACT;
end loop;
```

For statements are useful when repetition is over a predefined set of cases specified by a sequence of values of a control variable. However, when repetition is governed by occurrence of a computed data condition, such as convergence of a
function to a fixed value, then for statements are not appropriate. Such cases can generally be handled by a while statement. The following program fragment for computing the square
root of X illustrates use of the while statement.

Example 2.22. While statement

```
ROOT := 1.0;
while ABS(ROOT*ROOT-X) > .0001 loop      -- while this condition holds
  ROOT := 0.5 *(ROOT + X / ROOT);        -- perform this action
end loop;                                -- and repeat
```

The body of this while statement has a single assignment
statement which computes a new approximation to the square root
in terms of the previous one. The computation terminates when
the square of the current approximation is within .0001 of the
value of X.

Another example of the use of a while statement is the
following program for simulating division by repeated subtrac-
tion.

Example 2.23. While statement

```
QUOTIENT := 0;
while NUMBER >= DIVISOR loop           -- division
  NUMBER := NUMBER - DIVISOR;          -- by repeated subtraction
  QUOTIENT := QUOTIENT + 1;            -- count number of subtractions
end loop;
```

In a for statement the number of repetitions is the number
of elements in its range specification and is known on entry to
the for statement. In the present example, we do not know the
number of repetitions on entry to the while statement. In fact,
the purpose of the while statement is to compute the number of
repetitions (the final value of QUOTIENT). It is evident that
this could not easily be done with a for statement, and that the

more general <u>while</u> statement is, in this case, a more appro-
pirate iteration mechanism.

A final example of the use of <u>while</u> statements is the case
of reading and processing an arbitrary number of data items from
an input file until a termination symbol (end of file) occurs.

Example 2.24. While loop for file input

```
read next data item
while good data loop
  process data item
  read next data item
end loop;
```

Such an iteration can be performed by a <u>for</u> statement when
the number of data items is known ahead of time, but is more
appropriately performed by a <u>while</u> statement if termination of
the data stream is indicated within the data stream itself.

The <u>if</u>, <u>case</u> and <u>loop</u> statements are <u>compound statements</u>
which control the sequence in which component statements are to
be executed. In the next section we shall consider two more
primitive control structures - the <u>goto</u> and <u>exit</u> statements -
which simply specify transfer of control from one point in a
program to another.

2.6 Jump Statements (Exit and Go To Statements)

Control over the sequence in which statements are executed
may be specified either by compound statements such as the <u>if</u>,
<u>case</u>, and <u>loop</u> statements which control the order in which com-
ponent statements are executed, or by simple transfer of control
statements which specify a label to which control is to be
transferred.

A label is represented by the notation <<L>>. Transfer of
control to a labelled statement may be accomplished by a <u>goto</u>
statement. Use of the <u>goto</u> statement is illustrated by the
following example of searching through an array for an element
V.

Example 2.25. The goto statement

```
K := 0;
for I in 1..N loop
  if A(I) = V then
    K := I;
    go to FOUND;
  end if;
end loop;
<<FOUND>>
if K = 0 then
  perform action for no A(K) = V
else
  perform action for A(K) = V
end if;
```

Since the need to escape from a loop to the first statement beyond the end of the loop occurs frequently in practice, there is a special statement called the exit statement for accomplishing such transfer of control. The above example can be rewritten using the exit statement as follows.

Example 2.26. The exit statement

```
K := 0;
for I in 1..N loop
  if A(I) = V then
    K := I;
    exit;
  end if;
end loop;
if K = 0 then
    ...
```

The exit statement in the above program exits from the innermost enclosing loop statement and causes execution to continue with the next statement in sequence.

Exit statements may in general exit from several levels of enclosing loops by a statement of the form "exit L;" where L is the label of the loop statement to be exited. Exit statements may be conditional, as in the following version of the search program.

Example 2.27. Conditional exit statement

```
for I in 1..N loop
  K := I;
  exit when A(I) = V;
end loop;
```

This version of the search program is simpler than the previous one because we have been able to eliminate the if statement by specifying the condition as part of the <u>exit</u> statement. However, it takes a little longer to execute because K is set to the current value of I on every iteration, while the previous version sets K to I only when a match occurs. Moreover, this version does not adequately handle the case when no match occurs (it treats it in a way that is indistinguishable from a match of the last element).

The forms of the <u>exit</u> statement may be summarized as follows.

Example 2.28. Forms of exit statement

```
exit;                        -- unqualified form, exit innermost enclosing loop
exit L;                      -- exit loop labelled L
exit when condition;         -- exit innermost loop when condition holds
exit L when condition;       -- exit from loop L when condition holds
```

The <u>exit</u> statement handles a large fraction of transfer of control situations where a <u>goto</u> statement might otherwise be needed. However, the following example of a bubble sort program requires jumping back to the beginning of the loop whenever two elements are out of order. Such a jump is handled more appropriately by a <u>goto</u> statement than an <u>exit</u> statement.

Example 2.29. Bubble sort with goto statement

```
<<SORT>> for I in 1..N-1 loop      -- loop executed once for each interchange
            if A(I) < A(I+1) then  -- comparison determines if interchange necessary
               TEMP := A(I);       -- number of interchanges is proportional to N²
               A(I) := A(I+1);     -- comparisons per interchange proportional to N
               A(I+1) := TEMP;     -- total number of comparisons proportional to N³
               go to SORT;         -- try loop again after interchange
            end if;                -- if loop complete without any interchanges
         end loop SORT;            -- then vector is sorted
```

The above program is a very inefficient sorting program. It takes a time proportional to N^3 for sorting N elements,* while the best sorting programs take a time proportional to N log N. However, it is included here to illustrate the case when a <u>goto</u> statement cannot easily be replaced by an <u>exit</u> statement. It illustrates also the fact that programs where a <u>goto</u> statement appears to be necessary may often, by a radical redesign, be replaced by more efficient or better-structured programs in which no <u>goto</u> is needed.

Goto statements may jump out of compound statements but cannot jump out of subprograms or modules. Thus "visibility rules" for labels are slightly different from visibility rules for identifiers. Subprograms and modules can access nonlocal identifiers

---

*The number of interchanges is proportional to N^2, and the number of comparisons for each interchange is proportional to N. So the total number of comparisons is proportional to N^3.

declared in a textually enclosing environment, but cannot jump
to labels of a textually enclosing environment.

The following example illustrates how the exit statement and
loop statement may be combined to test for termination in the
middle of the loop.

Example 2.30. File processing with exit statement

```
loop
   get data item
   exit when (end of file)
   process data item
end loop;
```

The while statement may be simulated by a loop whose body
begins with an "exit when condition;" statement. Other control
structures such as the Pascal "do..until condition;" statement
can be realized by a loop whose last statement is an "exit when
condition;" statement. Thus the combination of loop and exit
statements provides great flexibility in constructing control
structures appropriate to particular applications.

2.7 Programming Examples (Computing Prime Numbers)

In this section we shall ring the changes on programs for
computing prime numbers. This application is sufficiently chal-
lenging to allow us to illustrate some interesting control structures, but is at the same time sufficiently familiar to require
little explanation. We shall start by considering a program for
testing a number N for primality, continue with a program for
generating successive primes which makes use of a knowledge of
all primes up to the square root of the number being tested for
primality, and finally consider a program for printing prime
factors of successive integers.

The program fragment below tests whether N is prime by first
testing whether N is divisible by 2 and then testing for divisibility of N by successive odd numbers up to the square root of
N. It consists of an if-then-else statement whose then branch
is a simple assignment statement and whose else branch contains
a loop statement with an inner if-then-else statement. It
assumes that N is an integer greater than 2.

Example 2.31. Nested branching and iteration statements

```
if N mod 2 = 0 then          -- test if N is divisible by 2
  PRIME := FALSE;            -- if so, set PRIME to FALSE, skip to end
else                         -- if N is not divisible by 2
  FACTOR := 3;               -- set FACTOR to 3
  loop                       -- and loop
    if FACTOR**2 > N then    -- test if FACTOR > SQRT(N)
      PRIME := TRUE;         -- if so, set PRIME to TRUE
      exit;                  -- and exit
    elsif N mod FACTOR = 0 then  -- test if N is divisible by FACTOR
      PRIME := FALSE;        -- if so, set PRIME to FALSE
      exit;                  -- and exit
    end if;                  -- end of inner if statement
    FACTOR := FACTOR+2;      -- next factor to be tested
  end loop;                  -- end of loop statement
end if;                      -- end of outer if statement
```

The loop statement of the above program has an interesting
structure. It contains an if part which tests for termination,
an elsif part which tests for divisibility by a factor and no
else part. Thus if neither the if condition nor the elsif condition is true, the if statement has no effect and FACTOR is incremented so that divisibility by the next odd number can be tested.
Note that, in this special case, the statement "FACTOR :=
FACTOR+2;" could have been specified as the else branch of the
if statement.

The inner if statement can be replaced by two conditional
exit statements. The resulting program is less efficient because
it includes an extra assignment to PRIME in its inner loop, but
is included here to illustrate an alternative control structure.

Example 2.32. Primality with flags and conditional exits

```
if N mod 2 = 0 then              -- if N is divisible by 2
  PRIME := FALSE;                -- set PRIME to FALSE and skip to end
else                             -- otherwise
  FACTOR := 3;                   -- set FACTOR to 3
  loop                           -- and loop
    PRIME := TRUE;               -- exit with PRIME := TRUE
    exit when FACTOR**2 > N;     -- when FACTOR > SQRT(N)
    PRIME := FALSE;              -- exit with PRIME := FALSE
    exit when N mod FACTOR = 0;  -- when N is divisible by FACTOR
    FACTOR := FACTOR+2;          -- consider next factor to be tested
  end loop;                      -- end of loop
end if;                          -- end of if statement
```

Still another method of primality testing, illustrated
below, uses composite logical conditions and a while statement
to test for termination. It performs an average of one-third
fewer tests of the form N mod FACTOR = 0 than the previous
program because it takes advantage of the fact that every third
odd number is divisible by 3.

Example 2.33. More efficient primality testing

```
if N mod 2 = 0 or N mod 3 = 0 then    -- if N is divisible by 2 or 3 set PRIME
   PRIME := (N<4);  -- to TRUE if N = 2 or 3, to FALSE if N > 3, and then exit
else                                  -- otherwise
   PRIME := TRUE;                     -- set PRIME to TRUE provisionally
   FACTOR := 5;                       -- and FACTOR to 5
   while FACTOR**2 <= N loop          -- loop while FACTOR < SQRT(N)
      if N mod FACTOR = 0 or N mod (FACTOR+2) = 0        -- if N is divisible by
         PRIME := FALSE;              --- FACTOR or FACTOR+2 set PRIME to FALSE
         exit;                        -- and exit
      end if;                         -- FACTOR+4 is divisible by 3
      FACTOR := FACTOR+6;             -- and can be omitted
   end loop;                          -- PRIME is TRUE on normal exit
end if;                               -- and FALSE on abnormal exit
```

Comparison of the three versions of testing for primality above illustrates both the inherent variety of ways of solving a computational problem and the richness and flexibility of Ada control structures in providing different methods of organizing the solution of even relatively simple problems.

The above program fragments for primality testing can be embedded in a function with an integer input parameter N whose primality is to be tested and a Boolean result which is TRUE if N is prime and FALSE otherwise.

Example 2.34. Function for testing primality

```
function ISPRIME(N: INTEGER) return BOOLEAN is  -- function with INTEGER
   FACTOR: INTEGER;         -- parameter, BOOLEAN result, two local variables
   PRIME: BOOLEAN;          -- FACTOR and PRIME
begin                       -- and a statement sequence which is
   -- any one of the three previously given
   -- program fragments for primality testing
   return PRIME;            -- followed by a return statement
end ISPRIME;                -- and an end statement
```

A call of the function ISPRIME may appear in any context in which a Boolean value is expected. In the following example ISPRIME is called in the condition part of an if statement which counts the number of primes in the range M through N.

Example 2.35. Calls of the function ISPRIME

```
COUNT := 0;
for I in 2..1000 loop       -- count number of primes
   if ISPRIME(I) then       -- test Ith number for primality
      COUNT := COUNT+1;      -- if I is prime, increase count by 1
   end if;
end loop;
```

61

The function ISPRIME provides a resource to users whose implementation is hidden from them. In particular, changes in implementation which do not affect the computational effect of a function are transparent to the user. Thus the user of a prime program need not be concerned which of the three versions of the prime program occurs in the procedure body, since the functional effect will be the same.

If we wish to enumerate all primes rather than merely test a given number for primality, we can save time by testing only for divisibility by previously computed primes (up to the square root of the number being tested). In the following program the first 100 computed primes are saved in the vector PRIMES. This program will store 3 in PRIMES(1), 5 in PRIMES(2), and 547 in PRIMES(100), and could compute all primes up to $557^2 = 310249$, since all integers less than 310249 have a prime ≤ 547 as a factor.

Example 2.36. Compute sequence of primes

```
PUT(2);                        -- print the fact that 2 is prime
PUT(3);                        -- and the fact that 3 is prime
PRIMES(1) := 3;                -- store 3 in PRIMES vector
N := 1;                        -- which initially has size 1
K := 5;                        -- and initialize number to be tested
while K < 300_000 loop         -- iterate while K < 300000
   I := 1;                     -- and initialize index of PRIMES vector
   while PRIMES(I)**2<= K loop  -- inner loop over previous primes
      if K mod PRIMES(I) = 0 then -- tests for prime factor
         go to L;              -- and escapes if one is found
      end if;                  -- if this prime does not divide K
      I := I+1;                -- try the next prime in PRIMES vector
   end loop;                   -- and repeat
   PUT(K);                     -- print K if it is prime
   if N < 100 then             -- and if it is one of first 100 primes
      N := N+1;                -- increment length of vector
      PRIMES(N) := K;          -- and store current prime
   end if;
<<L>> K := K+2;                -- increment K by 2
   end loop;                   -- and test next odd number for primality
```

The control structure of this program is a while loop which contains an inner while loop with a goto statement that escapes from the inner while loop into the middle of a statement sequence in the outer while loop. Normal exit from the inner while loop (when the number is prime) causes the execution of some bookkeeping statements (for recording the prime number). The normal and abnormal exit paths then join up, and the goto statement is used to effect the abnormal exit from the inner while loop to the point where the two control paths join. The goto statement is a natural mechanism for realizing transfer of control from an "abnormal" control path back to an arbitrary point in the normal control path. Another mechanism which accomplishes the same effect is to set a flag when the abnormal event occurs and to

62

test the flag when it is necessary to distinguish between the normal and abnormal case. This approach is used in the next example.

The next example, which prints out the prime factors of successive integers, is similar in its underlying structure to the previous program. It differs from the previous program in having an inner loop to compute multiple factors of a given prime. The goto jump of the previous program is replaced by a FLAG which is set to FALSE when a factor is found, and later tested. This program is typical of programs with deeply nested control structures and illustrates the interaction between for loops, while loops, exit statements and if statements.

Example 2.37. Compute table of prime factors for successive integers

```
procedure PRIME_FACTORS(MAXNUM: INTEGER) is
   N: INTEGER := 0;                   -- number of primes in PRIMES vector
   I: INTEGER;                        -- index in PRIMES vector
   FLAG: BOOLEAN;                     -- indicates if current integer is prime
   M: INTEGER;                        -- partially factored current integer
   PRIMES: array(1..100) of INTEGER; -- holds previously computed primes

begin
   PRIMES(1) := 2;                    -- install first element of PRIMES
   for K in 2..MAXNUM loop            -- loop over successive integers
     FLAG := TRUE;
     M := K;                          -- store K in "working" location
     I := 1;                          -- initialize index of PRIMES vector
     while PRIMES(I)**2 <= M loop     -- loop over successive prime factors
       while M mod PRIMES(I)=0 and PRIMES(I)/=M loop -- loop for given prime factor
         PUT(PRIMES(I));              -- print prime factor
         M := M/PRIMES(I);            -- divide M by prime factor
         FLAG := FALSE;               -- set flag to indicate factor
       end loop;                      -- and try this factor again

       I := I+1;                      -- try next prime as a factor
     end loop;                        -- end of loop for finding all prime factors
     if FLAG and N < 100 then         -- condition for inserting prime in PRIMES vector
       N := N+1;                      -- if N < 100
       PRIMES(N) := K;                -- add K to PRIMES vector
     end if;
     PUT(M)                           -- print last prime factor
     PUT(NEWLINE);                    -- and start new line
   end loop;                          -- end of for loop, factor next integer
end PRIME_FACTORS;
```

The PRIME_FACTORS procedure is the largest program considered so far and includes not only the statements which perform the computation but also the declarations which define the variables

used in the computation and a procedure parameter. In the
remaining sections of this chapter we shall examine in greater
detail the structure of declarations, procedures, functions and
parameters. We shall use mainly toy examples in order to illustrate language features in a simple setting. The reader should
not expect any further programs as large as the PRIME_FACTORS
program in the remainder of this chapter, but there will again
be larger illustrative programs in later chapters.

2.8   Declarations of Identifiers

The identifiers used in the PRIME_FACTORS procedure can be
classified into the following categories:

1. Reserved words, which are underlined in the program for
    clarity, but which would appear as identifiers in actual
    programs. Reserved words cannot be redeclared by the
    programmer.
2. System-defined identifiers such as INTEGER, BOOLEAN,
    TRUE. These identifiers could in principle be redec-
    lared to have different meanings, but it is undesirable
    to do so.
3. Identifiers defined in other program units such as PUT
    and NEWLINE, which are assumed to be declared in an
    accessible library input-output package·
4. Identifiers declared in the given program unit. These
    identifiers may in turn be classified as follows:

    a) Declarations of simple variables and constants, such
        as the integer variables N, I, M and the Boolean
        variable FLAG.
    b) Declarations of structured variables such as the
        array PRIMES.
    c) Declarations of subprogram parameters, such as the
        integer parameter MAXNUM.
    d) Declarations of procedure identifiers, such as the
        identifier PRIME_FACTORS.

Ada is a strongly typed language in which every identifier
must have a meaning that is predefined, previously defined in
some other program unit, or explicitly defined by a declaration
in the given program unit. We shall explore in some detail the
mechanisms for explicit declaration of identifiers. The mechanisms for declaring simple variables and constants are considered
in greater detail in the remainder of the present section. The
mechanisms for declaring subprograms and parameters are discussed in later sections of the present chapter. The mechanisms
for declaring structured data types and other programmer-defined
data types are discussed in the next chapter.

Variables and constants are referred to in Ada as objects.
Declarations for variables and constants are referred to as
object declarations to distinguish them from subprogram

declarations and type declarations. The general form of an object declaration is as follows:

identifier_list: [constant] typespec [:= expression];

Thus an object declaration may have the following components:

1. An identifier list consisting of at least one identifier followed by a colon. The identifiers name the objects being declared by the object declaration.
2. The optional reserved word constant. If it is present then the declared identifiers are constants whose value must be specified by an initializing expression. Otherwise the declared identifiers are variables and the initializing expression is optional.
3. A required type specification which determines the type of the declared identifiers. The type determines the set of values which may be taken by the identifiers and the operations applicable to the identifiers.
4. An assignment token followed by an optional initializing expression whose type must be compatible with the type specification. Initializing declarations are generally required for constant declarations (except in the case of deferred constants (see examples 1.23, 1.24, 3.80, 3.82)).
5. A semicolon which terminates the object declaration.

We have already encountered many object declarations in previous examples. Nevertheless we include some additional examples.

Example 2.38. Object declarations

```
I,J: INTEGER;                   -- declaration of two integer variables I, J
COUNT: INTEGER := 0;            -- initialized declaration of integer variable
FLAG: BOOLEAN := TRUE;          -- initialized declaration of Boolean variable
LENGTH: FLOAT := 4.5;           -- initialized floating-point variable
SQUARE: FLOAT := LENGTH*LENGTH; -- initializing expression
```

The declarations of any given declarative part are elaborated sequentially. The last declaration above illustrates that variables such as LENGTH, declared and initialized in a previous declaration, may be immediately used in a subsequent declaration. However, such variables (or constants) must always be textually declared and initialized before they are used. Thus, if the last two declarations were interchanged, the resulting program would be illegal because the variable LENGTH would not yet have been initialized at the time that its value was required to initialize SQUARE.

Constants must be initialized at declaration time and cannot be modified by assignment.

Example 2.39. Constant declarations

```
LIMIT: constant INTEGER := 1000;
PI: constant FLOAT := 3.1416;
MAX_AREA: constant FLOAT := PI*FLOAT(LIMIT)**2;
```

In the last example above the integer constant LIMIT is converted to the type FLOAT so that it can be used to compute the value of a floating-point expression. This expression could alternatively have been written as "PI * FLOAT(LIMIT ** 2)", which squares the integer variable LIMIT before converting the result to floating-point.

In the above examples the types of all declared objects were predefined types whose value set and applicable operations are determined by the system. Object declarations for programmer-defined data types will be considered in the next chapter.

2.9 Program Units and Block Structure

Program units are the mechanism for associating declarations which define the attributes of identifiers with the statements in which the identifiers are used.

A program unit consists of a declarative part in which local identifiers of a program unit are declared and an imperative part (statement sequence) in which both locally declared identifiers and accessible nonlocal identifiers may be used. It is convenient to distinguish three kinds of program units.

1. Subprograms - which are declared by subprogram declarations in the declarative part of a program unit and invoked by a subprogram call.
2. Modules - which are declared in the declarative part of a program unit. Modules have a specification part which specifies the resources made available by the module to the user. These resources may be used wherever the module is textually accessible.
3. Blocks - which must appear in the statement sequence of a textually enclosing program unit and have the syntactic status of a statement.

Program units govern the textual extent (scope) over which local identifiers of the program unit are accessible. Questions of scope will be illustrated first for blocks and later for other program units.

The syntax of blocks is as follows:

```
[declare
     sequence of declarations of local identifiers]
begin
     sequence of statements
     which may use both local and nonlocal identifiers
end;
```

That is, a block has an optional declarative part in which
local identifiers may be declared, followed by a sequence of
statements which may use both local identifiers declared in the
declarative part of the block and accessible nonlocal identifiers.

The distinction between local and nonlocal identifiers can
be illustrated by the following block for interchanging the
values of two integer variables.

Example 2.40. Swapping revisited

```
declare
  TEMP: constant INTEGER := X;   -- TEMP is initialized integer constant
begin
  X := Y;                        -- X and Y are nonlocal variables
  Y := TEMP;                     -- TEMP is a locally declared variable
end;
```

In this example local variable TEMP is an initialized constant which remains constant for any given instance of execution
of the block but may have different values for different instances of execution. X and Y are nonlocal variables which must be
declared by accessible declarations in a textually enclosing
program unit.

The scope of a declared identifier extends from its point of
declaration to the end of the program unit in which it is
declared. Any attempt to use an identifier outside its scope
is illegal.

The following example illustrates an "inner block" with a
local variable Y and nonlocal variable X, nested in an "outer
block" in which X is declared. In the inner block, both X and Y
are known and may be used. In the outer block only X is known
and uses of Y are illegal.

Example 2.41. Nested blocks

```
declare                          -- outer block
  X: INTEGER;                    -- declare X local to outer block
begin                            -- body of outer block
  X := 2;                        -- assign to X
  declare                        -- inner block
    Y: INTEGER;                  -- declare Y local to inner block
  begin                          -- body of inner block
    Y := 4;                      -- assign to Y
    X := X+Y;                    -- X can be used in inner block, X becomes 6
  end;                           -- exit from inner block, delete Y
  PUT(X+1);                      -- output the value 7
  PUT(X+Y);                      -- illegal, Y is unknown in outer block
end;                             -- exit from outer block, delete X
```

The above example illustrates that program units normally act
as one-way membranes which allow nonlocal names declared in a

textually enclosing environment to be used within the program unit, but do not allow locally declared names to be used outside the program unit.

We shall next examine the case of name conflicts between declared identifiers. The rules for resolving name conflicts differ for subprogram identifiers (which may be overloaded and disambiguated at compile time - see section 3.1) and other identifiers (for which name conflicts are simply not permitted).

It is illegal to have multiple declarations of an identifier (other than a subprogram identifier) in a given declarative part. However, the same identifier may be redeclared in several different declarative parts. The case when an identifier is redeclared in a nested declarative unit is examined in greater detail below.

When an identifier declared in an outer program unit is redeclared in an inner program unit, the inner declaration <u>hides</u> the similarly named identifier of the outer program unit, as in the following example.

<u>Example 2.42. Nested redeclaration of identifier</u>

```
declare
  X,Y: INTEGER;                  -- declare X and outer Y
begin
  X := 2;                        -- assign to X
  Y := 3;                        -- assign to outer Y
  declare
    Y: INTEGER;                  -- declare inner Y
  begin
    Y := 15;                     -- assign to inner Y
    PUT(X+Y);                    -- use inner Y, output the value 17
  end;                           -- delete inner Y on exit from inner block
  PUT(X+Y);                      -- use outer Y, output the value 5
end;
```

The inaccessibility of an outer identifier declaration in an inner block in which it is redeclared follows from the fact that each declaration causes an object to be created on entry to the block in which the declaration occurs. Thus entry to the inner block in the above example causes a new object Y to be created and causes uses of Y during execution of the inner block to refer to this object. The inner instance of Y is deleted on exit from the inner block, so that uses of Y after exit from the inner block will again refer to the outer Y.

Identifier declared in a block may be regarded as bound variables in the sense that replacing all occurrences of the identifier by some other unused identifier does not change the computational effect. The next example is obtained from the previous one by replacing occurrences of Y in the inner block by T.

Example 2.43. Renaming of local identifiers

```
declare                               -- outer block
  X,Y: INTEGER;
begin
  X := 2;
  Y := 3;
  declare                             -- inner block
    T: INTEGER;                       -- replace Y by identifier T
  begin
    T := 4;                           -- replace all uses of Y by T
    PUT(X+T);
  end;
  PUT(X+Y);                           -- no replacement in outer block
end;
```

The above program is less confusing than that of example
2.42 because different objects which inadvertently have the same
name in example 2.42 have different names in the present example.
Good programming practice suggests that use of the same declarative name for more than one object of a nested program structure should be avoided wherever possible.

For named program units, such as procedures, redeclaration
of an identifier in an inner program unit does not altogether
hide the outer declaration of that identifier, because the outer
identifier can be accessed by qualifying the identifier name by
the name of the procedure.

Example 2.44. Nonlocal access by qualified name

```
procedure OUTER is
  X,Y: INTEGER;             -- declare X and Y
begin
  X := 2;
  Y := 3;
  declare
    Y: INTEGER;             -- redeclare Y
  begin
    Y := OUTER.Y+Z;         -- qualified name denotes outer Y, Y becomes 5
    PUT(Y+OUTER.Y);         -- the value 8 is printed
  end;
  PUT(X+Y);                 -- the value 5 is printed
end;
```

Program units may be nested inside other program units to an
arbitrary level of static nesting. The declaration associated
with a given use of an identifier may be determined by examining
successive textually enclosing declarative environments enclosing the point of use, starting with the local declarative environment, and picking the first declaration for the given identifier that is found. Thus the declaration associated with a given
use of an identifier is the innermost textually enclosing declaration for that identifier.

2.10   Procedures and Parameters

The general format for procedure specification is as follows:

procedure name [parameter specification] is
    [local declarations]
begin
    sequence of statements
end [name];

Procedures are introduced by the reserved word procedure, followed by the procedure name, followed by a parameter specification which is omitted when there are no parameters. This constitutes the procedure specification, and is followed by local declarations (if any) and the sequence of statements which specifies the computation.

The procedure PRINT_CUBES below has no parameters and therefore no parameter specification, and has a local variable CUBE and three statements.

Example 2.45. A parameterless procedure

procedure PRINT_CUBES is
    CUBE: INTEGER;
begin
    for I in 1..100 loop
        CUBE := I**3;
        PUT(CUBE);
    end loop;
end CUBE;

The first two lines constitute the declarative part of this procedure and declare PRINT_CUBES to be the name of this procedure and CUBE to be a local variable of the procedure. The body of the procedure is a for loop which computes and prints the cubes of successive integers.

Procedure parameters have a type, and also a binding mode which specifies how the parameter information is transmitted between the environment of invocation and the environment of execution of the procedure.

The following simple procedure for adding two integers has two input parameters (the numbers to be added) and one output parameter (the result).

Example 2.46. Procedure declaration with input and output parameters

procedure ADD(I,J : in INTEGER; K: out INTEGER) is
begin
    K := I+J;
end;

70

The information between the keyword <u>procedure</u> and the keyword <u>is</u> is the procedure specification, and specifies the procedure name and the type and binding mode of each procedure
parameter. The procedure specification is the interface between
implementers and users of the procedure. It contains all the
information needed by the user of a procedure to use the procedure correctly. In particular, it contains the procedure name,
the number of procedure parameters, and the type and binding
mode of each parameter. The following call of the ADD procedure
requires the user to know the procedure name and the types of
the parameters.

Example 2.47. Call of ADD procedure

ADD(X,Y,Z);   -- add values of X and Y and store result in Z

This call causes the variables X, Y, Z (declared as integer
variables in the environment of call) to be associated with the
parameters I, J, K of the procedure declaration. The value X+Y
is computed and then stored in the environment of call as the
value of the result variable Z.

The parameters I, J, K of the procedure definition are <u>bound</u>
<u>variables</u> in the sense that they may be uniformly replaced by
other nonconflicting names in the procedure definition without
affecting the meaning of the procedure. The parameter names
used in the procedure definition are irrelevant to the user, and
parameters of a procedure definition are therefore referred to
as <u>formal parameters</u>. Identifiers used in a procedure call are
called <u>actual parameters</u> and determine values to be used as
arguments in the case of input parameters and locations to be
used for returning results in the case of output parameters.

The user need not know the <u>names</u> of formal parameters but
must know the <u>type</u> and <u>binding mode</u> of formal parameters. The
compatibility of type between actual and formal parameters may
be checked by the compiler at compile time. The binding mode
is relevant to the user because actual parameters of the input
mode may be expressions (such as X+5), while actual parameters
of the output mode must be variables. Actual input parameters
must be initialized prior to the call in which they occur, but
this cannot in general be checked at compile time.

The following example includes an ADD procedure whose formal
parameters I, J, K have been replaced by the nonconflicting
names FIRST, SECOND, RESULT and a call of the ADD procedure
whose actual input parameters are expressions.

Example 2.48. Parameters which are expressions

```
procedure USE_ADD is
   X,Z: INTEGER;        -- local variables used as actual parameters of ADD
   procedure ADD(FIRST,SECOND: in INTEGER; RESULT: out INTEGER) is  -- renamed
                        -- formal parameters
   begin
      RESULT := FIRST+SECOND;
   end ADD;
begin
   X := 7;
   ADD(4,X+5,Z);        -- actual input parameters may be expressions
   PUT(Z);              -- actual output parameters must be variables
end USE_ADD;
```

The correspondence between actual and formal parameters is determined in the above example by their position in the calling sequence. Ada also permits this correspondence to be specified by explicitly naming the formal parameters, as in the following procedure call.

Example 2.49. Named actual parameters

```
ADD(SECOND := X+5, FIRST := 4, RESULT =: Z);
```

Explicit naming of formal parameters allows the order of actual parameters to be independent of the order of formal parameters in the procedure definition. Moreover, formal parameter names can be a useful reminder of the function of the formal parameters in the procedure definition, especially to persons unfamiliar with the program. However, such explicit naming means that a change of formal parameter names within the procedure may require changes of those names at points of use, so that modularity is weakened.

Explicit formal parameters allow actual parameters to be omitted where this makes semantic sense. Consider, for instance, the following redefinition of the ADD procedure with the two input parameters initialized to the value 1.

Example 2.50. Initialized formal parameters

```
procedure NEW_ADD(FIRST,SECOND: in INTEGER := 1; RESULT: out INTEGER) is
begin
   RESULT := FIRST+SECOND;
end;
```

The new ADD function may be used as before to add two actual input parameters and return a result. However, if one of the input parameters is omitted, the default value of 1 is used for the omitted parameter and the successor function is obtained.

Example 2.51. Default initialization of unmentioned parameters

ADD(FIRST := 4; RESULT =: Z);   -- omitted parameter value is 1, Z becomes 5

   Explicit formal parameters require not only the formal parameter name but also its binding mode to be explicitly specified.
The binding mode of in and out parameters is respectively specified by ":=" and "=:". There is also a third binding mode,
in out, specified by ":=:".

2.11 Parameter Binding Modes

   The semantics of the three parameter binding modes supported
by Ada is defined in the reference manual as follows:

in   The parameter acts as a local constant whose value
          is provided by the corresponding actual parameter

out   The parameter acts as a local variable whose value
          is assigned to the corresponding actual parameter
          as a result of the execution of the subprogram

in out   The parameter acts as a local variable and permits
          access and assignment to the corresponding actual
          parameter.

   The semantics of each binding mode is defined independently
of whether parameter binding is implemented by computing with a
local copy of the actual parameter value or by accessing the
actual parameter in the calling environment. Thus actual in
parameters which are variables can be implemented either by read-
only access to a local copy of the value made at the time of
procedure entry or by read-only access to the nonlocal actual
parameter variable in the calling environment. Out parameters
may be implemented as local variables whose value is assigned
to the actual parameter variable on exit, or as direct references
to the nonlocal actual parameter variable. In out parameters may
be implemented as local variables initialized on entry and copied
out on exit or as references to the nonlocal actual parameter
variable.

   The above semantics insures that parameter binding is
implementation-independent in the sense that it is independent
of whether parameter binding is implemented by copying or sharing. It allows the compiler to perform time and/or space optimizations depending on whether copying or sharing is more efficient. The user is provided with a simple implementation-
independent abstract model of parameter binding.

   However, this view of parameter binding requires that programs whose computational effect differs for the copying and
sharing implementation of parameter binding be regarded as
undefined. It makes illegal a whole class of procedures which
would be perfectly legal in languages which recognize the

difference between copying and sharing of procedure parameters, and requires computations naturally specified by such procedures to be specified in some other way. Moreover, the legality of parameter binding cannot in general be guaranteed by the compiler. The problem of whether the computational effect of a program differs for copying and sharing semantics is in general undecidable. A compiler must either tag as illegal a class of programs which includes legal as well as illegal programs, or allow some illegal programs to be tagged as legal, thereby giving rise to problems of portability of such programs between different implementations.

The seriousness of the above drawbacks depends in part on the degree to which useful programs are excluded by the parameter binding semantics and in part on the degree to which the inability to completely realize the semantics is a practical rather than theoretical problem. The answers to these questions require more experience in writing programs in the language and running them through production compilers.

We have illustrated in and out parameters earlier and will briefly illustrate in out parameters by considering procedure calls for previously discussed procedures.

Example 2.52. Calls of in out parameters

```
SWAP(X :=: A, Y :=: B);
SORT(VECT);
```

Our old friend the SWAP procedure has two in out parameters (say X, Y) whose values are both accessed and assigned to. The SORT procedure of chapter 1 has a vector parameter whose elements are both accessed to determine their relative magnitude and assigned to in order to produce the sorted vector.

In both cases the parameter acts as a local variable which permits access and assignment to the corresponding actual parameter. The semantics is independent of whether the computation is performed on local copies of actual parameters or in the locations of the calling program where the actual parameters are stored. Both the SWAP and SORT programs do nothing that causes a difference of computational effect for copying or sharing semantics. However, there could be a difference in computational effect in multitasking situations where some other task has access to actual parameter locations. Thus legality of the SWAP and SORT procedures depends not only on the procedure definitions but also on certain restrictions which must be satisfied in the calling environment.

2.12   Functions and Value-Returning Procedures

Procedures in general have side effects in the sense that they change the values of nonlocal variables. For example, the call "SWAP(A,B)" has the side effect of changing (interchanging) the values of the nonlocal variables A and B.

Ada distinguishes between <u>procedures</u> which affect their environment by means of side effects and <u>functions</u> which are not allowed to have side effects but affect their environment by returning a result which may be used as an operand in an expression. The previously given procedure ADD may be specified as a function as follows.

Example 2.53. ADD function

<u>function</u> ADD(X,Y: <u>in</u> INTEGER) <u>return</u> INTEGER <u>is</u>
<u>begin</u>
  return(X+Y);   -- return an integer result
<u>end</u>;

The above ADD function has one fewer parameter than the corresponding procedure and instead returns a result which syntactically is an operand in an expression.

Example 2.54. Call of ADD function

Z := 2*ADD(A,B) + 1;   -- twice sum of A and B plus one

A function may have only <u>in</u> parameters, cannot assign to global variables, and can affect its environment only through the result which it returns. These restrictions permit optimizations to be performed such as "F(X)+F(X) = 2*F(X)", which may considerably reduce the amount of work in expression evaluation.

Functions may call themselves recursively, as in the following example.

Example 2.55. Recursive function

<u>function</u> FACT(I: INTEGER) <u>return</u> INTEGER <u>is</u>
<u>begin</u>
  <u>if</u> I = 1 <u>then</u>
    <u>return</u> 1;
  <u>else</u>
    <u>return</u> I*FACT(I-1);   -- recursive call of FACT
  <u>end</u> <u>if</u>;
<u>end</u> FACT;

This example illustrates that there may be more than one textual point of return from a function to the calling program. A call FACT(I) with I ≠ 1 causes recursive evaluation of I*FACT(I-1) while attempting to compute the value to be returned, and causes return of the value 1 when I = 1. Thus a call of FACT(3) would cause recursive calls of FACT(2) and FACT(1), evaluation of FACT(1) as 1 and unravelling of the recursion.

Example 2.56. Call of the factorial function

```
FACT(3) = 3*FACT(2)           -- first level of recursion
        = 3*2*FACT(1)         -- second level of recursion
        = 3*2*1               -- third level of recursion
```

The general format for function specification is as follows:

function name[parameter-spec] return type-spec is
    [local variable declarations]
begin
    sequence of statements including return statements
end;

Note that both the parameter specification and local variable declarations may be absent in function specifications, just as in procedures. However, the type of the value returned by a function must always be specified.

There are cases when it is useful to permit functions with global variables - for example, when it is desired to count the number of times a particular function is executed. Such functions are realized in Ada by value-returning procedures. The following value-returning procedure computes factorial N and increments a global variable COUNT which counts the number of function executions.

Example 2.57. Factorial as a value-returning procedure

```
procedure FACT(I: INTEGER) return INTEGER is
begin
  COUNT := COUNT+1;              -- increment global variable
  if I = 0 then
    return 1;
  else
    return I*FACT(I-1);
  end if;
end FACT;
```

In order to minimize the interaction of global variables of value-returning procedures and function calls of such procedures, the restriction is imposed that value-returning procedures may be called only in scopes where global variables of the procedure are not accessible.

Value-returning procedures behave functionally like procedures, but the order of evaluation of calls of such procedures cannot be optimized. Optimizations such as "F(X)+F(X) = 2*F(X)" cannot be performed (in the FACT example this would result in a smaller value of COUNT and this might in some context make a critical difference to the course of the computation.

If F is a function and P is a value-returning procedure, then F(X)+F(X)+P(X) can be optimized to 2*F(X)+P(X) while

F(X)+P(X)+F(X) cannot be optimized. Value-returning procedures occurring within an expression partition the expression into sub-expressions such that optimization can be performed within a sub-expression but not across partition boundaries.

The above examples illustrate that functions, procedures and blocks share a common syntactic structure. They have a body consisting of a sequence of statements and a declarative part with declarations of local identifiers. They may contain non-local identifiers which must be declared in a textually enclos-ing declarative part. Blocks are specified and executed in line in the body of some other program structure. Procedures and functions are specified in a declarative part (or as separately compiled program units) and subsequently are invoked in a body in which the declaration is accessible.

Functions may also be invoked in initialization specifica-tions in the declarative part of a program unit. The purpose of the declarative part of a program unit is fundamentally dif-ferent from that of the associated body, and there is a rigid syntactic separation between declarative parts and bodies in all program units. But the fact that initialization computations in a declarative part are in principle as powerful as computa-tions which can occur in the body of a program unit somewhat blurs this distinction.

2.13   Assertions

An _assert_ statement consists of the keyword _assert_ followed by a condition. _Assert_ statements are normally executed in line at the point where they occur and cause the associated condition to be evaluated. If the condition is TRUE execution proceeds normally to the next statement. If the condition is FALSE an error action (determined by the exception ASSERT_ERROR) may be initiated.

An _assert_ statement requires the associated condition to be true whenever it is executed. It provides the programmer with an explicit means for supplementing execution-time checks pro-vided by the system. The following example illustrates a number of contexts in which assert statements might be useful.

Example 2.58. Plausible assert statements

```
assert X /= 0;              -- check X prior to division by X
assert LENGTH1 = LENGTH2;   -- check length equality (of two vectors)
assert I in 1..100;         -- check that index is in range
```

The last statement involves a new form of relation which is true if the value determined by the left-hand side is in the set determined by the right-hand side and false otherwise.

An <u>assert</u> statement may be viewed dynamically as providing a conditional escape mechanism from a computation. However, it is also useful to view an <u>assert</u> statement as providing a static invariant which must always be true if the program is to be correct. If the environment contains a program verifier, then it is sometimes possible to prove that a given condition will always hold at the given point of execution. In this case the assertion has been checked statically and need not be checked dynamically during execution.

Assertions may be used to aid a program verifier in proving correctness of a program by suggesting intermediate assertions which, if they can be proved true, imply the correctness of the program. If we can find assertions that are not only necessary but also sufficient for a program to correctly perform its task, then it is useful to include them in test versions of the program even if they cannot be proved, since dynamic verification of the correctness of the assertion in even a small number of test cases will help to increase our confidence in the correctness of the program.

Execution of <u>assert</u> statements may be suppressed by suppression of the exception ASSERT_ERROR. Thus assertion checking may be used as a debugging tool and switched off during production runs or during time-critical computations.

3

DATA DESCRIPTION

3.1 Actions and Objects

Programs specify a sequence of <u>actions</u> on a collection of <u>data objects</u>. Actions are specified by expressions and statements. Data objects are specified in Ada by declarations.

In writing programs we may adopt an <u>action-oriented</u> view in which description of the algorithm is of central concern, and description of the data objects on which the algorithm operates is regarded as incidental. Alternatively, we may adopt an <u>object-oriented</u> view in which the description of the objects of computation is decided upon first and algorithms are viewed as auxiliary entities needed to describe the behavior of objects.

The action-oriented view is appropriate to one-shot scientific computations where the complexity lies in the algorithm and the data structures are relatively simple. The object-oriented view is appropriate to system programming and embedded computer applications where data structures represent the state of a system which evolves over time.

Early languages like Fortran were action-oriented (as reflected by the term "algorithmic languages"). However, large computer applications increasingly require an object-oriented view which starts with a description of real-world objects such as ships, airplanes, banks or cities by data structures, and then considers algorithms for operating upon the data objects.

Ada has powerful facilities for both algorithm and data description. However, language mechanisms for algorithm description were already well developed in earlier languages like Fortran. The biggest difference between Ada and earlier languages like Fortran is therefore in the area of data description.

The present chapter will describe the Ada type definition facilities for numeric types, enumeration types, array types, record types and access types (pointer types). Before doing so, the following global features of the Ada type system will be discussed:

1. Predefined types - which have a predefined value set and applicable operations.
2. Derived types - which are defined in terms of previously defined types.
3. Constraints - which constrain the value set of a type but do not affect the set of applicable operations.
4. Anonymous type definitions - which define a type in terms of its attributes rather than in terms of a previously defined type. Type equivalence rules for anonymous types.
5. Subtypes - which may constrain a parent type but are considered to be of the same type as the parent type.
6. Attribute enquiries - which may be used by the programmer to determine type attributes.
7. Classification of types - into scalar types, structured types and access types.

3.2   The Ada Type System

3.2.1   Predefined types

A data type determines a <u>set of values</u> which may be taken by data objects of the data type and a <u>set of operations</u> applicable to objects of the data type.

Ada has a number of <u>predefined</u> data types whose value set and applicable operations are determined by the system. The predefined types of Ada include INTEGER, FLOAT and BOOLEAN. These data types have already been extensively used, but are illustrated again in the following example.

Example 3.1.   Predefined types

```
procedure PREDEFINED_TYPES is
   I,J: INTEGER := 1;        -- integer variables initialized to literal 1
   X,Y: FLOAT := 1.0;        -- floating variables initialized to literal 1.0
   A,B,C: BOOLEAN := TRUE;   -- Boolean variables initialized to literal TRUE
begin
   I := 2*J+5;               -- integer literals, variables and operators
   X := 3.5+Y/2.5;           -- floating-point literals, variables and operators
   C := (not B) or A;        -- Boolean variables and operators
end;
```

Each predefined type has an associated set of <u>literals</u> which may be used to represent values of the data type. Integer literals consist of a string of digits. Floating-point literals contain a decimal point or the symbol E. The data type BOOLEAN has just the two literals TRUE, FALSE. The literals of each predefined type are syntactically distinct.

The set of <u>operators</u> of each data type are logically (but not necessarily syntactically) distinct from those of any other type. Both INTEGER and FLOAT use the "+" operator symbol for addition. But the + operator for integer operands is semantically distinct from the + operator for floating-point operands. The ambiguity at the user level caused by <u>syntactic overloading</u> of operator symbols can be detected at compile time by checking the operand types of each operator. Thus a compiler can recognize that a + symbol between two integer operands represents integer addition, a + symbol between two floating-point operands represents floating-point addition, and a + symbol between two operands of different type is a programmer error. Since integer and floating-point addition are generally implemented by different machine-language instructions, the compiler will probably generate different code in both the intermediate and target language for integer and floating-point addition operators.

3.2.2 Derived types

The type definition mechanism of Ada may be used to define <u>derived types</u> which have the same value set and operators as the parent types from which they are derived, but represent logically distinct classes of objects. In the following example we introduce the derived type WEIGHT which has the same value set and applicable operations as the data type INTEGER. This requires the language to treat weights and integers as logically distinct kinds of data objects and precludes adding of weights and integers or assignment of weights to integer variables.

Example 3.2. Derived types

```
procedure DERIVED_TYPES is
   type WEIGHT is new INTEGER;  -- WEIGHT is new type derived from INTEGER
   I: INTEGER := 0;       -- initialized integer variable
   W: WEIGHT := 0;        -- variable of type WEIGHT initialized to integer literal
begin
   W := W+1;              -- legal because WEIGHT inherits literal 1 and operator +
   W := W+I;              -- illegal because W and I are of different types
   W := I;                -- illegal because W and I are of different types
   W := WEIGHT(I);        -- legal, WEIGHT(I) is of type WEIGHT
   I := INTEGER(W)+1;     -- legal, INTEGER(W) is of type INTEGER
   W := W*W;              -- weights can be multiplied since * is inherited
end;
```

The example illustrates that the derived type WEIGHT inherits both literals and operators from its parent type INTEGER. The literal 1 in the expression "W+1" is interpreted as being of the type WEIGHT by virtue of its context, and the operator + is interpreted as being the addition operator for objects of type WEIGHT because it has operands of type WEIGHT. Thus the derived type WEIGHT causes an overloading of integer literals as well as overloading of operators such as the + operator. In this case the machine-language implementation of addition of weights is likely to be identical with that for addition of integers. The compiler need only check for the legality of source language programs. The code generated in the target language is likely to be the same as that which would have been generated if W had been declared an INTEGER variable.

The derived type mechanism can be used to build up a tree structure of related types, as illustrated in figure 3.1 below.

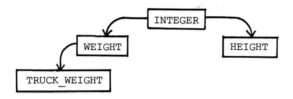

Figure 3.1. Tree structure of derived types.

Type conversion functions are automatically defined for conversion among adjacent nodes of such a tree structure, but cannot be used for indirect conversion between nonadjacent nodes.

Example 3.3. Type conversion for derived types

```
procedure TYPE_CONVERSION is
   type WEIGHT is new INTEGER;
   type HEIGHT is new INTEGER;
   type TRUCK_WEIGHT is new WEIGHT;
   I: INTEGER := 0;
   W: WEIGHT := 0;
   H: HEIGHT := 0;
   TW: TRUCK_WEIGHT := 0;
begin
   H := INTEGER(I);    -- legal conversion between "adjacent" derived types
   H := HEIGHT(W);     -- illegal conversion between "nonadjacent" types
   H := HEIGHT(INTEGER(W));            -- legal sequence of conversion
   TW := TRUCK_WEIGHT (WEIGHT(I));  -- legal sequence of conversions
   H := HEIGHT(INTEGER(WEIGHT(TW))); -- legal sequence of conversions
end TYPE_CONVERSION;
```

The derived type facility allows the user to distinguish between logically distinct classes of objects. But the rule that all literals and operators are inherited from the parent type is too permissive. For example, it does not really make sense to multiply weights and assign the result to a variable of type WEIGHT as in "W := W*W;". The derived type inheritance mechanism is too permissive to properly handle computations involving conversion among units, as illustrated by the following example.

Example 3.4. Conversion between units

```
procedure UNITS is
   type LENGTH is new FLOAT;      -- length is a basic unit
   type AREA is new FLOAT         -- product of lengths should yield an area
   type TIME is new FLOAT;        -- time is a basic unit
   type VELOCITY is new FLOAT;    -- length/time should yield velocity
   L1,L2: LENGTH := 0.0;
   A1,A2: AREA := 0.0;
   T1,T2: TIME := 0.0;
   V: VELOCITY;
begin
   L1 := L1+L2;                   -- legal addition of lengths
   L1 := L1*L2;                   -- product of lengths is a length
   A1 := L1*L2;                   -- illegal, since product is of type LENGTH
   V := L1/T1;                    -- illegal mixing of types
end UNITS;
```

The two illegal statements of the previous example can be
made legal by function specifications which overload the * and /
operators as follows.

Example 3.5. Functions for unit conversion

```
procedure OVERLOAD is
   function "*" (X,Y: LENGTH) return AREA is
   begin
      return AREA(FLOAT(X*Y));
   end "*";
   function "/" (L: LENGTH; T: TIME) return VELOCITY is
   begin
      return VELOCITY(FLOAT(L)/FLOAT(T));
   end "/";
begin
   A1 := L1*L2;     -- multiply lengths to produce area
   V := L1/T1;      -- divide length by time to produce velocity
end OVERLOAD;
```

The permissive inheritance rules for derived types have the
virtue of simplicity and are more likely to be used by application programmers than a more complex set of inheritance rules
which handles units correctly.

However, if the user wishes to define derived types with
selective inheritance rules, this can be accomplished with a
little more work on the part of the user by embedding functions
such as those above in a library package, as described in
Chapter 4.

3.2.3 Constraints

The value set of a type may be restricted by means of constraints associated with a type definition. For example, the
value set of the type WEIGHT could have been restricted by one
of the following range constraints.

Example 3.6. Constrained derived type definitions

```
type WEIGHT is new INTEGER range 0..1000;   -- integer in range 0..1000
type WEIGHT is new INTEGER range 0..MAXWEIGHT; -- value supplied at run time
type WEIGHT is new INTEGER range 0..INTEGER'LAST; -- any nonnegative integer
```

Constraints are illustrated above for integers but may be applied to a wide variety of types. They will be discussed in the context of each type as it is introduced.

3.2.4 Anonymous type definitions and type equivalence

The general syntax of type declarations is as follows

type typename is type-definition;

A type definition may be either a derived type definition or an anonymous type definition. Derived type definitions define the new type in terms of a previously named type and possibly a constraint, and have the following syntax:

new typename [constraint];

Anonymous type definitions define a new type directly in terms of the attributes of the new type. For example, the derived type definition "new INTEGER range 1..1000" can be expressed without use of the typename INTEGER by the anonymous type definition "range 1..1000". The three derived type declarations of the previous example may be expressed by the following anonymous type declarations.

Example 3.7. Type declarations with anonymous type definitions

```
type WEIGHT is range 0..1000;
type WEIGHT is range 0..MAXWEIGHT;
type WEIGHT is range 0..INTEGER'LAST;
```

Anonymous type definitions are used above to declare new type names. They may also be used in object declarations to directly declare the type of an object.

Example 3.8. Anonymous object declarations

```
I: range 0..1000;            -- I is integer variable of anonymous type
A: array(1..1000) of INTEGER; -- array object of anonymous type
SEX: (M,F);                  -- anonymous SEX object
```

Every type definition in Ada introduces a distinct new type. Each anonymous type declaration must therefore be regarded as introducing a distinct type. Thus A and B below have the same type, while the type of C is regarded as different from that of A and B because it is defined by a different type definition.

Example 3.9. Type equivalence for anonymous types

```
A,B: array(1..100) of INTEGER;    -- A, B have the same type
C: array(1..100) of INTEGER;      -- type of C differs from type of A, B
```

Anonymous types provide a useful abbreviation in certain contexts and may avoid needless introduction of superfluous type names. However, they should be used with caution because they can give rise to inadvertent type incompatibilities. In particular, anonymous types should not be used in procedure parameters because the parameter assumes a unique anonymous type, and there is no way of calling the procedure with a type-compatible actual parameter.

Example 3.10. Problem of anonymous subprogram parameters

```
A: array(1..100) of INTEGER;               -- A has anonymous type
procedure T(X: array(1..100) of INTEGER);  -- type of X differs from A
T(A);                         -- illegal call, type of A incompatible with X
                              -- since X is anonymous we cannot convert type
                              -- of A to type of X
```

Since anonymous type specifications of procedure parameters can never be used they are in fact syntactically illegal (compile-time errors). The types of procedure parameters must always be specified by named types, such as VECTOR in the following example.

Example 3.11. Type equivalence for named types

```
type VECTOR is array(1..100) of INTEGER;
A,B: VECTOR;            -- A, B are of type VECTOR
C: VECTOR;              -- C is of the same type as A and B
procedure T(X: VECTOR); -- X is of the same type as A, B, C
T(A);                   -- legal call, A and X have the same type
```

Thus two variable identifiers in Ada have the same type if they are declared to be of the same named type or if they are declared in the same anonymous type declaration.

3.2.5 Subtypes

Subtypes in Ada are abbreviations for a type name and associated constraint. They are introduced by subtype declarations which are similar in form to derived type declarations. However, variables of different subtypes of a given type may be freely mixed with each other and with variables and literals of the parent type.

Example 3.12. Subtypes and range checking

```
procedure SUBTYPES is
   subtype SMALL is INTEGER range -100..100;      -- subtype declaration
   S,T: SMALL := 0;          -- S, T are variables of subtype
   I,J: INTEGER := 0;        -- INTEGER is the parent type
begin
   S := 50;        -- legality can be checked at compile time
   S := S+10;      -- may require run-time range check
   I := S;         -- assignment is always legal
   S := I;         -- may require run-time range check
   I := S+J;       -- type and subtype variables can be freely mixed
   S := S*S-T*T;   -- subtype constraints may be exceeded during expression
end SUBTYPES;      -- evaluation.  Need be checked only on assignment
```

This example illustrates that constraints may sometimes be checkable at compile time (as in "S := 50;") or may require checking at run time (as in "S := S+10;"). Mixing of subtypes in assignment statements is always legal, but may require range checking. Expressions (such as "S*S-T*T") are evaluated as though they were of the parent type, but the subsequent assignment to S requires a range check.

The type conversion and range-checking requirements between a type, its subtype and its derived types are illustrated in figure 3.2.

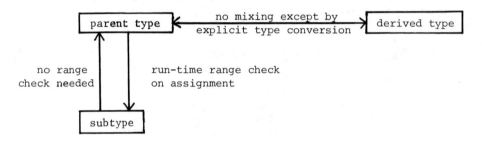

Figure 3.2. Range checking and explicit type conversion

Note that subtype declarations in which the parent type has no constraints are a mechanism for renaming the parent type.

Example 3.13. Renaming function

```
subtype INT is INTEGER;      -- INT is a new name for INTEGER
```

A subtype declaration has the following syntax:

```
subtype newname is typename [constraint];
```

The new type name of a subtype must be defined in terms of a type name. Thus the following subtype definition is illegal.

Example 3.14. Subtypes must be defined in terms of named types

subtype WEIGHT is range 0..1000; -- illegal because subtype must be defined
                                  -- in terms of a type name

The definition of WEIGHT as a constrained integer type (or subtype) provides a more realistic characterization of the attributes of weights and allows certain errors, such as negative weights, to be caught by the system. However, range errors cannot in general be caught at compile time. Range constraints may require the compiler to insert additional code for checking at run time. Computations with constrained variables in an inner loop may noticeably slow down a computation. The language permits range checking to be suppressed (see section 1.18).

Constraints are illustrated above for integers but are applicable to a wide variety of data types, and require different notations for different classes of data types. They will be discussed in the context of each class of types as it is introduced.

3.2.6 Attribute enquiries

Data types determine a set of attributes possessed by data objects of the type. These attributes are sometimes needed by the programmer during the course of a computation, and may be accessed by attribute enquiries.

Attribute enquiries are composite names of a special form. They consist of a type or object name followed by a single quote mark followed by an attribute name.

Example 3.15. Attribute enquiries

```
INTEGER'FIRST       -- first (most negative) integer value
INTEGER'LAST        -- last (largest) integer value
WEIGHT'LAST         -- last value of data type WEIGHT
VECTOR'FIRST        -- first index of data type VECTOR
VECTOR'LENGTH       -- length of VECTOR type
V'LENGTH            -- length of VECTOR object V
```

Attribute enquiries are read-only variables (constants) and return values which may be used to control the course of a computation. For example, the attributes V'FIRST, V'LAST may be used to control the index of iteration of a for loop over elements of a vector V.

87

Example 3.16. Use of attribute enquiries to control iteration

```
for I in V'FIRST..V'LAST loop            -- first to last index of V
   SUM := SUM+V(I);
      -- or some complicated computation
      -- involving V
end loop;
```

Each class of declared object has characteristic attribute enquiries associated with it, which will be described when that class of objects is considered. Appendix A of the reference manual contains a list of 45 language-defined attribute enquiries.

3.2.7 Classification of types

The data types of Ada can be classified into three categories:

1. Scalar types whose associated data objects have no components. These include numeric, Boolean, character and enumeration types.
2. Structured types, such as arrays and records, whose associated data objects have components which are selectable by selectors.
3. Access types, whose associated data objects are created dynamically by executing allocation commands in the statement sequence of a program unit.

The scalar types of Ada may further be classified as follows:

1. Integer types which may be used for exact computation.
2. Enumeration types which have a finite value set defined by enumeration of their elements. The types BOOLEAN and CHARACTER may be classified as enumeration types.
3. Floating-point types which may be used for approximate computation with a specified relative accuracy (number of significant figures).
4. Fixed-point types which may be used for approximate computation with a specified absolute accuracy (number of decimal places).

Integer types have a value set which is ordered and which has a minimum and maximum element. Every element other than the maximum has a unique successor, and every element other than the minimum has a unique predecessor.

Ordered value sets with minimum and maximum elements and successor and predecessor functions are referred to as discrete ranges. A data type whose value set is a discrete range is said to be a discrete type.

In Ada both integer types and enumeration types have discrete ranges. Floating-point and fixed-point types have value sets which are ordered, but are not discrete types because they do not have successor and predecessor functions defined over the value set. Floating- and fixed-point types are sometimes referred to as <u>real types</u>.

Discrete ranges may be used as index sets of arrays, and as ranges of iteration statements. In Ada both integer and enumeration types can be used for indexing and iteration, but floating- and fixed-point types cannot.

Scalar types may conveniently be classified into discrete types and real types as indicated in figure 3.3.

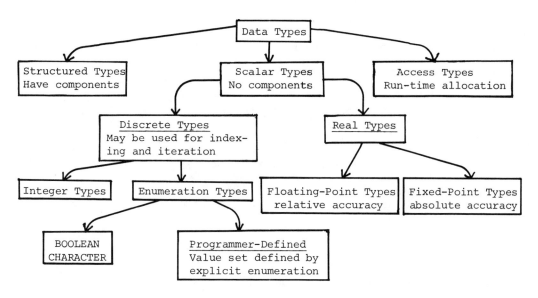

Figure 3.3. Classification of data types.

In the remaining sections of this chapter we shall consider first type definition mechanisms for various kinds of scalar types and then type definition mechanisms for structured types and access types.

3.3 Numeric Types

In defining numeric types we start from the notion of numbers as abstract mathematical objects which can be operated on by abstract algebraic operators. However, the finiteness of computers requires range restrictions to be placed on the value set of numeric types. In the case of floating- and fixed-point types an accuracy restriction as well as a range restriction is required.

Ada supports <u>predefined</u> integer and floating-point types with range and accuracy restrictions generally determined by the word size of the implementation. There is no predefined fixed-point type.

89

The need for <u>programmer-defined</u> numeric types stems in part from the need to ensure <u>portability</u> among different implementations, and in part from the need of applications for logical distinctions among entities with the same value set and for range and accuracy guarantees for numeric value sets.

3.3.1 Integer types

The predefined type INTEGER has an implementation-defined range whose smallest (most negative) value is given by the attribute enquiry INTEGER'FIRST and whose maximum value is given by INTEGER'LAST. An implementation may also provide the predefined type LONG_INTEGER with a greater range than INTEGER and SHORT_INTEGER with a smaller range than INTEGER.

The programmer has no control over the range of the predefined integer data types. Programs which contain them may not be portable between implementations. The programmer may wish to define integer data types with explicit range constraints both in the interests of portability and because range constraints (such as non-negativity) may arise naturally in an application. The example below has a type INDEX with a range constraint that might be used to limit the size of arrays, a type NATURAL with a range constraint which requires variables of the type to be natural numbers, and a type SHORT_INT with a range constraint which allows variables of the type to be implemented in a 16-bit computer word.

Example 3.17. Declaration and use of integer types

```
procedure INTEGER_TYPES is
    type INDEX is range 1..100;          -- index range
    type NATURAL is range 1..INTEGER'LAST; -- positive integer
    type SHORT_INT is range -32768..32767; -- short (16-bit) integer
    I,J: INDEX;                           -- two index variables
    N1,N2: NATURAL;                       -- two natural number variables
    S1,S2: SHORT_INT;                     -- two short integer variables
begin
    I := 80;                  -- assign to index variable
    I := I+1;                 -- requires run-time range check
    I := INTEGER'SUCC(I);--  SUCC and PRED are defined for integers
    S1 := S2*S2;              -- requires run-time range check
    N1 := I;                  -- illegal mixing of types
end INTEGER TYPES;
```

A data type will be called an <u>integer type</u> if its value set is a subrange of integers and its operations are the integer operations. Integer types may be defined by derived types from predefined types (as in section 3.2.2) or by anonymous integer type definitions (as in section 3.2.4). For any integer type T the smallest and larges values can be determined by the attribute enquiries T'FIRST, T'LAST. Thus LONG_INTEGER'LAST yields the value of the largest long integer.

Integer literals consist of a string of digits, possibly separated by underscore symbols (as in 1_234_567). The general syntax of integers is as follows:

    digit{[underscore]digit}

Ada permits based integer literals in any base between 2 and 16. Based integer literals have the following syntax:

    base # extended-digit{[underscore] extended-digit}

where an extended digit for bases greater than 10 may use the symbols A..F to represent the respective digits 10..15.

Example 3.18. Based integer literals

```
2#1101                  -- represents 13
2#1101_1011             -- represents 219
16#D                    -- represents 13
16#DB                   -- represents 219
```

The operators applicable to integer types are listed in table 3.1 in order of decreasing precedence.

```
exponentiation operator:  **                -- highest precedence
multiplying operators:    * / mod
unary operators:          + -
adding operators:         + -
relational operators:     = /= < <= > >=  -- lowest precedence
```

    Table 3.1 Precedence of integer operators

The operators generally behave in the expected way. Certain nonstandard behavior of the exponentiation, division and mod operators is pointed out below.

The exponentiation operator for integers must have an integer as its first operand and a non-negative integer as its second operand.

Example 3.19. Behavior of exponentiation operator

```
2**3            -- has value 8
2**3.5          -- illegal - no non-integer exponents
2**-3           -- illegal - no negative exponents
2**I            -- legality may require run-time check
```

The division operator truncates towards zero.

Example 3.20. Behavior of integer division

```
7/4                       -- has value 1
-7/4                      -- has value -1
7/4 + 7/4                 -- has value 2
```

The division and mod operators are related by the identity

A = (A/B)*B + A mod B

Thus if A is -7 and B is 4 then

-7 = (-7/4)*4 + (-7 mod 4)

so that -7 mod 4 = -3, and the remainder A mod B is in general a negative number when A/B is negative.

This means that mod in general does not satisfy the identity

A mod B = (A-B) mod B

Example 3.21. Behavior of mod operator

```
3 mod 4                   -- has value 3
(3-4) mod 4               -- has value -1
(I-J) mod 4               -- value depends on sign of I-J
```

Thus the mod function should be used with caution when there is a possibility of A/B being negative, since it does not behave entirely as expected.

3.3.2 Floating-point types

Floating-point types have a precision and a range, as illustrated by the following type definition.

Example 3.22. Floating-point type definition

digits 8 range -1E30..1E30;

Type definitions may be used to declare named types having the attributes of the type definition, as in the following example.

Example 3.23. Floating-point type declaration

type MY_FLOAT is digits 8 range -1E30..1E30;

The precision and range specification of a type define minimum requirements for an implementation. The actual precision

92

and range will be determined by the characteristics of the object computer and may exceed these specifications. For example, the specification "digits 8 range -1E30..1E30" requires at least 28 bits for the mantissa and 8 bits for the exponent. It could be efficiently implemented in a 36-bit word. However, in a computer with a 32-bit word, the implementation of this type would require two words, and might for example be implemented by a 32-bit mantissa (over 9 digits of precision), an 8-bit exponent and 24 unused bits.

The predefined type FLOAT has a system-defined precision and range which is generally determined by the hardware. The precision and accuracy of FLOAT can be constrained, as in "FLOAT digits 8 range -1E30..1E30". New constrained types can be defined in terms of previously named types by derived type declarations.

Example 3.24.   Nonportable derived type declaration

type MY_FLT is new FLOAT digits 8 range -1E30..1E30;

This derived type declaration has the same semantic effect as the type declaration of the previous example provided the predefined type FLOAT has at least the precision and range specified by the constraints. However, if FLOAT has an accuracy of less than 8 digits, then the declaration of MY_FLT would be illegal. This example illustrates that programs with constrained predefined types may be nonportable.

The following example illustrates a derived type declaration which is guaranteed to be portable because it is defined in terms of a programmer-defined type (MY_FLOAT) whose range and precision are explicitly defined to be greater than that of the constraint.

Example 3.25. Portable derived type declaration

type MY_FLT is new MY_FLOAT digits 6 range -1E30..1E30;

The following example illustrates both styles of declaration, and includes some examples of legal and illegal floating-point assignment statements.

Example 3.26. Declaration and use of floating-point types

```
procedure FLOAT_TYPES is
   type MY_FLOAT is digits 8 range -1E30..1E30;
   type MY_FLT is new MY_FLOAT digits 6 range -1E30..1E30;
   X,Y,Z: MY_FLOAT := 0.0;    -- user-defined accuracy and range
   P,Q,R: MY_FLT;             -- derived type definition
begin
   X := 1.53+2.53E-1;         -- constant expression, evaluated at compile time
   Y := 2.0*X**2;             -- multiplication and exponentiation
   Y := X**3.51;              -- illegal, only integer exponents permitted
   R := 2*P+1;                -- illegal, cannot use integer literals
   Z := R;                    -- illegal, cannot mix types
end FLOAT_TYPES;
```

The syntax of floating-point literals may be summarized as follows:

```
[sign]integer.integer[E exponent]  -- 3.5, 3.5E-1
[sign]integer E exponent            -- 1E2, 1E-2
```

That is, a floating-point literal is a number literal with a decimal point optionally followed by an exponent, or an integer followed by an exponent. The exponent part consists of the symbol E and an integer optionally preceded by a + or - sign.

The set of operations on floating-point numbers includes all operations on integers with the exception of mod. The precedence of operations is the same for floating-point numbers as for integers.

The exponentiation operator for floating-point numbers may take negative as well as non-negative integers as its second operand, but cannot take floating-point values as operands.

The syntax of floating-point type declarations may be summarized as follows:

```
type typename is digits P[range L..R];
type typename is new oldtype digits P[range L..R];
```

where P is a static integer expression specifying the number of digits, and L and R are static floating-point expressions specifying the minimum (most negative) and maximum values of the range.

Note that the range (which determines the number of bits required to specify the exponent) is optional in a type declaration. Only the precision (determined by the number of bits in the mantissa) need be specified.

If T is a floating-point type then the attribute enquiries T'DIGITS, T'SMALL and T'LARGE specify the precision, smallest

positive element and maximum element of the type T. Thus
FLOAT'DIGITS specifies the precision of the predefined type
FLOAT.

The predefined types LONG_FLOAT with precision greater than
FLOAT and SHORT_FLOAT with precision less than FLOAT may, but
need not, be defined in the language. Their precision can be
determined by appropriate attribute enquiries, and could be
defined to be the same as FLOAT for implementations which do not
support these predefined types.

3.3.3 Fixed-point types

Fixed-point types have precisely the same set of literals
and operations as floating-point types. However, the accuracy
of fixed-point types is defined in absolute terms rather than in
relative terms. The accuracy of fixed-point types is referred
to as the delta.

Example 3.27. Fixed-point type definition

delta .01 range -100.0..100.0;

The above type definition can be used in a type declaration
which associates a name with the type definition.

Example 3.28. Fixed-point type declaration

type MY_FIXED is delta .01 range -100.0..100.0;

A derived type with a delta of .1 can be defined as follows:

Example 3.29. Fixed-point derived type declaration

type MY_FIX is new MY_FIXED delta .1;

Since the range constraint is omitted it is assumed to be
the same as the type from which it is derived.

Fixed-point types guarantee that numbers will be represented
to at least the accuracy specified by the delta. However, they
do not guarantee that numbers are stored exactly. The accumula-
tion of small errors to yield an inexact value may be illustrated
by the following example.

Example 3.30. Declaration and use of fixed-point types

```
procedure FIXED_TYPES is
   type MY_FIXED is delta .1 range -100;
   X,Y: MY_FIXED;
begin
   X := 1.1;
   Y := 1.1+2.1+3.1;
   PUT(X);                          -- value of 1.1 is guaranteed
   PUT(Y);                          -- value of 6.3 is not guaranteed
end FIXED_TYPES;
```

The above declaration for MY_FIXED guarantees that numbers such as 1.1 will be represented to an accuracy of delta = .1, so that PUT(X) in the above example will print the correct value. However, the fractional part corresponding to a delta of .1 might, for example, be represented by a four-binary-digit fractional part. In this case .1 would be represented by 2/16 = .125, .2 would be represented by 3/16 = .1875, .3 would be represented by 5/16 = .3125, etc. The sum 1.1 + 2.1 + 3.1 would be computed as 1.125 + 2.125 + 3.125 = 6.375 which, when printed, would yield 6.4. On the other hand, if the fractional part is represented by five or more binary digits, the individual numbers would be stored with greater accuracy and this particular sequence of additions would yield the correct value of 6.3.

This example illustrates that fixed-point data types cannot be used for exact computations such as payroll computations, where the sum of a column of figures must exactly balance.

Multiplication and division of fixed-point expressions by integers is permitted.

Example 3.31. Multiplication by integers

```
2*X+X/3               -- legal if X is fixed-point
                      -- but not if X is floating-point
```

It is easy to lose accuracy in fixed-point computations if the numbers are smaller than expected or to exceed capacity if the numbers are larger than expected. Floating-point types provide more flexibility than fixed-point types for most numeric computations. The fixed-point facility is essentially a "poorman's" floating-point for computers which have no hardware-supported floating-point or where space is so critical that storage for exponents is unaffordable.

3.4   Enumeration Types

Enumeration types have a finite number of values and may be defined by explicitly listing the values in a type definition. A type DIRECTION with four values can be defined as follows.

Example 3.32. Enumeration type declaration

type DIRECTION is (NORTH,SOUTH,EAST,WEST);

     The use of enumeration types in computation can be illustrated by the following function for "turning left" which has a parameter of type DIRECTION and returns a result of type DIRECTION.

Example 3.33. Function with enumeration type parameter and result

```
function TURN_LEFT(D: DIRECTION) return DIRECTION is
begin
  case D of
    when NORTH => return WEST;
    when SOUTH => return EAST;
    when EAST => return NORTH;
    when WEST => return SOUTH;
  end case;
end TURN_LEFT;
```


     This example illustrates that functions which perform a different computation for each value of an enumeration type may typically be handled by a case statement. It illustrates also the ease with which Ada allows us to define and use an abstract concept like direction.

     We shall take this example a little further and define a function CHANGE_COURSE which takes a direction and a TURN specification as parameters and returns a new direction as a result. In order to do this it is convenient to define the following data type.

Example 3.34. Another enumeration type

type TURN is (LEFT,RIGHT,STRAIGHT,REVERSE);

     The function CHANGE_COURSE may be defined in terms of the data types DIRECTION and TURN as follows.

Example 3.35. Function with two enumeration type parameters

```
function CHANGE_COURSE(D: DIRECTION: T: TURN) return DIRECTION is
begin
  case T of
    when LEFT => return TURN_LEFT(D);
    when RIGHT => return TURN_RIGHT(D);
    when STRAIGHT => return D;
    when REVERSE => return TURN_ABOUT(D);
  end case;
end CHANGE_COURSE;
```

The function TURN_LEFT used in the CHANGE_COURSE function has already been defined. The functions TURN_RIGHT and TURN_ABOUT may be defined using a case statement which is similar to that used to implement the TURN_LEFT function.

Further use of the enumeration data types DIRECTION and TURN may be illustrated by defining a function MANEUVER which takes an old and a new direction as its arguments and computes the turn required to change from the old to the new direction.

Example 3.36. Building up vocabulary for "navigation"

```
function MANEUVER(OLD,NEW: DIRECTION) return TURN is
begin
  if NEW = TURN_LEFT(OLD) then
    return LEFT;
  elsif NEW = TURN_RIGHT(OLD) then
    return RIGHT;
  elsif NEW = TURN_ABOUT(OLD) then
    return REVERSE;
  elsif NEW = OLD then
    return STRAIGHT;
  end if;
end MANEUVER;
```


This example is implemented by an if statement with four branches corresponding to the four possible relations between the parameters OLD and NEW. We cannot use a case statement because the branches of a case statement can contain only statically determined value sets and not conditions to be tested at execution time.

The above examples illustrate how type and subprogram declarations may be used to build up a vocabulary of abstract concepts in an application domain (in this case "navigation").

In order to further illustrate enumeration types, we shall switch our domain of discourse from navigational concepts and consider an enumeration type DAY with the seven days of the week as its values.

Example 3.37. Days of the week

```
type DAY is (MON,TUE,WED,THU,FRI,SAT,SUN);
```


Use of the type DAY may be illustrated by the function HOURS_WORKED which takes a parameter of the type DAY and returns the number of hours worked as its value.

Example 3.38. HOURS WORKED function

```
function HOURS_WORKED(D: DAY) return INTEGER is
begin
   case D of
      when MON|TUE|WED|THU|FRI => return 8;
      when SAT|SUN => return 0;
   end case;
end HOURS_WORKED;
```

The sequence of values of an enumeration type is considered to be ordered ("TUE < SAT" has the value TRUE). The function HOURS_WORKED could alternatively have been specified as follows.

Example 3.39. An implementation which uses ordering relations

```
function HOURS_WORKED(D: DAY) return INTEGER is
begin
   if D < SAT then
      return 8;
   else
      return 0;
   end if;
end HOURS_WORKED;
```

Note that this style of specification could not have been implemented with a case statement. The clause "when D < SAT => return 8;" is illegal because the condition following the keyword when must be statically determined and the condition D < SAT can be determined only at run time.

The set of elements of an enumeration type is a discrete range with a lower bound, upper bound and linear ordering. Discrete ranges which are enumeration types have many of the properties of discrete ranges of integers. For example, the notation MON..FRI can be used to denote a subrange of the type DAY just as 1..10 is used to denote a subrange of integers. Subranges of enumeration types may be used to control the iteration of for statements, as in the following example.

Example 3.40. Iteration over enumeration range

```
for I in MON..FRI loop
   A(I) := A(I)+1;
end loop;
```

The above example also illustrates that the index type of an array may be an enumeration type, as in the following anonymous type declaration for A.

99

Example 3.41. Array with enumeration index type

A: array(DAY) of INTEGER;

Subranges of an enumeration type may be used as constraints
in a derived type definition or as range constraints of a directly defined type, just as for integers.

Example 3.42. Subranges of an enumeration type

type WEEKDAY is new DAY range MON..FRI;
subtype WEEKDAY is DAY range MON..FRI;

Enumeration types have many predefined attributes which may
be interrogated by attribute enquiries. Some of the permitted
attribute enquiries are illustrated in the following example.

Example 3.43. Enumeration types

```
procedure ENUMERATION_TYPES is
   type DAY is (MON,TUE,WED,THU,FRI,SAT,SUN);
   D1,D2: DAY;                   -- D1, D2 are objects of type DAY
begin
   D1 := MON;                    -- assign literal MON to D1
   D1 := DAY'FIRST;              -- same effect as previous statement
   D2 := DAY'SUCC(D1);           -- successor function for type DAY
   if D1 /= DAY'FIRST then       -- test for legality
      D1 := DAY'PRED(D1);        -- of predecessor function
   end if;
end ENUMERATION_TYPES;
```


This example illustrates that the first element of a variable V of enumeration type T can be determined by the attribute
enquiry T'FIRST (as in DAY'FIRST). Last elements may similarly
be determined by T'LAST. The successor function attribute
T'SUCC and predecessor function attribute T'PRED for variables
of an enumeration type are also illustrated.

Other attribute enquiries available for enumeration types
include T'ORD(X) which gives the ordinal position of X in the
enumeration type (DAY'ORD(TUE) = 2), and T'VAL(I) which gives
the value of the Ith enumeration literal (DAY'VAL(2) = TUE).
The functions ORD and VAL are inverses: T'VAL(T'ORD(X)) = X and
T'ORD(T'VAL(I)) = I.

Elements of an enumeration type (called enumeration literals) can be identifiers or character literals. In the following
example the set of values of the type HEX_LETTER is different
from the set of literals of the type GRADE.

100

Example 3.44. Enumeration literals

type HEX_LETTER is ("A","B","C","D","E","F");
type GRADE is (A,B,C,D,E,F);

However, enumeration types with the same literals may be
defined, as in the following example.

Example 3.45. Overloading of enumeration literals

type COLOR is (RED,BLUE,WHITE,BLACK);
type LIGHT is (RED,AMBER,GREEN);
type LANGUAGE is (RED,GREEN,YELLOW,BLUE);

The literals RED, GREEN and BLUE in the above example are
overloaded. In most instances of use the syntactic ambiguity of
such overloading can be resolved because the context will require
a specific type. However, when this is not the case (as in
"for I in RED..GREEN loop") the type of the constant must be
explicitly indicated using the type conversion notation.

Example 3.46. Disambiguation of overloaded literals

for I in LANGUAGE(RED)..LANGUAGE(GREEN) loop

3.5 Boolean and Character Data Types

     The predefined data type BOOLEAN may be regarded as an
enumeration type with the two literals FALSE, TRUE. The predefined logical operators not, and, or, xor have operands and
values of this enumeration type. Like other enumeration types,
the value set of Boolean types is a discrete range so that
FALSE < TRUE, BOOLEAN'FIRST has the value FALSE and
BOOLEAN'SUCC(FALSE) has the value TRUE. Examples of expressions
and statements with Boolean data objects have been given in
Chapter 2.

     The predefined type CHARACTER may be regarded as an enumera-
tion type with the standard 128 ordered ASCII character literals.
The character set and textual ordering (collating sequence) are
defined in the language reference manual (Appendix C) by the
following derived type definition.

Example 3.47. The enumeration type CHARACTER

```
type CHARACTER is
  ( NUL,  SOH,  STX,  ETX,  EOT,  ENQ,  ACK,  BEL,
    BS,   HT,   LF,   VT,   FF,   CR,   SO,   SI,
    DLE,  DC1,  DC2,  DC3,  DC4,  NAK,  SYN,  ETB,
    CAN,  EM,   SUB,  ESC,  FS,   GS,   RS,   US,
    " ",  "!",  """",  "#",  "$",  "%%",  "&",  "'",
    "(",  ")",  "*",  "+",  ",",  "-",  ".",  "/",
    "0",  "1",  "2",  "3",  "4",  "5",  "6",  "7",
    "8",  "9",  ":",  ";",  "<",  "=",  ">",  "?",
    "@",  "A",  "B",  "C",  "D",  "E",  "F",  "G",
    "H",  "I",  "J",  "K",  "L",  "M",  "N",  "O",
    "P",  "Q",  "R",  "S",  "T",  "U",  "V",  "W",
    "X",  "Y",  "Z",  "[",  "\",  "]",  "^",  "_",
    "`",  "a",  "b",  "c",  "d",  "e",  "f",  "g",
    "h",  "i",  "j",  "k",  "l",  "m",  "n",  "o",
    "p",  "q",  "r",  "s",  "t",  "u",  "v",  "w",
    "x",  "y",  "z",  "{",  "|",  "}",  "~",  DEL);
```

Thus letters appear after digits in the collating sequence. The digit "0" is the 49th element in the collating sequence (CHARACTER'ORD("0") has the value 49), while the letter "A" is the 66th element (CHARACTER'ORD("A") has the value 66). Arithmetic operators appear before letters and digits, and small letters appear after capital letters. Character positions which do not correspond to characters of the extended character set contain mnemonic identifiers.

The data type STRING, denoting an array of characters, is a predefined type of the language whose semantics will be discussed after array data types have been discussed.

The predefined binary operator & is applicable to arguments of the type CHARACTER or STRING, and produces a string as a result.

3.6 Array Types

An array is a data structure with a set of components of similar type which may be selected by indexing. Array types may be constructed from an underlying component type and index type by means of a type constructor designated by the keyword array.

Example 3.48. Array type definition

```
array(1..100) of INTEGER      -- component-type INTEGER, index-type 1..100
```

Declaration and accessing of array data types is illustrated in the following example.

Example 3.49.

```
procedure ARRAYS is
   type VECTOR is array(1..100) of INTEGER; -- index type is subrange of integers
   type MATRIX is array(1..N,1..M) of INTEGER;   -- two-dimensional array
   V: VECTOR;                               -- an object of type VECTOR
   M: MATRIX;                               -- an object of type MATRIX
begin
   V(3) := 7;              -- assignment to element of a vector
   M(I,J) := V(3)+1;       -- assignment to element of a matrix
end ARRAYS;
```

Arrays in Ada may be manipulated either by access to components as in the previous example or by operations on the complete array. We can define array-valued literals (called aggregates), assign array aggregates to array variables, and assign values of array variables to arrays of compatible size.

Example 3.50. Positional array aggregates

```
declare
   type VECTOR is array(1..5) of INTEGER;
   V,W: VECTOR := (0,0,0,0,0);        -- initialize to array literal
begin
   V := (1,2,3,4,5);                  -- assign literal array to V
   W := V;                            -- assign value of array V to W
end;
```

Complete array assignments such as "W := V;" are legal only if the types of W and V are the same and the number of elements in V is the same as the number of elements in W.

The literals in the above example are called positional aggregates because the association between array components and array values is indicated by a position in a list. Ada also supports nonpositional array aggregates where the association between component names and values is explicitly indicated.

Example 3.51. Nonpositional array aggregates

```
(1..3 => 1, 4..5 => 0) -- nonpositional aggregate with value (1,1,1,0,0)
(1..3 => 1, others => 0) -- alternative representation of same value
(1|3|5 => 1, others => 0) -- nonpositional aggregate with value (1,0,1,0,1)
(MON..FRI => 8, others => 0) -- literal (8,8,8,8,8,0,0) for "array(DAY)
                           -- of INTEGER"
(N => W, S => E, E => N, W => S) -- initialization for "array(DIRECTION) of
                      -- DIRECTION" which corresponds to turning left
```

The use of nonpositional aggregates can be illustrated by the following implementation of the function TURN_LEFT in terms of an initialized array whose index set and value set are directions.

Example 3.52. Use of nonpositional array aggregates

```
function TURN_LEFT(D: DIRECTION) return DIRECTION is
   NEW_D: constant array(DIRECTION) of DIRECTION
       := (N => W,              -- initialize components of
            S => E,             -- constant array NEW_D
            E => N,             -- by a nonpositional aggregate
            W => S);            -- insensitive to ordering of components
begin
   return NEW_D(D);            -- new direction is found by
end TURN_LEFT;                 -- table look-up in array NEW_D
```

The above example suggests the implementation of symbol tables by arrays whose index and value sets are enumeration types. The index set constitutes the set of "keys" of the symbol table. Table look-up is accomplished simply by indexing the identifier which names the symbol table array by the element of the index set which constitutes the key, while updating of a symbol table entry can be accomplished by assigning a new value to the given entry.

Example 3.53. Enumeration type index sets and symbol tables

```
TABLE: array(INDEX_SET) of VALUE_SET;    -- anonymous table declaration
function TABLE_LOOK_UP(KEY: INDEX_SET) return VALUE_SET is
begin
   return TABLE(KEY);
end TABLE_LOOK_UP;
procedure UPDATE(KEY: in INDEX_SET; VALUE: in VALUE_SET) is
begin
   TABLE(KEY) := VALUE;
end UPDATE;
```

The above symbol table operations are both simple to define and efficient to execute. Enumeration type index sets allow the user to refer to sets of objects which arise in applications directly by their names, and avoids the encoding of names into integers which would be required if index sets were restricted to subranges of integers.

The array TABLE is a nonlocal data structure accessible to both the TABLE_LOOK_UP function and the UPDATE procedure. In the next chapter we shall see how groups of subprograms using a common data structure may be implemented as a package which hides the common data structure but makes procedures which operate on the common data structure accessible to the user.

The above examples illustrate assignment to individual elements of an array and to complete arrays. It is also possible to assign to a contiguous subsequence of elements of an array. Such contiguous subsequences are called slices.

Example 3.54. Slices of arrays

```
procedure SLICES is
   V: array(1..100) of INTEGER;   -- anonymous declaration of V
begin
   V(5..9) := (0,0,0,0,0);        -- assign aggregate to slice
   V(15..19) := V(5..9);          -- assign slice to slice
   V(6..10) := V(5..9);           -- illegal, assignment between overlapping
                                  -- slices is forbidden
   V(6..10) := V(I..J);  -- requires run-time check to determine legality
end SLICES;
```

Slices of vectors are indicated by the vector name followed by a discrete range which must be a subrange of the vector. Aggregates and slices of compatible size may be assigned to slices, but assignment between overlapping slices is forbidden.

Attribute enquiries for one-dimensional array types and array objects include enquiries concerning the first index, last index and length.

Example 3.55. Attribute enquiries for vectors

```
VECTOR'FIRST    -- lower bound of index for VECTOR type
VECTOR'LAST     -- upper bound of type index
VECTOR'LENGTH   -- number of components of VECTOR type
V'FIRST         -- lower bound of index for object V
V'LAST          -- upper bound of index for object V
V'LENGTH        -- number of components of index for object V
```

Use of the above attribute enquiries may be illustrated by a program fragment for computing the inner product of two vectors.

Example 3.56. Inner product of two vectors

```
assert V'FIRST = W'FIRST;        -- vectors must have equal lengths
assert V'LENGTH = W'LENGTH;
PRODUCT := 0;
for I in V'FIRST..V'LAST loop
   PRODUCT := PRODUCT+V(I)*W(I);
end loop;
```

For indices of arrays with multiple dimensions an attribute enquiry is subscripted by an index position number.

Example 3.57. Attribute enquiries for matrices

```
MATRIX'FIRST(I)      -- lower bound of Ith index of MATRIX type
MATRIX'LAST(I)       -- upper bound of Ith index of MATRIX type
MATRIX'LENGTH(I)     -- length of Ith index of MATRIX type
M'FIRST(I)           -- lower bound of Ith index of matrix object
M'LAST(I)            -- upper bound of Ith index of matrix object
M'LENGTH(I)          -- length of Ith index of matrix object
```

Use of the above attribute enquiries may be illustrated by
a program fragment for multiplying the Ith column of matrix M1
by the Jth column of matrix M2, where the number of columns of
M1 equals the number of rows of M2.

Example 3.58. Multiply Ith row of M1 by Jth column of M2

```
assert M1'LENGTH(2) = M2'LENGTH(1);    -- # columns of M1 = # rows of M2
PRODUCT := 0;
for K in M1'FIRST(2)..M1'LAST(2) loop  -- iterate on column index of M1
  PRODUCT := PRODUCT+M1(I,K)*M2(K,J)
end loop;
```

Ada permits slicing of one-dimensional subarrays of multidimensional arrays. The following example illustrates assignment of a slice of the second row of the matrix M to a slice of
the vector V.

Example 3.59. Slices of one-dimensional submatrices

```
V(5..9) := M(2)(6..10);      -- 5-element slice of 2nd row of matrix M
```

In this example M(2) identifiers the second row of M and
M(2)(6..10) determines a slice of this row. Slices of columns
cannot be specified. For three dimensions we can specify a one-
dimensional slice by fixing the first two index components and
specifying a subrange of the third component. Thus if M3D is
a three-dimensional matrix then the following statement assigns
a slice of the (5,2) subarray of M3D to a slice of the vector V.

Example 3.60. Slice of multidimensional matrix

```
V(5..9) := M3D(5,2)(6..10);       -- slice of (5,2) subarray of M3D
```

In general we can define submatrices of multidimensional
matrices by fixing early dimensions and letting later dimensions
vary. One-dimensional submatrices defined in this way can be
sliced, but slicing of other one-dimensional subarrays of a
multidimensional matrix is not possible.

3.7 Array Types With Unspecified Bounds

An array type definition has the following syntax:

array(index-type{,index-type}) of typename [constraint];

where each index type may be specified either by a type name or by a discrete range specification (such as 1..10).

If the index type is a discrete range specification then the bounds of the array are determined at the time of elaboration of the type declaration.

Example 3.61. Index types specified by discrete ranges

```
type VECT is array(1..10) of INTEGER;  -- bounds determined at compile time
type VECT1 is array(1..N) of INTEGER;  -- dynamic bounds determined at
                                       -- elaboration time
V1: VECT;          -- all objects of type VECT have same dimensions
V2: VECT 1;        -- bounds need not be specified in object declarations
```

If the index type is a type name, then the array type is said to have unspecified bounds which are restricted to be a subrange of the index type. Bounds for such arrays must be specified in each object declaration.

Example 3.62. Array types with unspecified bounds

```
type INDEX is range 1..100;
type VECTOR is array(INDEX) of INTEGER;
V1: VECTOR(1..100);    -- V1 has 100 elements
V2: VECTOR(1..10);     -- V2 has 10 elements
V3: VECTOR(1..200);    -- illegal - bounds not within subrange
V4: VECTOR;            -- illegal - bounds must be specified
V5: VECTOR(I..J);      -- run-time legality check may be required
```

Bounds for an object declaration for an array with unspecified bounds can be taken from an initializing literal.

Example 3.63. Bounds specified by initialization

```
V6: VECTOR := (2,4,6,8,10);  -- bounds on V6 determined by initializing literal
                             -- V(1) = 2, ..., V(5) = 10
```

Array types with unspecified bounds are particularly useful in subroutines having array parameters which may take on different values on different instances of call. The formal parameter VECTOR of the following summation function has unspecified bounds and allows the actual bounds of the vector to be summed to be transmitted as part of the actual parameter specification.

107

Example 3.64. Array parameters with unspecified bounds

```
function SUM(A: in VECTOR) return INTEGER is
  X: INTEGER := 0;
begin
  for I in A'FIRST..A'LAST loop        -- bounds taken from actual parameter
    X := X+A(I);
  end loop;
  return X;
end SUM;
```

The bounds A'FIRST, A'LAST are evaluated on entry to the
for loop during execution of the function, and will take as
their values the bounds of the actual parameter vector being
summed. Thus, in the following example, the for loop will be
executed 100 times the first time SUM is called and 10 times the
second time SUM is called (assuming the declarations of the
previous example).

Example 3.65. Call of function with array parameter

```
VALUE := SUM(V1) + 2*SUM(V2);     -- V1 has 100 elements, V2 has 10 elements
```

For this example to work it is necessary that not only the
array name but also the array bounds information is passed to
the called subprogram at procedure call time. In many earlier
languages (like Algol 60) it was necessary to pass array bound
information by additional parameters, resulting in calls such as
"SUM(A,N)". The Ada view that array bound information is implicitly supplied as part of the actual parameter provides a consistent view of array parameters as abstract objects which may
be passed to subprograms in much the same way as scalar objects.

The passing of array bounds information (dope vectors) for
arrays with more than one dimension may be illustrated by a procedure MATMULT for matrix multiplication (of floating-point
matrices) which has two input parameters and one output parameter of the type MATRIX.

108

Example 3.66. Matrix multiplication procedure

```
procedure MATMULT(A,B: in MATRIX; C: out MATRIX) is
   TEMP: FLOAT;
begin
   assert A'LENGTH(2) = B'LENGTH(1);     -- # columns of A = # rows of B
   for M in A'FIRST(1)..A'LAST(1) loop -- outer loop, iterate over rows of A
    for N in B'FIRST(2)..B'LAST(2) loop -- middle loop, iterate on columns of B
     TEMP := 0.0;
     for K in A'FIRST(2)..A'LAST(2) loop    -- inner loop, inner product of
       TEMP := TEMP+A(M,K)*B(K,N);          -- Mth row of A and Nth column of B
     end loop;                         -- end inner loop
     C(M,N) := TEMP;                   --- assign to element of C
    end loop;                          -- end middle loop
   end loop;                           -- end outer loop
end MATMULT;
```

Declaration of the type MATRIX and of a call of the procedure with matrix parameters X, Y, Z of compatible type is illustrated below.

Example 3.67. Call of matrix multiplication procedure

```
procedure MATMULT_CALL is
   type NATURAL is range 1.. INTEGER'LAST;
   type MATRIX is array(NATURAL,NATURAL) of FLOAT;
   X: MATRIX(1..20,1..30);
   Y: MATRIX(1..30,1..10);
   Z: MATRIX(1..20,1..10);
   procedure MATMULT(A,B: in MATRIX; C: out MATRIX) is separate;
begin
   -- read in or otherwise initialize X and Y
   MATMULT(X,Y,Z);
   -- print out or otherwise use the matrix Z
end MATMULT_CALL;
```

3.8 Strings

Strings are specified in the predefined environment as arrays with unspecified bounds having the following declarations.

Example 3.68. Predefined string declarations

```
type NATURAL is INTEGER range 1..INTEGER'LAST;
subtype STRING is array(NATURAL) of CHARACTER;
```

Concatenation of strings is also defined in the predefined environment as a function with the following semantic effect.

Example 3.69. Concatenation function

```
function "&"(X,Y: STRING) return STRING is
   RESULT: STRING(1..X'LENGTH+Y'LENGTH);
begin
   RESULT(1..X'LENGTH) := X;              -- assign X to slice of RESULT
   RESULT(X'LENGTH+1..RESULT'LAST) := Y;  -- assign Y to slice of RESULT
   return RESULT;
end "&";
```

   The concatenation function for strings is a predefined
function. However, the above function specification indicates
how concatenation could be realized in the language.

   The use of string data types and the concatenation function
is illustrated in the following example.

Example 3.70. Some operations on strings

```
procedure USE_STRINGS is
   LINE: STRING(1..100);
   TEXT: STRING(1..1000);
   STR: STRING(1..10);
   V1,V2: STRING := "ABCDE";       -- length determined by initalization
begin
   STR := V1 & V2;                 -- length of STR must exactly match
   LINE(1..V1'LAST) := V1;         -- assign to slice of longer string
   L := V1'LENGTH + V2'LENGTH;     -- sum of string lengths
   LINE(I..I+L-1) := V1 & V2;      -- assign to slice of longer string
end USE_STRINGS;
```

   The constant "ABCDE" is an array aggregate (of length 5)
of the type STRING, and determines not only the value but also
the length of the initialized strings V1, V2. The string STR to
which V1 & V2 is assigned must be exactly the sum of the lengths
of V1 and V2. It is often more convenient to assign computed
string values to slices (substrings) of longer strings, as
illustrated by the two assignments to slices of the string LINE.

   The above technique of assigning strings to slices of string
arrays corresponds to the substring facility of languages like
PL/I.

3.9   Record Types

   Record data types define structures whose components may be
named by selectors. The declaration for the record data type
DATE below has three components named by the selector types
DAY, MONTH, YEAR.

110

Example 3.71. Record declaration

```
type DATE is
  record
    DAY: INTEGER range 1..31;
    MONTH: (JAN,FEB,MAR,APR,MAY,JUN,JUL,AUG,SEP,OCT,NOV,DEC);
    YEAR: INTEGER range 0..2000;
  end record;
```

A record declaration defines a "structure template" from which record data objects may be created by object declarations. Declaration, accessing and assignment of record objects are illustrated by the following example.

Example 3.72. Creation and initalization of records

```
procedure USE_RECORDS is
  X: DATE;                          -- uninitialized object of type DATE
  Y: DATE := (15,JUN,1979);         -- initialized object of type DATE
begin
  X.DAY := 15;                      -- assign to record component
  X.MONTH := JUN;
  X.YEAR := 1979;
  X := Y;                           -- assign value to complete record
  X := (15,JUN,1979);              -- assign positional aggregate
  X := (MONTH=>JUN,DAY=>15,YEAR=>1979); -- assign nonpositional aggregate
end USE_RECORDS;
```

The above example illustrates several different ways of assigning a value to a record variable, including initialization at declaration time, assignment to individual components, assignment from a record variable of similar type, assignment of positional aggregates (in which the correspondence between values and components is determined by a position in a value list) and nonpositional aggregates (in which the association of values and field names is explicitly indicated).

The use of records in computation may be illustrated by defining a procedure TOMORROW which is given a record parameter of type DATE and (if the date is valid) computes "tomorrow's" date. The procedure specification for TOMORROW is as follows.

Example 3.73. Specification of TOMORROW

```
procedure TOMORROW(D: in out DATE);
```

In order to define TOMORROW we need a function VALID to check whether a given date is valid. The function VALID will use a function DAYS_IN_MONTH to determine the number of days in the given month, which in turn uses a function LEAP to determine if the given year is a leap year. The specification of VALID, DAYS_IN_MONTH and LEAP will be as follows.

111

Example 3.74. Specification of auxiliary procedures

```
function VALID(D: DATE) return BOOLEAN;
function DAYS_IN_MONTH(M: MONTH, IS_LEAP: BOOLEAN) return DAY;
function LEAP(Y: YEAR) return BOOLEAN;
```

The identifiers DAY, MONTH, YEAR are used above as type names which name the types of associated record components. Each of these type names must be introduced by an explicit type declaration, and the record declaration for DATE must be redefined to have new component names whose type is no longer anonymous.

Example 3.75. Revised data type specifications for DATE

```
type DAY is range 1..31;
type MONTH is (JAN,FEB,MAR,APR,MAY,JUN,JUL,AUG,SEP,OCT,NOV,DEC);
type YEAR is range 0..2000;
type DATE is
   record
      D: DAY;
      M: MONTH;
      Y: YEAR;
   end record;
TODAY: DATE;                  -- TODAY is an object of type DATE
```

The use of named types rather than anonymous types for component declarations means that components can be passed as actual parameters to procedures which have actual parameters of the given type.

The rule for leap years is that a year is a leap year if it is a multiple of 4 but not a multiple of 100. The function LEAP may therefore be defined as follows.

Example 3.76. Computing leap years

```
function LEAP(Y: YEAR) return BOOLEAN is
begin
   return (Y mod 4 = 0) and not (Y mod 100 = 0);
end;
```

The function DAYS_IN_MONTH can be implemented by a case statement with three branches corresponding to 30-day months, 31-day months and February.

Example 3.77. Computing days in the month

```
function DAYS_IN_MONTH(M: MONTH: IS_LEAP: BOOLEAN) return DAY is
begin                                -- thirty days hath September...
   case M of
      when SEP|APR|JUN|NOV => return 30;
      when FEB =>
         if IS_LEAP then
            return 29;
         else
            return 28;
         end if;
      when others => return 31;
   end case;
end DAYS_IN_MONTH;
```

The function VALID is passed a parameter of the type DATE whose components are known to satisfy the constraints determined by the component types DAY, MONTH and YEAR. The only check required is that the value of the DAY component does not exceed that permitted by the MONTH component.

Example 3.78. Validating today's date

```
function VALID(TODAY: DATE) return BOOLEAN is
begin
   return TODAY.D <= DAYS_IN_MONTH(TODAY.M, LEAP(TODAY.Y));
end VALID;
```

Now that the above auxiliary functions have been defined, the procedure TOMORROW may be defined as follows:

Example 3.79. Foretelling tomorrow's date

```
procedure TOMORROW(TODAY: in out DATE) is
   LY: constant BOOLEAN := LEAP(TODAY.Y);
begin
   if not VALID(TODAY) then
      PUT("INVALID DATE")
   elsif TODAY.D < DAYS_IN_MONTH(TODAY.M, LY) then
      TODAY.D := TODAY.D+1;            -- not last day of month
   elsif TODAY.M < DEC then
      TODAY.D := 1;                    -- last day of month
      TODAY.M := MONTH'SUCC(TODAY.M);  -- but not last month of year
   elsif TODAY.Y < YEAR'MAX then
      TODAY := (1,JAN,TODAY.YEAR+1);   -- last day of year
   else
      PUT("BEYOND THE END OF TIME")    -- run out of years
   end if;
end TOMORROW;
```

The above examples illustrate subprograms which use record data types as parameters, and indicate how types and values of

113

components may be used within such subprograms. Record types allow the user to think abstractly about record objects and also to manipulate components of record objects. In the above examples the implementer of a procedure like TOMORROW must be aware of the component structure of dates, but the user of this procedure may think of the DATE parameter as an abstract object.

Record types may have constant components, as in the following example.

Example 3.80. Records with deferred constants

```
type CONST_YEAR is
   DAY: INTEGER range 1..31;
   MONTH: MONTH_NAME;              -- previously defined enumeration type
   YEAR: constant INTEGER range 1..2000;  -- deferred constant
end record;
```

A constant component (such as YEAR) which is not given an explicit assignment in the type definition is called a deferred constant. Deferred constants can have their values assigned only by a complete record assignment.

Example 3.81. Assignment to deferred constants

```
declare
   X: CONST_YEAR;                  -- uninitialized record
   Y: CONST_YEAR := (20,JUL,1980); -- Y is initialized to (20,JUL,1980)
begin
   X.DAY := X.DAY+1;              -- legal, component is integer subtype
   X.MONTH := OCT;               -- legal, component is enumeration type
   X.YEAR := 1984;               -- illegal, constant cannot be reassigned
   X := Y;                       -- complete record assignment is legal
end;
```

3.10 Variant Records

Record types discussed in the previous section have components of fixed type and structure. Nonconstant components may be modified by component assignment, and complete record assignments may modify both constant and nonconstant components.

Ada allows record types to have components which may vary not only in size but also in structure. Such records are called variant records. Two essentially different kinds of variation are permitted in variant records.

1. Variation in size. Records may have components which are dynamic arrays whose size may be changed by assignment to the complete record.
2. Variation in type. Records may have components whose type and selector name may be changed by assignment to the complete record.

114

Records of varying size may be illustrated by the record
VARYING_ARRAY with a component SIZE which is a deferred constant
and a second component BUFFER whose size depends on the value of
the first component.

Example 3.82. Record types of varying size

```
type VARYING_ARRAY is
  record
    SIZE: constant INTEGER range 1..N;    -- deferred constant (discriminant)
    BUFFER: array(1..SIZE) of INTEGER;    -- array whose size depends on
  end record;                             -- discriminant
```

Data objects of type VARYING_ARRAY may but need not be
initialized at declaration time.

Example 3.83. Object declarations for records of varying size

```
VA1: VARYING_ARRAY;                     -- uninitialized varying array
VA2: VARYING_ARRAY := (3,(1,2,3));      -- positional initialization
VA3: VARYING_ARRAY := (SIZE => 4,BUFFER => (0,0,0,0)); -- nonpositional
                                                       -- initialization
VA4: VARYING_ARRAY := (2,(1,2,3));      -- illegal, incompatible values
```

Any given object of the type VARYING_ARRAY may have its
size modified by assignment to the complete record during execution. The component BUFFER cannot be changed in size by component assignment, but assignment to the components of BUFFER or to
the complete BUFFER is permitted.

Example 3.84. Assignment to records of varying size

```
VA1 := (4,(2,4,6,8));      -- assign a complete record literal
VA1 := VA2;                -- assign a complete record variable
VA1.BUFFER := (0,0,0);     -- legal if VA1.SIZE has value 3
VA1.BUFFER(1) := 7;        -- assign to first component of buffer
VA1.SIZE := 4;             -- illegal assignment to constant component
for I in 1..10 loop
  VA1 := (I,(1..I => 0));  -- assign to VA1 a sequence
end loop;                  -- of records of different sizes
```

The SIZE component is called a discriminant because it
discriminates among records of different sizes. The value of the
discriminant completely determines the record structure. Variant records in general have one or more discriminants whose
values completely determine the record structure.

Constrained variant records whose size cannot be changed by
complete record assignment can be created by imposing a constraint on the discriminant at object declaration time.

Example 3.85. Discriminant constraints

```
V: VARYING_ARRAY(20);      -- constraint which fixes size of object V
W: VARYING_ARRAY(M);       -- constraint evaluated at run time
```

The discriminant SIZE may be regarded as a "type parameter" of VARYING_ARRAY, which controls its structural variation. Variant records provide a mechanism for defining parametrized types. This view will be further explored in the next section after records with variant type components have been discussed

Records with components of varying type have a discriminant of an enumeration type whose value set may be used to discriminate among alternative branches of a <u>case</u> statement. In the PERSON record type below, the discriminant SEX has two possible values M, F which respectively discriminate between a field called HEIGHT of type INTEGER for males and a field called PREGNANT of type BOOLEAN for females.

Example 3.86. Records of varying type

```
type PERSON is
  record
     SEX: constant (M,F);            -- discriminant which discriminates
     case SEX of                     -- among components of varying type
       when M => HEIGHT :INTEGER range 1..1000;
       when F => PREGNANT: BOOLEAN;
     end;
```

The set of values of a type discriminant must be statically determined (at compile time). The discriminant component must appear before the variant component in which the discriminant is used. A variant record may in general have several type and size discriminants as well as regular components.

The rules for declaration, initialization and assignment to records with varying component types are similar to those for records of varying size.

116

Example 3.87. Declaration and use of varying type records

```
procedure USE_PERSON is
   MAN: PERSON := (M,70);     -- initialized PERSON
   WOMAN: PERSON(F);          -- constrained record with unmodifiable discriminant
   ANYONE: PERSON;            -- uninitialized PERSON
begin
   ANYONE := (F,TRUE);        -- assign complete record
   ANYONE.PREGNANT := FALSE;     -- assign compatible value
   ANYONE.HEIGHT := 68;       -- illegal, incompatible value
   ANYONE.SEX := M;           -- illegal assignment of discriminant
   MAN := (F,FALSE);          -- legal sex change
   MAN := ANYONE;             -- legal complete record assignment
   WOMAN := (F,TRUE);         -- legal
   WOMAN := (M,70);           -- illegal, WOMAN has fixed sex
end USE_PERSON;
```

The restriction that the discriminant of a variant record cannot be changed without changing the complete record provides an assurance that the type of the variant will always agree with the type of the discriminant. However, security of variant records also requires a check on accessing a variant component that the type is consistent with that expected. This check can be programmed by a case statement which parallels the structure of the variant record.

Example 3.88. Programmed check of discriminant

```
case X.SEX
   when M => action for male variant
   when F => action for female variant
end case;
```

When the check on the discriminant is not explicitly programmed by the programmer, a run-time check may have to be implicitly supplied by the compiler.

Example 3.89. Implicit run-time check of discriminant

```
X.HEIGHT := X.HEIGHT+1;   -- may require implicit run-time check that X.SEX = M
```

A run-time check may have to be supplied by the system even when a check is supplied by the programmer.

Example 3.90. Side effects which may invalidate programmed check

```
case X.SEX
   when M => X.HEIGHT := 65;          -- no run-time check needed
      -- procedure with potential side effects which might change X
      X.HEIGHT := 75;                 -- run-time check needed
   when F => X.PREGNANT := TRUE;      -- no run-time check needed
end case;
```

The above example illustrates that when an action for a given variant has uncontrollable side effects between the time the discriminant is checked and the time the variant is used, then run-time checks on accessing must be reintroduced.

The security of a variant record could also be breached if it is shared between tasks A and B and there is a record assignment in task B while the record is being used in task A. The security of variant records shared among concurrent tasks cannot be handled by run-time discriminant checks, and must be handled by the programmer by providing adequate mutual exclusion and protection with available concurrent programming primitives.

3.11 Discriminants and Type Parameters

The discriminant components of a record are in a sense redundant because the information they contain is present in the components which they discriminate and could in principle be made available by attribute enquiries.

However, the discriminants make explicit the structure variation of a record in a form in which it can be used to check the validity and security of operations before they are applied.

The discriminants of a record also serve to "parametrize" its structure.

Example 3.91. Constrained types

```
Z: VARYING_ARRAY(SIZE => 20);
P: PERSON(SEX => M, FAMILY_SIZE => 5);
```

These constrained types specify the discriminant constraints by explicitly naming the discriminating attributes. This notation parallels the notation for procedure parameters and emphasizes the parametric nature of such information.

Variant records in general have one discriminant for each varying component. The second constrained type above assumes a complex PERSON record with a component SEX of varying type and a component FAMILY_SIZE of varying size.

There are some important analogies between constrained record parameters and subprogram parameters.

Subprograms have formal parameters and may be called with several different sets of actual parameters. Discriminants of varying records serve as implicit formal parameters. Object declarations in the form of constrained records supply actual parameter values for discriminants.

The relation between a subprogram declaration and subprogram call may be compared to the relation between a type declaration

and an object declaration. A subprogram declaration, like a
type declaration, may be viewed as a template which may give
rise to multiple calls during execution in much the same way
that a type declaration gives rise to multiple objects during
execution. Both procedure calls and object declarations are
implemented by allocating data structures which may differ for
different instances.

It is natural to have parameters for type definitions whose
values are supplied at object declaration time by analogy with
procedures. Ada does not provide general type parametrization
facilities, but discriminants in variant records provide effec-
tive parametrization in a special case.

One difference between procedures and types is that procedures have a body which is hidden from the user while components
of record types are automatically accessible whenever the record
name is accessible. Ada supports a mechanism for hiding the
internal data structure of types, and providing access to type
components only through user-defined operations. This mechanism
is defined in chapter 4.

Arrays with unspecified bounds also have a rudimentary type
parametrization facility, where the parameter is a subrange.

Example 3.92. Size parameters for array types

```
LINE: STRING(1..80);        -- 1..80 is a subrange parameter
S: STRING(1..N);            -- N is evaluated at elaboration time
M: MATRIX(1..20,1..20);     -- a two-dimensional array requires two subrange
                            -- parameters
```

Thus whenever Ada provides types whose structure is not
compile-time determined it tries to provide "structure parameters" which allow the structure to be frozen at object declaration time.

3.12 Access Types

Access types provide a mechanism for the dynamic creation
of data objects and data structures during statement execution.
Like other programmer-defined data types, they are introduced
by type declarations. Access type declarations have the following syntax:

```
type T is access type-specification;  -- declares T to be
                            -- an access type for objects of
                            -- the given type specification
```

Example 3.93. Access type declarations

```
type INT_POINTER is access INTEGER;    -- access type for integer objects
type ARRAY_POINTER is access array (1..5) of INTEGER;  -- access type for
                            -- array objects
```

Access types differ from other data types in the mechanism for declaring data objects. An object declaration for non-access types such as "X: INTEGER;" serves two functions:

1. It defines the identifier X to be a name for integer values;
2. It creates (allocates) an integer object (memory cell) and associates this integer object with the identifier X.

These two functions are performed by separate language mechanisms for access types. Names of access variables are introduced by declarations which look very much like object declarations.

Example 3.94. Declaration of access variables

```
PTR1,PTR2: INT_POINTER;   -- two access variables for naming integers
A1,A2: ARRAY_POINTER;     -- two access variables for naming arrays
```

Declarations of access variables create names for objects of a given type without creating any data objects. Data objects of an access type (called access objects) are separately created by allocation expressions with the following syntax:

new access-type-name (initializing-expression)

Access objects of the two previously defined types may be defined as follows.

Example 3.95. Creation of anonymous access objects

```
new INT_POINTER(3)    -- creates an access object of type INT_POINTER and
                      -- initializes it to the integer value 3
new ARRAY_POINTER (0,0,0,0,0)   -- creates an array access object
                      -- initialized to (0,0,0,0,0)
```

The allocation expression "new INT_POINTER(3)" creates an anonymous initialized integer access object and returns as its value a reference to this object which may be assigned to access variables of compatible type by assignment statements.

Example 3.96. Assignment of access objects to access variables

```
PTR1 := new INT_POINTER(3);     -- assign integer access object to PTR1
A1 := new ARRAY_POINTER((0,0,0,0,0)); -- assign array access object to A1
```

Allocation and initialization of access variables can also be accomplished at declaration time.

Example 3.97. Initialized access variable declarations

```
PTR1: INT_POINTER := new INT_POINTER(3);   -- initialized declaration
A1: ARRAY_POINTER := new ARRAY_POINTER((0,0,0,0,0));
```

The declaration "X: INTEGER;" determines an immutable correspondence between the identifier X and an associated integer object which remains unchanged throughout the lifetime of X. In contrast, the declaration "PTR1: INT_POINTER;" creates just a name, and allows a sequence of different integer objects to be associated with PTR1 by a sequence of assignment statements.

Example 3.98. Dynamic assignment of access objects

```
PTR1 := new INT_POINTER(3);  -- create integer access object, associate with PTR1
PTR2 := new INT_POINTER(57); -- create and assign second integer access object
PTR1 := PTR2;  -- assign to PTR1 reference to the second access object
             -- PTR1 and PTR2 now "share" second access object"
A1 := new ARRAY_POINTER((0,0,0,0,0)); -- create and assign array access object
A2 := new ARRAY_POINTER((1,2,3,4,5)); -- and a second access object
A1 := A2;  -- A1 gets a reference to second array access object
         -- A1 and A2 now "share" the same array access object
```

Execution of this sequence of six assignment statements yields the association between access variables and access objects indicated in figure 3.4.

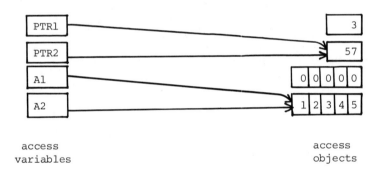

access
variables

access
objects

Figure 3.4.   Relation between access variables and access objects.

Figure 3.4 illustrates the following properties of access objects:

1. Sharing of an access object by more than one access variable;
2. Inaccessible access objects - not referred to by any access variables.

Access types provide a mechanism for referring to objects by more than one name. Multiple naming of objects is referred to as aliasing, since each name may be regarded as an alias for its object. Aliasing makes it difficult to keep track of the effects of assignment because updating of the value of a variable Y changes the value of all aliases of Y. However, aliasing is important in applications such as information retrieval

121

where the essence of the problem is to permit reference to an object by its attributes in several different ways. We shall return to this subject later.

Inaccessible objects present a problem because they are "deadwood" which can never again be used in the computation but continue to take up memory resources. Implementations of languages which support access variables require a garbage collection mechanism which reclaims the memory taken up by inaccessible objects so that it can be reused.

Access variables are always created at the time of entry to the program unit in which they are declared and deleted on exit from the scope of the program unit. Creation and deletion of access variables is in a last-in-first-out order and may be implemented in a stack along with object declarations for non-access variables.

In contrast, access objects are dynamically created and are not subject to a last-in-first-out creation and deletion discipline. A separate memory area, sometimes called a heap, is set aside for allocation and garbage collection of access objects.

Access objects have two kinds of values:

1. A reference value which, in implementation-dependent terms, may be thought of as the pointer to the memory cell which represents the access object;
2. A data value which, in implementation-dependent terms, is the content of the memory cell. Ada permits access to the data value of an object Y by the notation Y.all.

The distinction between assignment of reference values and data values may be illustrated as follows.

Example 3.99. Reference values and data values

```
PTR2 := PTR1;  -- PTR2 is assigned the reference value of the object assoc-
               -- iated with PTR1; PTR2 and PTR1 share the same access object
PTR2.all := PTR1.all;  -- PTR2 is assigned a new data value which is a copy
                       -- of the data value of PTR1
```

The notation ".all" is motivated by the fact that access objects are often structured data objects such as arrays and records. In this case "A.all" permits access to all components of the structured data object A.

Example 3.100. Reference and data values for arrays

```
A1 := new ARRAY_POINTER((0,0,0,0,0));  -- assign initialized object to A1
A1.all := (1,2,3,4,5);  -- update all components of A1
A2 := A1;               -- update the reference value of A2
A2 := new ARRAY_POINTER(A1.all);  -- A2 gets new object initialized to data
                                  -- value of A1
A2.all := A1.all;       -- data value of A1 is assigned to A2
```

The operation ".all" is sometimes referred to as a dereferencing operation since it converts a reference value into a data value.

For structured data objects we must consider access not only to complete structures but also to components. Strictly speaking, the notation "A1.all(I)" should be used to refer to the Ith component of the access array A1. However, the dereferencing operation ".all" is omitted in the case of component selection, so that the notation for selection of a component of an access array A1 is precisely the same as that for access to a directly declared array of the same name.

Example 3.101. Component accessing for array access objects

```
A1 := new ARRAY_POINTER((0,0,0,0,0));
A1(3) := 17;          -- we need not write A1.all(3) := 17;
for I in 1..5 loop
   A(I) := 2*I;       -- assignment to access array
end loop;             -- looks just like assignment to non-access array
```

Access arrays may themselves have components of an access type, as in the following type declaration.

Example 3.102. Access array with access values

```
type POINTER_ARRAY is access array(INTEGER) of INT_POINTER;
A: POINTER_ARRAY;
```

Creation of an initialized access object for the pointer array A may be accomplished as follows.

Example 3.103. Initialization of access array and access values

```
A := new POINTER_ARRAY(1..20 => new INT_POINTER(0));
```

This assignment statement involves two levels of allocation corresponding to the two instances of the keyword new:
1. Allocation of an array access object with 20 components which are names of integers and assignment of the reference value for this object to A.
2. Allocation of an integer access object and assignment of the reference value for that object to each of the 20 array indices.

There is a special value null which may be assigned to access values of any type and indicates that the access value does not point to any object. Initialization of components of the array A to null allows the creation of an array of names of integers which do not initially point to integer objects. Components of the array can then be selectively associated with integer objects by assignment to components.

123

Example 3.104. Selective initialization of access values

```
A := new TWO_LEVEL_ACCESS(1..100 => null);  -- create array of names
A(1) := new INT_POINTER(3);      -- selectively create integer access objects
A(5) := A(1);                    -- or share previously created objects
for I in 1..100 loop             -- or selectively initialize complete array
   if P(I) then                  -- create data object A(I) if P(I) is true
     A(I) := new INT_POINTER(F(I));  -- initialize to value F(I)
   end if;
end loop;
```

Now that we have introduced access arrays with components that are access types, we will consider access records with components that are access types. The following type declaration of an access record describes a person in terms of a varying-size name, and a father, mother and spouse who are persons.

Example 3.105. Record structure with recursively defined access types

```
type PERSON is
  access record
    SIZE: constant INTEGER;   -- deferred constant
    NAME: STRING(1..SIZE);    -- varying-size name
    FATHER: PERSON;           -- three recursively defined components
    MOTHER: PERSON;
    SPOUSE: PERSON;
  end record;
```

An instance of this record type can be created and initialized as follows.

Example 3.106. ADA - an example of a recursive name

```
ADA_AUGUSTA: PERSON := (3, "ADA",
                        LORD_BYRON,
                        LADY_BYRON,
                        LORD_LOVELACE);
```

Lord Byron, Lady Byron and Lord Lovelace are assumed to be previously created persons. There is thus an apparent difficulty, since a complete definition of ADA_AUGUSTA would require an infinite regress through her ancestry. Fortunately, the Bible comes to our rescue and enables us to postulate a "first person" with no father, mother or spouse.

Example 3.107. Null as a placeholder for dynamically developed information

```
ADAM: PERSON := new PERSON (4,"ADAM",null,null,null);
EVE: PERSON := new PERSON (3,"EVE",null,null,ADAM);
```

This provides only a highly speculative basis for defining the ancestry of ADA_AUGUSTA. But it does illustrate the usefulness of the access value null as a placeholder for information that may but need not be dynamically developed later.

An access type is said to be <u>recursively defined</u> if it is defined in terms of itself. The access type <u>PERSON</u> is an example of a recursively defined access type with three recursively defined components. Any recursively defined access type potentially involves an infinite regress but can be finitely defined by initializing undeveloped components to <u>null</u>.

Components of access records may be accessed using the standard record accessing mechanism.

<u>Example 3.108. Record accessing and relational aliasing</u>

ADA_AUGUSTA.FATHER has the **value** LORD_BYRON
EVE.SPOUSE has the value ADAM

EVE.SPOUSE uniquely identifies ADAM and may be thought of as an alias for ADAM which identifies ADAM not by a direct name but in terms of his relationship with EVE. Record structures with recursively defined access components are useful in applications concerned with relationships among a collection of objects, such as persons, cities or aircraft. Each of the objects may be defined by an access record, and relations between an object A and object B are indicated by a defined component in object A which "points to" the value B.

3.13 List Processing

List structures are an important class of data structures definable as record structures with access components of recursive type. List elements with a value field and a pointer field which either points to the next element or has the value <u>null</u> can be defined as follows.

<u>Example 3.109. Declaration of a list element</u>

<u>type</u> ELEMENT <u>is</u> <u>access</u>
  <u>record</u>
    VALUE: INTEGER;   -- value field
    NEXT: ELEMENT;   -- points to next element or has value <u>null</u>
  <u>end</u> <u>record</u>;

List processing in Ada will be illustrated by a program for building a list of N such elements. Two auxiliary access variables called HEAD and CURRENT will be used, and will respectively point to the first element and current element of the list. The list that we want to build is illustrated in figure 3.5 below.

The access variables HEAD and CURRENT are of type ELEMENT, and can be declared as follows.

125

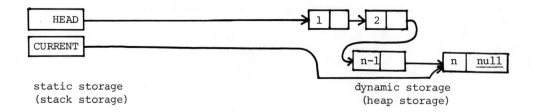

static storage　　　　　　　　　　　dynamic storage
(stack storage)　　　　　　　　　　(heap storage)

Figure 3.5.　List with variable number of elements.
Access to list is controlled by the
access variables HEAD and CURRENT.

Example 3.110.　Two names of list elements

HEAD, CURRENT: ELEMENT := null;

The above state of affairs represents a list with no
elements.　A list with one element can be created by allocating
a list element and assigning to both HEAD and CURRENT a reference to the created element.

Example 3.111.　One-element list

```
HEAD := new ELEMENT(1,null);  -- create list element, assign to null
CURRENT := HEAD;              -- CURRENT must also point to created element
```

Creation of the N-1 remaining elements of the list may be
accomplished by a loop which creates successive elements,
assigns a reference to the newly created element to the NEXT
field of the previous element, and updates the value of CURRENT.

Example 3.112.　Two-element list

```
for I in 2..N loop
   CURRENT.NEXT := new ELEMENT(I,null);  -- create next element; update
                                         -- NEXT field of previous element
   CURRENT := CURRENT.NEXT;              -- update current element pointer
end loop;
```

In this example the two statically created variables HEAD
and CURRENT are used to manage an arbitrarily long list of
dynamically created list elements.　Storage for the variables
HEAD and CURRENT is allocated at the time that their declarations are elaborated on entry to the block in which they are
declared, while storage for list elements is allocated dynamically in a dynamic storage area (heap).

Deletion of the access variables HEAD and CURRENT occurs on
exit from the scope of the program unit in which they are

126

declared. Dynamically created list elements can be deleted
after they become inaccessible using garbage collection tech-
niques.

Garbage collection may be an unacceptably time-consuming
form of storage management in certain time-critical computations. Ada provides a mechanism for avoiding garbage collection
by allowing a user to define a maximum number of created objects
of the given type (called a collection). A collection has
fixed maximum storage requirements, and can be allocated on the
stack as part of the activation record in which the associated
access type is declared. However, in predeclaring the maximum
number of created objects of an access type, we sacrifice both
the ability to let the maximum size be determined dynamically
by the requirements of the implementation, and the possibility
of garbage collection to delete created objects which become
inaccessible. The degree to which collections are used in
practice will depend in part on the efficiency and effectiveness
of the garbage collection mechanism provided by the implementation.

3.14   Tree-Structured Symbol Tables

As another example of programming with access types, consider a search and update program for "ordered" trees whose nodes
have integer values. Each node may have a left branch to a node
with a smaller integer value and a right branch to a node with a
larger integer value, as in Figure 3.6.

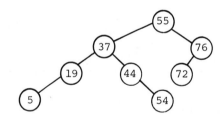

Figure 3.6.   Symbol table with integer keys.

Nodes of the tree may be represented by an access record
with an integer field and two pointer fields.

Example 3.113.   Tree-structured node declaration

```
type NODE is access
   record
      KEY: INTEGER;
      LEFT, RIGHT: NODE;
   end record;
ROOT: NODE := null;
```

We will write a function FIND which, when given an integer argument, returns with the value TRUE when the integer is found in the tree and returns with the value FALSE otherwise. This function may be specified as follows.

Example 3.114. Specification of tree-searching function

function FIND(I: INTEGER) return BOOLEAN;

The implementation of FIND below assumes that both the data type NODE and the object ROOT of type NODE are defined in the environment of FIND and accessible as non-local variables.

Example 3.115. Implementation of tree-searching function

```
function FIND(I: INTEGER) return BOOLEAN is
  N: NODE := ROOT;          -- N is initialized to the global variable ROOT
begin
  while N /= null loop      -- while current node exists
    if I < N.KEY then       -- if number less than key
      N := N.LEFT;          -- go to left successor
    elsif I > N.KEY then    -- if number greater than key
      N := N.RIGHT;         -- go to right successor
    else
      return TRUE;          -- if number equals key
    end if;                 -- return TRUE
  end loop;
  return FALSE;             -- if I is not in tree return FALSE
end FIND;
```


If this function is called with the tree of figure 3.6 and the integer 41, it will examine 55 and execute "N := N.LEFT;", examine 37 and execute "N := N.RIGHT;", examine 44 and execute "N := N.LEFT;" and then escape from the while loop and return with the value FALSE.

We will consider next a value-returning procedure called UPDATE which performs precisely the same function as FIND when the integer argument is in the tree, but adds a new node for that integer argument when the argument is not in the tree. Thus a call of UPDATE with argument 41 would insert a new node into the tree as the left branch of the node "44".

The procedure UPDATE has the same arguments as FIND, and examines the same sequence of nodes as FIND to determine whether a given integer argument is in the tree. But it needs access to the terminating node to perform updating, and therefore checks for termination in a more complex manner.

Example 3.116. Tree updating procedure

```
procedure UPDATE(I: INTEGER) return BOOLEAN is
N: NODE := ROOT;
begin
  if N = null then                    -- if tree is empty
    ROOT := new NODE(I,null,null);    -- insert its first node
    return FALSE;                     -- and return FALSE
  else                                -- otherwise (if tree has at least 1 node)
    loop                              -- perform main search loop
      if I < N.KEY then               -- case when I<N.KEY, branch left
        if N.LEFT := null then        -- if null, then terminate
          N.LEFT := new NODE(I,null,null);  -- insert new node
          return FALSE;               -- and return FALSE
        else                          -- otherwise (if N has left successor)
          N := N.LEFT;                -- prepare to look at next node
        end if;
      elsif I > N.KEY then            -- case when I>N.KEY, branch right
        if N.RIGHT = null then        -- if null then terminate
          N.RIGHT := new NODE(I,null,null);  -- insert new node
          return FALSE;               -- and return FALSE
        else                          -- otherwise (if N has right successor)
          N := N.RIGHT                -- prepare to look at next node
        end if;
      else                            -- case when I=N.KEY, value already exists
        return TRUE;                  -- return TRUE without updating
      end if;
    end loop;
  end if;
end UPDATE;
```

The UPDATE procedure can be used both to build up the set
of tree elements and to search for elements in a tree. It is a
prototype for symbol table construction and lookup functions.

However, symbol tables generally have both key and value
fields. The above example will be modified so that it can deal
with symbol tables whose keys are alphabetic character strings
and whose values are integers.

We shall permit the key to be a character string with a
varying number of characters. Thus nodes of the tree must be
implemented by variant records with a discriminant field which
specifies the size of the key field.

Example 3.117. Node with varying-size keys

```
type NODE is access
  record
    SIZE: constant INTEGER;     -- discriminant of KEY field
    KEY: STRING(1..SIZE);       -- varying-size key field
    VALUE: INTEGER;             -- value field
    LEFT, RIGHT: NODE := null;  -- left and right successors
  end record;
ROOT: NODE := null;
```

Symbol tables constructed out of the above nodes will be lexically ordered on the varying-size key field, as indicated in Figure 3.7.

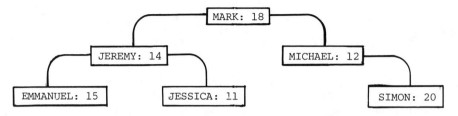

Figure 3.7. Symbol table with keys and values.

A function FIND will be defined for such symbol tables, which is given a character string as an argument, returns a pointer to the node containing the character string if there is one, and returns the value NULL otherwise.

Example 3.118. FIND function for separate keyword values

```
function FIND(S: STRING) return NODE is
  N: NODE := ROOT;
begin
  while N /= null loop
    if S < N.KEY then
      N := N.LEFT
    elsif S > N.KEY then
      N := N.RIGHT;
    else
      return N;            -- return N when S = N.KEY
    end if;
  end loop;
  return null;            -- return null if S not in symbol table
end FIND;
```


Note that we would actually prefer to return a value of type INTEGER when the node with key S is in the symbol table. However, this raises a problem because a function must return a value of fixed type, and the type returned when the key does not correspond to a symbol table entry must correspond to the type when it does. There are other solutions to this problem, such as singling out a dummy integer value (such as 0), or making use of the exception mechanism when the symbol is not in the symbol table. An alternative version of this program is presented in Chapter 4.

The UPDATE procedure could be implemented using a minor perturbation of the previous UPDATE procedure. However, in the following implementation we separate the tree-searching phase from the creation and attachment of a new node to the tree, thereby providing the reader with a different perspective on the structure of the program.

130

Example 3.119. Revised UPDATE function

```
procedure UPDATE(S: STRING; V: INTEGER) is
   M,N: NODE := ROOT;
   FOUND: BOOLEAN := FALSE;
   TEMP: NODE;
begin
   while N /= null loop                    -- while a node exists
      M := N;                              -- remember current node
      if S < N.KEY then                    -- if less than key
         N := N.LEFT;                       -- go to left successor
      elsif S > N.KEY then                 -- if greater than key
         N := N.RIGHT;                      -- go to right successor
      elsif S = N.KEY then                 -- if equal to key
         FOUND := TRUE;                     -- set FOUND to TRUE
         N.VALUE := V;                      -- update node
         exit;                              -- and exit
      end if;
   end loop;
   if not FOUND then                       -- if not found create new node
      TEMP := new(NODE(VALUE => V, SIZE => S'LENGTH, KEY => S);
      if M := null then                    -- if tree is empty
         ROOT := TEMP;                      -- assign new node to root
      elsif S < M.KEY then                 -- if less than terminal key
         M.LEFT := TEMP;                    -- then new left branch
      elsif S > M.KEY then                 -- if greater than terminal key
         M.RIGHT := TEMP;                   -- then new right branch
      end if;
   end if;
end UPDATE;
```

The subprograms FIND and UPDATE make use of the data type NODE and the variable ROOT of the type NODE. These variables are shared by the subprograms FIND and UPDATE, because the function FIND must have access to the symbol table created by UPDATE in order to retrieve information inserted into the symbol table by UPDATE.

However, no other subprogram needs to know the representation of symbol tables so that nodes and the root of the tree should be defined in an environment that is accessible only to FIND and UPDATE and no other subprograms.

Such hiding of shared information may be accomplished using the package mechanism of Chapter 4. In section 4.5 we shall define a symbol table package which hides the representation of symbol tables, but makes the functions FIND and UPDATE available as computational resources to the user.

4

MODULARITY AND PROGRAM STRUCTURE

4.1 Review of Data and Subprogram Packages

Modules allow the user to separate the specification of computational resources from their implementation. Ada supports two kinds of modules called packages and tasks. Task modules are the units of concurrent computation and will be discussed in Chapter 5. Packages may be used to define logically related collections of resources for sequential computation, and are the subject of the present chapter.

Packages may have two textually distinct parts which may be written by different programmers and separately compiled:

1. A package specification which determines the resources made available by a package to the user. The package specification should be written before programs which use the package, and must be compiled before (or concurrently with) program units which use the package.
2. A package body which "implements" resources provided by the package. The package body may contain implementation-dependent resources hidden from the user. It can be written and compiled independently of the specification. It can be replaced by a "functionally equivalent" package body without requiring the recompilation of programs which use the package.

The relation between package specifications and package bodies is illustrated in figure 4.1.

Packages containing only type and object declarations do not need a package body, because there are no implementation details to be hidden from the user, and will be considered first. The simplest packages are those containing only object declarations.

```
┌─────────────────────────────────────┐
│ Package specification:              │   The user can "see" specification
│ Visible part                        │   Enough information to use resources
├─────────────────────────────────────┤   Declare and use data types
│ May include:                        │   Call procedures, etc.
│   data type declarations            │   Must be compiled before (or concur-
│   data object declarations          │   rently with) program units which
│   subprogram specifications         │   use the package
│   "private" data types              │
│   nested package specifications     │
└─────────────────────────────────────┘

┌─────────────────────────────────────┐
│ Package body:                       │   May be separately compiled
│ Hidden part                         │   May be written and compiled much
├─────────────────────────────────────┤     later than specification
│ May include:                        │   May be replaced by "equivalent"
│   implementation of subprograms     │     implementation without reprogram-
│     defined in visible part         │     ming or recompilation of other
│   declarations of local var-        │     program units
│     iables and auxiliary            │   Packages containing only type and
│     subprograms needed to           │     object declarations do not need
│     implement user subprograms      │     a package body
│   initialization specifications     │
└─────────────────────────────────────┘
```

Figure 4.1. Separation between package specification and
             package body.

Example 4.1. Package with only object declarations

```
package COMMON is
   X: INTEGER;
   Y: INTEGER;
   V: array(1..100) of INTEGER;
end;
```


    Packages which contain only object declarations are like the
named COMMON blocks of Fortran. However, they are more flexible
than Fortran COMMON blocks in a number of respects. Fortran
COMMON blocks are global to the program, have a permanent block
of storage allocated for them at load time, and must have all
components explicitly listed in every context of use. Packages
may be declared local to the declarative part of any program
unit, have storage allocated for them only on entry to the program unit in which they are declared, and may be used without
listing their components at any point within the scope of
declaration.

    The resources named in a package may be accessed anywhere in
the scope of the declaration using a dot notation similar to that
used in accessing records.

133

Example 4.2. Qualified access to objects in a package

```
COMMON.X := 0;
COMMON.Y := COMMON.X + COMMON.Y;
COMMON.V(1) := 37;
```

The similarity of notation for accessing packages and records reflects the fact that packages and record type declarations are both mechanisms for naming and grouping together logically related resources. However, there are several important differences between package specifications and record type declarations.

One important difference arises from the fact that a record type is a template from which instances must be created by object declaration, while a package specification directly declares a group of objects which may be accessed. Thus "COMMON.X := 53;" assigns a value to the X component of the package COMMON, while assignment to a component X of a record type first requires a record object to be created.

Example 4.3. Comparison of records and packages

```
procedure RECORD_COMPONENTS is
   type VULGAR is                    -- a record type is a template
     record                          -- objects of this type must be created
       X: INTEGER;                   -- before components may be accessed
       Y: INTEGER;
       Z: array(1..100) of INTEGER;
     end record;
   ME, YOU: VULGAR;                  -- declare two VULGAR objects
begin
   ME.X := 53;                       -- legal assignment to VULGAR object
   VULGAR.X := 53;            -- illegal attempt to assign to record type
end;
```

Another difference between package and record components is that dot qualification in accessing components of a package may be avoided by means of a use clause in the declarative part of a program unit.

Example 4.4. The use clause

```
declare;
   use COMMON;
begin
   X := 0;              -- X may be used instead of COMMON.X
   Y := Y+X;            -- Y may be used instead of COMMON.Y
   V(1) := 37;          -- V(1) may be used instead of COMMON.V(1)
end;
```

There is no corresponding mechanism in Ada for removing dot qualification for record accessing.

Perhaps the most important difference between package and record components is that package components are not restricted to data objects. The following package specification includes type declarations as well as object declarations.

Example 4.5. Package with type declarations

```
package WORK_DATA is
    type DAY is (MON,TUE,WED,THU,FRI,SAT,SUN);
    type TIME is delta 0.01 range 0.0..24.0;
    type WORK_WEEK is array(MON..SUN) of TIME;
    NORMAL_HOURS: constant WORK_WEEK := (MON..FRI => 8.0, SAT|SUN => 0.0);
end;
```

The package WORK_DATA makes available to the user not only the data object NORMAL_HOURS but also the data types DAY, TIME and WORK_WEEK. The function OVERTIME below, which is assumed to be declared in the scope of the package WORK_DATA, has a parameter of the type WORK_WEEK, and makes use also of the data types DAY and TIME and the nonlocal data object NORMAL_HOURS.

Example 4.6. Function which uses package declarations

```
use WORK_DATA;
function OVERTIME(ACTUAL: WORK_WEEK) return FLOAT is
OVER: FLOAT := 0.0;
begin
    for I in DAY loop
        OVER := OVER + FLOAT(ACTUAL(I)) - FLOAT(NORMAL_HOURS(I));
    end loop;
    return OVER;
end OVERTIME;
```

This function might in turn be used by a function SALARY to compute the total pay for a given pay rate and number of hours worked.

Example 4.7. Sharing of package declarations by several functions

```
function SALARY(RATE: FLOAT; HOURS: WORK_WEEK) return FLOAT is
PAY, EXCESS: FLOAT;
begin
    EXCESS := OVERTIME(HOURS);
    if EXCESS < 0.0 then              -- when EXCESS is negative
        PAY := (40.0+EXCESS) * RATE;  -- pay is at the normal rate
    else
        PAY := 40.0*RATE + 2.0*EXCESS*RATE;  -- overtime is paid
    end if;                           -- at twice the normal rate
    return PAY;
end SALARY;
```

The package WORK_DATA could be expanded to include the functions OVERTIME and SALARY, resulting in a package with a richer set of resources.

Example 4.8. Package with subprogram specifications

```
package WORK_PROGRAMS is
    type DAY is (MON,TUE,WED,THU,FRI,SAT,SUN);
    type TIME is delta 0.01 range 0.0..24.0;
    type WORK_WEEK is array(MON..SUN) of TIME;
    NORMAL_HOURS: constant WORK_WEEK := (MON..FRI => 8.0, SAT|SUN => 0.0);
    function OVERTIME(ACTUAL: WORK_WEEK) return FLOAT;
    function SALARY(RATE: FLOAT, ACTUAL: WORK_WEEK) return FLOAT;
end;
```

This package specification for WORK_PROGRAMS contains declarations, objects and subprograms, and is an example of a subprogram
package. A subprogram package has an associated package body
which contains the implementation of specified subprograms (such
as OVERTIME and SALARY), as well as any additional local variables
and subprograms needed to implement the specified subprograms.
The package body for the package WORK_PROGRAMS would essentially
have the following form.

Example 4.9. Package body with subprogram implementation

```
package body WORK_PROGRAMS is
    -- function declaration which implements OVERTIME (example 4.6)
    -- function declaration which implements SALARY (example 4.7)
end WORK_PROGRAMS;
```

Inclusion of previously specified text in a given program
text can be accomplished by defining the text to be included as
a text file and then using the INCLUDE pragma.

Example 4.10. The INCLUDE pragma

```
package body WORK_PROGRAMS is
    pragma INCLUDE(OVERTIME_FILE);
    pragma INCLUDE(SALARY_FILE);
end WORK_PROGRAMS;
```

This example would require the texts of the subprograms
OVERTIME and SALARY to have been defined as files named
OVERTIME_FILE and SALARY_FILE, using the facilities described in
chapter 14 of the reference manual. These facilities are really
text-editing rather than programming facilities and will not be
further described here.

4.2 Syntax of Package Declarations

A package specification has the following syntax.

Example 4.11. Syntax of package specifications

```
package name is
  declarations of visible resources
[private
  declarations of private data types]
end [name];
```

The optional private part may contain specifications of
"private" data types whose names are visible to the user but
whose internal structure is hidden from the user. Operations on
private data types may be supplied by the package, so that the
user can perform operations on private data types but does not
have access to their internal representation.

Packages whose resources include subprogram specifications
have a package body with the following syntax.

Example 4.12. Syntax of package bodies

```
package body name is
  [declarations of local resources]
  subprogram declarations which implement visible subprograms
[begin
  initialization part]
end [name];
```

The package specification may reside in the declarative part
of an enclosing program unit or be a stand-alone library package.
Elaboration of the package specification causes allocation of
variables declared in the visible part and assignment of any
initial values. Elaboration of the package specification also
causes local variables of the package body to come into existence
and causes execution of the initialization part of the package
body. The local variables of the package body remain in existence until exit from the scope of the package specification and
act as "own variables" of the package body. That is, local
variables remain in existence between calls of visible subprograms of the package body and may be used to "remember" state
information between calls of subprograms.

The body of a package may be compiled separately from its
specifications. Since all information needed to use a package is
contained in the specification, the package body can be written
independently of modules which use the package, and can be rewritten and replaced even after the system is in use without affecting
other modules. However, the compiled package body must be available at run time whenever the package is used, since elaboration
of the package specification causes elaboration and initialization of the package body.

137

4.3   A Complex Number Package

The relation between package specifications and package bodies will be illustrated by a package for complex numbers, with operations for adding and multiplying complex numbers. The package specification below has a data type COMPLEX whose internal structure is visible to the user, addition and multiplication functions which take complex arguments and return complex values, and a multiplication function which multiplies a complex number by a scalar.

Example 4.13.   Package specification for complex numbers

```
package COMPLEX_NUMBERS is
  type COMPLEX is
    record
      RE: FLOAT := 0.0;
      IM: FLOAT := 0.0;
    end record;
  function "+"(X,Y: COMPLEX) return COMPLEX;
  function "*"(X,Y: COMPLEX) return COMPLEX;
  function "*"(X: FLOAT; Y: COMPLEX) return COMPLEX;
end COMPLEX_NUMBERS;
```

Before considering the package body for this package, we will illustrate how the resources of this package may be used.

Example 4.14.   Use of complex number specification

```
declare
  use COMPLEX_NUMBERS;
  X,Y,Z: COMPLEX;
begin
  X := (1.5,2.5);        -- assigns complex literal to X
  Y := X*X;              -- multiplication of complex numbers
  Z := X+Y;              -- addition of complex numbers
  Z := 2.7*Z;            -- multiplication by a floating-point number
  Z := 2*Z;              -- illegal - multiplication by integers not defined
  Z := Z*2.7;            -- illegal - post-multiplication by scalar not defined
end;
```

The illegal expressions 2*Z and Z*2.7 could be made legal by adding two more procedures to the package body.

Example 4.15.   Overloading of multiplication operator

```
function "*"(X: INTEGER; Y: COMPLEX) return COMPLEX;
function "*"(X: COMPLEX; Y: FLOAT) return COMPLEX;
```

This is not sufficient to handle all "reasonable" combinations of real and complex multiplication, since "Z*2" would still be illegal. However, the above examples illustrate both mechanism of overloading an operator such as * to handle additional types of arguments, and the fact that an attempt to handle all reasonable types might in certain contexts cause an exponential explosion in the number of subprograms.

The above package specification allows the user to independently manipulate components of complex numbers, as in the following example.

Example 4.16. Accessing of components of abstract objects

```
declare
  use COMPLEX_NUMBERS;
  X,Y: COMPLEX;
begin
  X.RE := 53.7;                -- arbitrary manipulation of components
  Y.IM := X.RE*36.9;           -- legal floating-point multiplication
end;
```

A complex number package which treats complex numbers as abstract objects should not permit arbitrary manipulation of components. This can be accomplished by declaring the data type COMPLEX to be private, and including a function MAKE_COMP which takes two floating-point arguments and returns a value of the type COMPLEX.

Example 4.17. Complex numbers with private data types

```
package COMPLEX_TYPE is
  type COMPLEX is private;
  function "+"(X,Y: COMPLEX) return COMPLEX;
  function "*"(X,Y: COMPLEX) return COMPLEX;
  function "*"(X: FLOAT; Y: COMPLEX) return COMPLEX;
  function MAKE_COMP(X,Y: FLOAT) return COMPLEX;
private
  type COMPLEX is
    record
      RE: FLOAT := 0.0;
      IM: FLOAT := 0.0;
    end record;
end COMPLEX_TYPE;
```

The private type declaration for COMPLEX allows the user to declare complex variables and to manipulate them by the operations provided in the package, but does not allow the user access to the components of complex numbers. The user does not know how complex numbers are represented and cannot therefore write complex literals. Thus a function for creating complex literals from floating components is provided in the package specification.

Since private data types are hidden, and hidden structures are generally specified as part of the package body, it is surprising that Ada requires the structure of the private data type to be specified in the specification rather than the body. The reason for this is that the compiler needs to know the structure of private data types in order to allocate storage for instances of private data types created by the user. Thus, in the following example, a compiler which has access to the structure of COMPLEX can directly allocate storage for the complex data objects X, Y, Z.*

Example 4.18. Use of abstract complex number package

```
declare
  use COMPLEX_TYPES;
  X,Y: COMPLEX;          -- allocate two complex objects with hidden structure
  Z: COMPLEX := MAKE_COMP(1.5,2.5);  -- initialize to created literal
begin
  X := MAKE_COMP(2.5,3.5);    -- initialization by assignment
  Y := X+Z;                   -- complex addition
  X.RE := Y.RE;               -- illegal attempt to assign to components
  if X = Y then               -- equality for complex numbers is defined
    X := Y+Z;                 -- complex addition
  else
    X := Y*Z;                 -- complex multiplication
  end if;
end;
```

Assignment, equality and inequality testing are normally defined automatically for all new types, including private types declared in a package. Thus "X := Y;", "X = Y" and "X /= Y" are legal for variables of private types such as COMPLEX above.

We have illustrated two styles of specification for complex number packages, but have not yet discussed the package body for implementing the functions promised to the user in the specifications. The package body is of no concern to the user of the package, and we are tempted to omit the discussion of the package body for complex numbers on the ground that it is

---

*If the specification of COMPLEX were in a separately compiled package body, the compiler could not assume that knowledge of the representation of the data type is available at the time of compilation of user modules. It would have to compile user modules on the assumption that code for allocating private data types would be supplied at load time. This would require a more complex loader but would not necessarily result in less efficient object code.

Inclusion of private data types in the package specification implies that a change in representation of the private data type will require recompilation of the program unit which contains the package specification, thus violating the principle that package specifications are recompiled only when there are specification changes which affect the user. This appears to be a very heavy price to pay for the simplification in compiling and loading that is achieved by including private declarations in the specification part.

140

irrelevant to the user. However, although the programmer need
not know the details of package bodies supplied by others,
every programmer is likely to build private applications packages, and must therefore be familiar with the mechanisms for
constructing package bodies.

The package body may be defined as follows.

Example 4.19. Body of complex number package

```
package body COMPLEX_TYPES is
    function "+"(X,Y: COMPLEX) return COMPLEX is   -- complex addition function
    begin
        return (X.RE+Y.RE, X.IM+Y.IM);   -- adds real and complex components
    end;
    function "*"(X,Y: COMPLEX) return COMPLEX is  -- complex multiplication
        R: FLOAT := X.RE*Y.RE - X.IM*Y.IM;  -- value of real component
        I: FLOAT := X.RE*Y.IM + X.IM*Y.RE;  -- value of imaginary component
    begin
        return (R,I);            -- return complex number with components R and I
    end;
    function "*"(X: FLOAT; Y: COMPLEX) return COMPLEX is -- scalar multiplication
        TEMP: COMPLEX;
    begin
        TEMP := (X*Y.RE, X*Y.IM);     -- multiply each component by scalar
        return TEMP;
    end;
    function MAKE_COMP(X,Y: FLOAT) return COMPLEX is  -- create complex number
    begin
        return (X,Y);              -- return complex number with given components
    end;
end COMPLEX_TYPES;
```

This package body contains only the implementations of
visible procedures, and no additional local declarations. Both
the visible and private parts of the package specification are
accessible within the body, so that the functions + and * can
access components such as X.RE and X.IM, and the function
MAKE_COMP can construct a literal of the type COMPLEX from its
floating-point components.

4.4 Generating "Secure" Keys

Private types may be used also in applications which require
security. Consider, for example, a security system based on
"keys" supplied by a key management package. The package must
be able to issue keys which are unique and cannot be forged.
This can be accomplished by declaring KEY to be a private data
type.

141

Example 4.20. Specification of key manager

```
package KEY_MANAGER is
  type KEY is private;
  procedure GET_KEY(K: out KEY);          -- get a unique unforgeable key
  function "<" (X,Y: KEY) return BOOLEAN;  -- define "<" for keys
private
  type KEY is new INTEGER range 0..INTEGER'LAST;
end KEY_MANAGER;
```

The function GET_KEY above provides the user with a unique unforgeable key.

Uniqueness of keys can be realized by including within the package body a variable of type KEY that is initialized to 1 and incremented by 1 whenever a new key is generated. Unforgeability is guaranteed because type conversion between objects of the private type KEY and other objects such as integers is illegal outside the package body. Thus the only way of creating objects of type KEY is by the GET_KEY procedure.

Although conversion between keys and integers is illegal outside the package body, it is permitted inside the package body because the fact that KEY is a derived integer type is known within the package body. The function "<" on objects of type KEY contains a statement which converts keys to integers so that the operation "<" on keys can be defined in terms of the corresponding operation on integers.

Example 4.21. Body of key manager

```
package body KEY_MANAGER is
  NEXT_KEY: KEY := 1;      -- own variable - exists between procedure calls
procedure GET_KEY(K: out KEY) is
begin
  K := NEXT_KEY;                  -- assign key value to out parameter
  NEXT_KEY := NEXT_KEY+1;         -- increment unique key value
end GET_KEY;
function "<"(X,Y: KEY) return BOOLEAN is
begin
  return INTEGER(X)<INTEGER(Y);   -- convert keys to integers
end "<";                          -- so that < for keys is defined
end KEY_MANAGER;                  -- in terms of < for integers
```

Although keys generated by the key manager are unique and unforgeable, they can be copied by assignment to a variable of the type KEY. Thus additional security measures will have to be taken in the program (probably a package) which makes use of the keys generated by the key manager to control access to other resources.

142

4.5   A Symbol Table Package

The symbol table programs FIND and UPDATE discussed at the end of Chapter 3 may be realized as a package with the following specification.

Example 4.22.   Specification of symbol table package

```
package SYMTAB is
   function FIND(S: STRING) return INTEGER; -- return value for key S
   procedure UPDATE(S: STRING; V: INTEGER); -- update value for key S
end SYMTAB;
```

The FIND function will be defined so that it returns the value associated with the key S if S is in the symbol table and returns the special value INTEGER'FIRST if S is not in the symbol table. It may be implemented by very slightly modifying the FIND procedure of Chapter 3.

Example 4.23.   FIND subprogram

```
function FIND(S: STRING) return INTEGER;  -- find key S, return integer value
   N: NODE := ROOT;          -- ROOT is nonlocal to FIND but local to package body
begin
   while N /= null loop      -- while current node not null
      if S < N.KEY then       -- if key parameter less than node
         N := N.LEFT;         -- move to left descendant
      elsif S > N.KEY then    -- if key parameter greater than node
         N := N.RIGHT;        -- move to right descendant
      else                    -- if key parameter equal to node
         return N.VALUE;      -- return value of node
      end if;
   end loop;                  -- end of while loop
   return INTEGER'FIRST;      -- if key not found in tree
end FIND;                     -- return special value
```

The text of the above FIND program must be included in a package body which contains a type declaration for NODE, a declaration of a variable ROOT, and the text of the UPDATE program. In the package body below it is assumed that FIND and UPDATE have been previously created and stored in files which are respectively called FIND_FILE and UPDATE_FILE.

Example 4.24. Body of symbol table package

```
package body SYMTAB is
   type NODE is access            -- a NODE is a variant record
      record
         SIZE: constant INTEGER range 1..INTEGER'LAST;
         KEY: STRING(1..SIZE);
         VALUE: INTEGER;
         LEFT, RIGHT: NODE := null;
      end record;
   ROOT: NODE := null;
   pragma INCLUDE(FIND_FILE);
      -- as given in the previous example
   pragma INCLUDE(UPDATE_FILE);
      -- very similar to that given at the end of Chapter 3
end SYMTAB;
```

A comparison of the COMPLEX_NUMBERS and SYMTAB package illustrates the two levels of hiding which can be associated with a data type. In the COMPLEX_NUMBERS package the type COMPLEX was private but its name was known to users. In the SYMTAB package we were able to hide both the name and the structure of the data type NODE.

These two levels of hiding serve two very different purposes. The private mechanism is useful for abstract data types where only specified abstract operations on objects of the data type are permitted, and for security, where the structure is "private" or "classified" but the name must be accessible. These two cases were illustrated by the complex number and key manager example. Total hiding arises when, as in the symbol table example, the structure is of no concern to the user but is merely a mechanism of implementation.

4.6 A List Processing Package

As a final example of packages we shall consider the implementation of list processing primitives of the language LISP. LISP has two kinds of primitive objects, respectively called atoms and lists. List elements in LISP have two access components each of which may point to an atom or a list. The required abstract properties of list elements may be realized by the following named record.

Example 4.25. The LISP data type

```
type LISP is access              -- the LISP data type is variant record
   record
      CHOICE: constant(LIST,ATOM);    -- whose discriminant may have two values
      case CHOICE of
         when LIST => CAR: LISP;      -- the LIST variant has two fields
                      CDR: LISP;      -- CAR and CDR of the type LISP
         when ATOM => VALUE: INTEGER; -- ATOM variant has INTEGER value field
      end case;
   end record;
```

We want to define a package which supports the following
LISP operations.

Example 4.26. Operations on LISP data structures

```
function CAR(X: LISP) return LISP;
function CDR(X: LISP) return LISP;
function CONS(X,Y: LISP) return LISP;
function ATOM(X: LISP) return BOOLEAN;
function EQ(X,Y: LISP) return BOOLEAN;
```

The function CAR is given an argument X of the type LISP.
If the CHOICE component has the value LIST then the value is
X.CAR. If the CHOICE component has the value ATOM, then an
exception NO_LIST declared and handled outside the subprogram
is raised.

Example 4.27. The function CAR

```
function CAR(X: LISP) return LISP is    -- the function CAR
begin
    if X.CHOICE = LIST then        -- returns the value of its CAR component
      return X.CAR;                -- if the argument is a LIST
    else
      raise NO_LIST;               -- and raises an exception
    end if;                        -- if the argument is an atom
end CAR;
```

The function CDR returns the value X.CDR if X.CHOICE =
LIST, and raises an exception if X.CHOICE = ATOM. Its implementation is similar to that of CAR.

Example 4.28. The function CDR

```
function CDR(X: LISP) return LISP is    -- the function CDR
begin
    if X.CHOICE = LIST then        -- returns the value of its CDR component
      return X.CDR;                -- if the argument is a LIST
    else
      raise NO_LIST;               -- and raises an exception
    end if;                        -- if the argument is an atom
end CDR;
```

The function CONS has two arguments of type LISP and
creates a new cell of type LISP with discriminant value LIST.

Example 4.29. The function CONS

```
function CONS(X,Y: LISP) return LISP is
begin
    return new LISP(CHOICE => LIST, CAR => X; CDR  => Y);
end;
```

The function ATOM returns the value TRUE if X.CHOICE = ATOM and the value FALSE if X.CHOICE = LIST.

Example 4.30. The function ATOM

```
function ATOM(X: LISP) return BOOLEAN is   -- the function ATOM
begin
   if X.CHOICE = ATOM then                 -- returns the value TRUE
      return TRUE;                         -- if its argument is an ATOM
   else
      return FALSE;                        -- and returns the value FALSE
   end if;                                 -- if its argument is a LIST
end ATOM;
```

The function EQ returns the value TRUE if both its arguments are atoms with the same value, returns the value FALSE if X and Y are unequal atoms and raises an exception if X and/or Y are not atoms.

Example 4.31. The function EQ

```
function EQ(X,Y: LISP) return BOOLEAN is   -- the function EQ
begin
   if X.CHOICE = ATOM and Y.CHOICE = ATOM then   -- returns the value TRUE
      return X.VALUE=Y.VALUE;        -- if its two arguments are equal atoms
   else                    -- the value FALSE if its arguments are unequal atoms
      raise NO_ATOM;                 -- and raises an exception
   end if;     -- if one or both of its arguments are non-atomic
end EQ;
```

The above list processing primitives all have arguments of the type LISP and some return results of the type LISP. The user must be permitted to create variables of the type LISP but should not be allowed access to the representation of list elements. The type LISP will therefore be declared as a private data type of the package specification.

146

Example 4.32. Specification of a LISP processing package

```
package LISP_PROCESSING is               -- package specification
  type LISP is private;                  -- with a private data structure
  NULLIST: constant LISP;     -- constant is initialized in private part
  function CAR(X: LISP) return LISP;  -- package has six list processing functions
  function CDR(X: LISP) return LISP;  -- which operate on the data structure
  function CONS(X,Y: LISP) return LISP;
  function ATOM(X: LISP) return BOOLEAN;
  function EQ(X,Y: LISP) return BOOLEAN;
  function MAKE_ATOM(X: INTEGER) return LISP;
private
  type LISP is access                    -- private data structure
  record                                 -- is a variant record
    CHOICE: constant(LIST,ATOM) := LIST; -- whose discriminant has 2 values
    case CHOICE of
      when LIST => CAR: LISP := null;    -- the LIST variant has a CAR
                  CDR: LISP := null;     -- and a CDR field of type LISP
      when ATOM => VALUE: INTEGER;       -- the ATOM variant has a VALUE
    end case;                            -- field of type INTEGER
  end record;
  NULLIST: constant LISP := null; -- representation of NULLIST known in
                                  -- private part
end LISP_PROCESSING;
```

The above specification includes the function MAKE_ATOM in addition to the previously specified LISP primitives. The function may be defined as follows.

Example 4.33. The MAKE_ATOM function

```
function MAKE_ATOM(X: INTEGER) return LISP is
begin
  return new LISP(CHOICE => ATOM, VALUE => X); -- return a new LISP element
end;                                           -- with an ATOM variant
```

A MAKE_LIST function is not needed, because the user can construct new list elements by CONS operations on NULLIST arguments.

Example 3.34. Creating list elements

```
declare
  use LISP_PROCESSING;
  L1: LISP := NULLIST; -- L1 is LISP variable with value NULLIST
  L2,L3: LISP;         -- L2, L3 are uninitialized variables of type LISP
begin
  L2 := CONS(L1,L1);   -- L2 is list with two NULLIST components
  L3 := CONS(MAKE_ATOM(53),NULLIST); -- L3 is list with ATOM and null components
```

The use of the CONS, CAR and CDR functions will be illustrated by showing how the list structure of figure 4.2 can be constructed and then accessed.

147

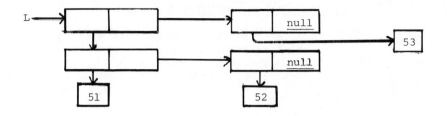

Figure 4.2.   Example of a list structure.

This program requires four CONS operations to create the four list elements and three MAKE ATOM operations to create the three atoms with values 51, 52, 53.

Example 4.35. Constructing lists

```
declare
  use LISP_PROCESSING;
  L,L1,L2: LISP;
begin
  L1 := CONS(MAKE_ATOM(53),NULLIST);      -- list element (53, null)
  L2 := CONS(MAKE_ATOM(52),NULLIST);      -- list element (52, null)
  L2 := CONS(MAKE_ATOM(51),L2);           -- list (51, (52, null)
  L := CONS(L2,L1);                       -- list of figure 4.2
  L1 := CAR(CAR(L));              -- L1 points to atom with value 51
  L2 := CAR(CDR(L));              -- L2 points to atom with value 53
end;
```

Now that we have illustrated the use of the LISP processing package, we shall define its package body. This contains the declarations which implement the functions of the package specification as well as an initialization part which contains declarations and handlers for the NO_LIST and NO_ATOM exceptions. These exception handlers print a message and then raise the LISP_ERROR exception, which is assumed to be declared and handled outside the LISP_PROCESSING package.

148

Example 4.36. Body of the LISP PROCESSING package

```
package body LISP_PROCESSING is          -- the package body
    -- text which implements CAR
    -- text of CDR
    -- text of CONS
    -- text of ATOM
    -- text of EQ
    -- text of MAKE_ATOM
end LISP_PROCESSING;
```

The above LISP_PROCESSING package is typical of packages
which define a group of common operations on an abstract data
type. The data type is abstract because it can be manipulated
only by the operations of the package and by no other operations. The LISP package illustrates the implications of allowing user access to the name of the type, but hiding the representation of the type.

It is instructive to contrast the symbol table package,
whose data structure is totally hidden in the package specification, with the list processing package, whose data structure is
private. In the case of the symbol table package the user is
concerned only with the correct retrieval and updating of
previously stored information. The data structure used to
accomplish this is of no concern to the user and can remain
totally hidden. In the case of the list processing package,
manipulation of the list structure is the name of the game, and
it is essential that the user be explicitly able to name and
traverse list structures. However, LISP is a high-level list
processing language which provides the user with abstract operations that are not dependent on the representation of list
elements. The list processing package above illustrates very
clearly the mechanisms by which such abstraction can be realized.

4.7   The Use Clause

Now that packages have been illustrated by a number of
examples, we shall consider some issues which arise in integrating packages and other program units into a complete program.
In particular, we shall consider mechanisms at the interface
between a program unit and its environment which change the set
of identifiers (names) that can be used within the program unit.
The first such mechanism to be considered is the use clause.

The use clause may be viewed as a renaming mechanism for externally declared identifiers. It augments the name space of the program unit in which it occurs by allowing shortened (unqualified) forms of certain already accessible names to be used. In some cases this reduces the amount of writing and makes a program more readable. However, in other cases name qualification can serve to disambiguate names that would otherwise be ambiguous, and can make programs more readable and maintainable by providing useful identifying mnemonics.

The packages WEIGHT and HEIGHT below, with identically named components ID and VALUE, are perhaps an extreme example of this. The use clause in the procedure INNER is in fact of no use at all because unqualified use of the component names ID and VALUE results in unresolvable ambiguities.

Example 4.37. Use statement which introduces ambiguous names

```
procedure OUTER is
  package HEIGHT is           -- package HEIGHT with ID and VALUE variables
    ID: INTEGER;
    VALUE: FLOAT;             -- VALUE component of package HEIGHT
  end HEIGHT;
  package WEIGHT is
    ID: INTEGER;
    VALUE: FLOAT;             -- VALUE component of package WEIGHT
  end WEIGHT;
  procedure INNER is
    use HEIGHT, WEIGHT;       -- augment name space with unqualified
  begin                       -- names of package components
    HEIGHT.VALUE := 65.3;     -- qualified names may still be used
    WEIGHT.VALUE := HEIGHT.VALUE ;   -- without ambiguity
    VALUE: = 63.5;  -- unqualified names are ambiguous and therefore illegal
  end INNER;                   -- this error can be caught by compiler
begin                         -- beginning of statement part for OUTER
  VALUE := 63.5;              -- this is illegal for a different reason
end OUTER; -- outside scope of use statement only qualified names are legal
```

Further insight into the effect of a use clause can be obtained by the following example which redeclares VALUE in the INNER procedure. This hides the outer ambiguous VALUE identifiers and causes references to VALUE in the INNER procedure to be to the inner INTEGER object. The outer ambiguous identifier ID is visible in the procedure, so that unqualified references to ID are ambiguous and therefore illegal. However, qualified references to outer identifiers such as HEIGHT.VALUE and HEIGHT.ID are legal.

Example 4.38. Redeclaration of names made visible by use clause

```
package OUTER is
   package HEIGHT is
      ID: INTEGER;
      VALUE: FLOAT;                 -- variable VALUE in package HEIGHT
   end HEIGHT;
   package WEIGHT is
      ID: INTEGER;
      VALUE: FLOAT;                 -- variable VALUE in package WEIGHT
   end WEIGHT;
   procedure INNER is
      use HEIGHT, WEIGHT;
      VALUE: INTEGER;               -- inner declaration of VALUE
   begin
      HEIGHT.VALUE := 65.3;         -- variable VALUE in package HEIGHT
      VALUE := 65;                  -- inner variable VALUE
      VALUE := 65.3;                -- illegal - type of RHS should be INTEGER
      OUTER.VALUE := 65.3;          -- illegal - ambiguous variable name
      ID := 23657;                  -- illegal - ambiguous variable name
   end INNER;
end OUTER;
```

In the following example, WEIGHT is declared in an inner declarative part, so that normal block-structure scope rules would allow VALUE to be used unambiguously in the procedure INNER. However, the language reference manual (section 8.4) states that "an identifier is made visible by a use clause if it is defined in the visible part of one and only one module made visible by an accessible use statement", so that VALUE is invisible in the procedure INNER according to the current language definition.

Example 4.39. Mnemonic value of qualified names

```
procedure HEIGHT_PROC is
   package HEIGHT is
      HEIGHT_ID: INTEGER;
      VALUE: FLOAT;
   end HEIGHT;
   procedure WEIGHT_PROC is
      package WEIGHT is
         WEIGHT_ID: INTEGER;
         VALUE: FLOAT;
      end WEIGHT;
      procedure INNER is
         use HEIGHT,WEIGHT;
      begin
         VALUE := 96.5;  -- illegal, VALUE is invisible, occurs in HEIGHT and WEIGHT
         WEIGHT.VALUE := 96.5;   -- same effect as previous statement
         HEIGHT.VALUE := WEIGHT.VALUE/2.0;
         WEIGHT_ID := 28537;    -- mnemonic identifiers have the same
         HEIGHT_ID := 28537;    -- psychological effect as qualified names
      end INNER;
   begin ...                       -- statement part of HEIGHT_PROC
      begin ...                    -- statement part of WEIGHT_PROC
   end WEIGHT_PROC;
end HEIGHT_PROC;
```

In this example the ID components of HEIGHT and WEIGHT have the unambiguous mnemonic names HEIGHT_ID, WEIGHT_ID. Use of these unqualified names has the same psychological effect as HEIGHT.ID, WEIGHT.ID. Thus, name qualification may be thought of as a useful mnemonic device in cases of contextual ambiguity.

These examples illustrate that the use clause is a relatively "passive" linguistic mechanism which merely provides abbreviated "aliases" for objects that would be accessible even if the use clause were not present. It does not do anything radical like augmenting the set of accessible objects.

The restricted clause, which is considered in the next section, is a more radical mechanism for modifying the name space than the use clause in the following two respects:

1. It can restrict as well as augment the set of accessible names in the program unit which it qualifies.
2. It changes not only the set of accessible names but also the set of accessible objects and computational resources.

4.8   Restricted Clauses

Ada program units normally act as one-way membranes which permit access within a program unit to identifiers declared in textually enclosing program units, but do not permit access from outside a program unit to identifiers declared within the program unit.

The restricted clause allows the programmer to restrict the set of nonlocal identifiers accessible within a program unit. The keyword restricted immediately preceding a subprogram or module declaration completely shuts off access to nonlocal identifiers.

Example 4.40. Total inaccessibility of nonlocal identifiers

```
restricted procedure P(X: in out INTEGER) is
   -- no access to nonlocal programmer-declared identifiers
   -- is permitted within the procedure P
   -- but predefined identifiers such as INTEGER, INTEGER'LAST
   -- are accessible
   -- communication between P and its environment
   -- is restricted to its parameter X
end P;
```

The keyword restricted may in general be followed by a visibility list of named program units.

Example 4.41.   Restricted visibility

restricted (Q) -- visibility list contains Q, Q must be name of an enclosing
procedure P is -- program unit or non-enclosing module
   -- accessibility of nonlocal identifiers
   -- is restricted to the nonlocal program unit Q
   -- if Q is a package then all its visible identifiers are accessible
   -- if Q textually encloses P then all identifiers declared in program
   -- units enclosing P but enclosed by Q are visible
end P;

     The effect of restricting accessibility within P to a non-
local program unit Q depends on the textual relation between P and
Q. Two possible textual relations between P and Q must be considered:

   1.   Q textually encloses the restricted program P. In this
        case all identifiers declared in program units enclos-
        ing P but enclosed by Q are accessible in P. But iden-
        tifiers declared in program units which textually enclose
        Q remain invisible.
   2.   Q does not textually enclose P, but is declared within
        a textually enclosing program unit, and would normally
        be accessible in the absence of restricted clauses. In
        this case Q must be a module (cannot be a subprogram).
        Its occurrence in the visibility list makes all the
        resources in the visible part of Q accessible in P, but
        other nonlocal declarations in the textually enclosing
        environment remain inaccessible.

     The visibility list of a restricted program unit may in
general contain one textually enclosing program unit satisfying
condition 1, and several non-enclosing modules satisfying condition 2.

     A restricted clause has the general form "restricted(P,M1,M2,
...,MK)" where the first parameter P may (but need not) be the name
of a textually enclosing program unit and the remaining names are
module names. Each name in a visibility list provides access to
a collection of resources (environment). The first name may provide access to a set of enclosing resources, while remaining names
provide access to sets of resources of non-enclosing modules.

     The following example, taken from the language rationale,
has a restricted procedure R with a visibility list (Q,E) consisting of an enclosing procedure Q and a non-enclosing package E
declared outside Q. Thus all nonlocal declared identifiers and
parameters out as far as Q are visible in R, and the visible components of the package E are visible in R. But the outer procedure
P, and declarations within P but not within Q or the visible part
of E, are not visible in R.

Example 4.42. Visibility for enclosing and non-enclosing program units

```
procedure P(X: INTEGER) is          -- P and X are not visible in R
   LP: BOOLEAN;                      -- LP is not visible in R
   package E is
      LE: BOOLEAN                    -- E is visible in R
   ...
   end E;
   package body E is
      LBE: BOOLEAN;
   ...
   end E;
   procedure Q(Y: INTEGER) is        -- Q textually encloses R
      LQ: BOOLEAN;
      restricted (Q,E)               -- restricted clause
      procedure R(Z: INTEGER) is     -- for procedure R
      begin
         -- the local identifiers of Q are visible:
            -- the procedure Q itself
            -- the parameter Y
            -- the local variable LQ
            -- the procedure R itself
            -- the parameter Z of R
         -- the package name E is visible:
            -- names such as E.LE can be used
            -- the clause "use E;" is legal
            -- as usual, LBE is not visible
         -- the names P, X and LP are not visible
      end R;
   begin
   ...
   end Q;
begin
...
end P;
```

A restricted clause may be used not only to restrict access
to normally accessible identifiers of the textually enclosing
environment. It may be used also to augment the set of accessible identifiers by including separately compiled program units
in the visibility list. For example, the procedure
QUADRATIC_EQUATIONS below makes use of the package TEXT_IO for
input-output and the package MATH_LIB for taking square roots.
The restricted clause augments the name space of
QUADRATIC_EQUATIONS with the identifiers declared in the visible
parts of the packages MATH_LIB and TEXT_IO. In this case the
keyword restricted is perhaps a misnomer. However, it seems
reasonable to use the same language mechanism for both restrict-
ing and augmenting the set of names in a name space.

Example 4.43. Quadratic equations procedure

```
restricted(MATH_LIB, TEXT_IO)      -- makes MATH_LIB, TEXT_IO accessible
procedure QUADRATIC_EQUATIONS is
  use TEXT_IO;              -- GET, PUT, NEWLINE are defined in TEXT_IO
  A,B,C,D: FLOAT;
begin
  GET(A); GET(B); GET(C);
  D := B**2 - 4.0*A*C;
  if D < 0.0 then
    PUT("IMAGINARY ROOTS");
  else
    declare
      use MATH_LIB;        -- SQRT is defined in MATH_LIB
    begin
      PUT("REAL ROOTS:");
      PUT((B - SQRT(D))/(2.0*A));
      PUT((B + SQRT(D))/(2.0*A));
      PUT(NEWLINE);
    end;
  end if;
end QUADRATIC_EQUATIONS;
```

The specifications of modules and subprograms on which a separately compiled program unit depends must be compiled before that program unit. Thus the specifications of MATH_LIB and TEXT_IO above must be compiled before the QUADRATIC_EQUATIONS procedure. The quadratic equations procedure must be recompiled if the specifications of MATH_LIB or TEXT_IO are changed, but not if the implementation of these packages is modified. Thus separation of the specification and implementation not only factors out information needed by the user from information needed to implement the desired resources, but also aids maintainability by explicitly indicating when changes of a given module may require changes in other modules which use the given module.

4.9 Generic Program Structures

Generic program structures, just like packages, are a mechanism for expressing abstract computational behavior. Packages express abstract behavior by hiding irrelevant implementation information and allowing the user to "see" only high-level computational resources. Generic program structures express abstraction by capturing the similarities among a group of computational tasks in a common program structure, and expressing the variability among tasks by parameters.

Parametrization was recognized as a basic mechanism for expressing computational abstraction very early in the game. It is the basic abstraction mechanism of subprograms. However, subprogram parametrization in Ada is restricted to variables. Computational similarities which can be captured in this way are expressed by varying a variable over the set of values of its type.

Generic program structures provide a more powerful form of parametrization. They allow parameters to be not only variables but also types and procedures. The following generic SWAP procedure, already discussed in Chapter 1, illustrates how the abstract notion of swapping, which is independent of the type of object being swapped, can be expressed by a generic procedure.

Example 4.44. Two kinds of parametrization

```
generic (type T)
procedure SWAP(X,Y: in out T) is
   TEMP: T;
begin
   TEMP := X;
   X := Y;
   Y := TEMP;
end SWAP;
```

This procedure declaration illustrates that generic procedures have two levels of parametrization:

1. Procedure parameters which must be variables. Actual parameters are substituted for formal parameters during execution at procedure call time.
2. Generic parameters specified in the generic clause which may be variables, types or subprograms. Substitution of actual for formal parameters must be performed at translation time.

Whereas ordinary procedures are called during execution, generic procedures are "called" at translation time. Translation-time "calls" of generic procedures are referred to as instantiations. An instantiation of a generic procedure may give rise to an instance of a program text in much the same way that a macro call gives rise to a program text in a macro assembler.

Two instances of the SWAP procedure which respectively swap integers and vectors may be created as follows.

Example 4.45. Instantiation of generic procedures

```
procedure SWAP_INT is new SWAP(INTEGER);
procedure SWAP_VECT is new SWAP(VECTOR);
```

Since swapping of vectors requires very different code from swapping of integers, it seems reasonable to generate two separate program texts for SWAP_INT and SWAP_VECT. Conceptually, every instantiation of a generic program structure is represented by a separate program text. However, generic instantiations are often sufficiently similar so that the optimization of representing them by the same program text becomes worthwhile.

Generic program structures may have generic subprogram parameters. The generic function INTEGRATE below has the function

156

to be integrated as a generic parameter, and the bounds of integration as function parameters.

Example 4.46. Generic subprogram parameters

```
generic (function F(X: FLOAT) return FLOAT)
function INTEGRATE(LOW,HIGH: FLOAT) return FLOAT is
  -- text of numerical integration function
  -- which computes the definite integral
  -- of a function F(X) supplied at instantiation time
  -- between bounds LOW, HIGH supplied at function call time
end INTEGRATE;
```

The generic INTEGRATE function might be part of a mathematical subroutine package. In order to use INTEGRATE for integrating a specific function, the function would have to be instantiated.

Example 4.47. Instantiation for subprogram parameters

```
function INTEGRATE_SIN is new INTEGRATE(SIN);
function INT_FOO is new INTEGRATE(USER_F);
```

Each instantiation is supplied with a function to be integrated (SIN, USER_F) that must be defined and accessible at the time the generic instantiation is elaborated, and must have parameter and result types compatible with those in the generic clause (SIN must have a FLOAT parameter and return a result of type FLOAT).

Elaboration of the instantiation produces a function with the parameters and result type of INTEGRATE. (INTEGRATE_SIN has two parameters LOW, HIGH of type FLOAT and produces a result of type FLOAT.)

Example 4.48. Call of instantiated generic functions

```
declare
  X,Y: FLOAT;
begin
  X := INTEGRATE_SIN(0.5,1.0);
  Y := INT_FOO(-1.0,1.0);
end;
```

When generic program structures have a type parameter, it is often necessary to supply subprograms for operating on objects of the type as additional parameters. Thus the following generic function for squaring objects of an arbitrary type T needs a multiplication operation for objects of type T as a second generic argument.

157

Example 4.49. Dependence of subprogram parameters on type parameters

```
generic (type T; function "*"(U,V: T) return T)
function SQUARING(X: T) return T is
  pragma INLINE;
begin
  return X*X;      -- * is squaring function for objects of type T
end SQUARING;
```

This squaring function can be instantiated for objects of the type INTEGER, COMPLEX, and MATRIX as follows.

Example 4.50. Instantiation with type and subprogram parameters

```
function SQUARE is new SQUARING(INTEGER,"*");
function SQUARE is new SQUARING(COMPLEX,"*");
function SQUARE is new SQUARING(MATRIX,MATMULT);
```

This example illustrates that we need not introduce a new function name for each type of argument taken by SQUARE, but can overload the function name SQUARE in much the same way that the function names + or * are overloaded.

Each instantiation is given both a type name which is to be substituted for the generic type parameter and a procedure name which is to be substituted for the generic procedure parameter. The procedure name * for integer squaring is identified with the system-defined integer multiplication operator. The * for complex squaring requires a multiplication operator for complex numbers to have been previously defined, for example by a complex number package such as that in section 3.3. A MATMULT function for multiplying matrices must also be defined if the instantiation of matrix squaring is to be legal.

Generic parameters, just like other parameters, can be initialized by explicit association between the formal parameter name and the parameter value.

Example 4.51. Explicit naming of generic parameters

```
function SQUARE is new SQUARING(T is COMPLEX, "*" is COMPLEX."*");
```

Generic parameters may have default initialization. Thus in the following generic clause "*"(U,V: T) return T is initialized to the default value T."*".

Example 4.52. Default initialization of generic parameters

generic (type T; "*"(U,V: T) return T is T."*")
function SQUARING(X: T) return T;
  -- text of procedure

Such initialization allows the second parameter value to be
omitted on instantiation whenever the value for a type T is T."*".

Example 4.53. Omission of parameters initialized to default values

function SQUARE is new SQUARING(T is INTEGER); -- default second parameter
                                                -- is INTEGER."*"
function SQUARE is new SQUARING(COMPLEX);   -- default second parameter
                                                -- is COMPLEX."*"
function SQUARE is new SQUARING(MATRIX,MATMULT); -- requires explicit initia-
                                                -- lization of second parameter

Thus the second parameter value can be omitted when instan-
tiating INTEGER and COMPLEX squaring, but must be present for
MATRIX squaring if the matrix multiplication operator is
MATMULT. If the matrix multiplication operator were * then the
second parameter value could be omitted also when instantiating
MATRIX squaring.

4.10 Generic Packages

There are two differences between subprograms and modules
which make the generic facility even more useful for modules
than for subprograms:

1. Subprograms have parameters while modules do not. Thus
    generic parameters merely provide a more powerful ver-
    sion of an already existing facility for subprograms,
    while they provide an entirely new facility for modules.
2. Subprogram declarations are effectively instantiated by
    being called, while module specifications do not permit
    the creation of multiple instances. Thus generic
    instantiation of subprograms provides a translation-time
    version of a facility that is already available at run
    time by means of the subroutine call mechanism, while
    generic instantiation of modules provides an entirely
    new facility.

As an example of a generic package, consider the symbol table
package of section 4.5. This package could be made more flexible
by allowing the type of symbol table values to be a generic parameter, and by including a maximum symbol table size as an additional parameter.

Example 4.54. A generic symbol table package

```
generic (type T; SIZE: INTEGER);
package SYMTAB is
   function FIND(S: STRING) return T;
   procedure UPDATE(S: STRING; V: T);
end SYMTAB;
```

The generic symbol table package allows us to instantiate symbol tables of different sizes and value types.

Example 4.55. Instantiation for different value types

```
package INT_TABLE is new SYMTAB(INTEGER, 100);
package FLOAT_TABLE is new SYMTAB(FLOAT, 100);
package PERSON_TABLE is new SYMTAB(PERSON, 50);
```

Parameters may have default initializations. In the following example, the SIZE parameter has a default initialization of 100, and need be explicitly mentioned only if an initialization different from 100 is required.

Example 4.56. Default initialization of one parameter

```
generic (type T; SIZE: INTEGER := 100)
package SYMTAB is
   -- text of SYMTAB specification
...
package INT_TABLE is new SYMTAB(INTEGER);
package PERSON_TABLE is new SYMTAB(PERSON, 50);
```

In the following example we initialize both the type and the SIZE fields.

Example 4.57. Default initialization of two parameters

```
generic (type T is INTEGER; SIZE: INTEGER := 100)
package SYMTAB is
   -- text of SYMTAB specification
```

This allows us to instantiate SYMTAB with zero, one or two parameters.

Example 4.58. Instantiation with zero, one or two parameters

```
package INT_TABLE is new SYMTAB;                  -- default type and size
package FLOAT_TABLE is new SYMTAB(FLOAT);         -- specified type, default size
package PERSON_TABLE is new SYMTAB(PERSON,50);    -- specified type and size
```

Default initialization allows us to combine the flexibility of providing variation when it is needed with the linguistic ease of parameters when they have a standard value.

The generic mechanism may be used to instantiate multiple copies of parameterless modules. For example, if we need only symbol tables with value type INTEGER and size 100, we can omit the size and type parameters from the specification and use instead the following parameterless generic package.

Example 4.59. Parameterless generic packages

```
generic package SYMTAB is        -- parameterless generic SYMTAB package
   -- text of package specification
...
package T1 is new SYMTAB;        -- can use T1.FIND, T1.UPDATE
package T2 is new SYMTAB;        -- and T2.FIND, T2.UPDATE
```

A parameterless generic package may be compared to a record type declaration. It is a template from which instances may be created by instantiation in much the same way that instances of records are created by object declarations. Components of instances of a generic package are accessed in much the same way as components of objects of a record type. However, record components are restricted to data objects, while components of generic packages can be type and procedure specifications.

The need to create multiple instances of a given module arises frequently in large applications. Consider, for example, a Navy simulation with large numbers of ships, each of which has an identical set of computational resources. In this case it is convenient to define a generic package SHIP which specifies the resources available on ships and allows as many ships to be created as are required for the simulation.

Example 4.60. Multiple instances of resource packages

```
generic package SHIP is          -- parameterless generic package
   -- specification of resources
   -- which constitute a ship
end;
package S is new SHIP;  -- multiple instances have same attributes (speed, guns)
package T is new SHIP;  -- but different attribute values
```

Objects such as ships are sources of asynchronously generated computations and events. They may be more appropriately simulated by concurrent processes (called tasks in Ada) than by packages.

Example 4.61. Parameterless generic task modules

```
generic task SHIP is
   -- specification of resources
   -- which constitute a ship
end;
```

Tasks in Ada are viewed as modules which provide the user with a collection of computational resources similar to those

161

provided by packages, but which have the additional property that
they may be executed concurrently with other modules. Tasks will
be discussed in detail in Chapter 5.

4.11   Program Structure and Name Space Modification

The mechanisms in a programming language for changing the
environment of accessible names are basic to the understanding
of program structure. The principal construct in Ada for changing the set of accessible names is the program unit.

The name space of a program initially includes the set of
reserved words (such as begin, for, procedure) and predefined
identifiers (such as INTEGER, INTEGER'LAST, TRUE, INLINE). This
initial name space is modified on entry to program units of the
program being executed, so that the set of accessible names at
any given point of execution is the initial name space modified
by names introduced by program units which have been entered but
not yet exited. The set of accessible names at a given point of
execution will be called the environment.

The mechanisms for modifying the environment of accessible
names at a program unit interface include the following:
1. Declarations of local identifiers in the declarative
    part of a program unit.
2. Parameter specifications, including formal subprogram
    parameters which are bound to actual parameters at sub-
    program call time, and generic subprogram and module
    parameters which are bound to actual parameters at
    compile time.
3. The restricted clause which restricts access to textual-
    ly enclosing declarations, but may also be used to
    expand the set of accessible names to visible identifiers
    of stand-alone compilation units and library modules.
4. The use clause which introduces abbreviations for certain
    nonlocal accessible names.

The syntactic mechanisms for modifying the environment of
names on entry to a program unit are illustrated in the following
example. Six distinct syntactic mechanisms for modifying the
name space are given, illustrating that Ada has more linguistic
mechanisms for controlling the name space than previous languages
such as Algol 68, Pascal or even PL/I. Each mechanism has a different purpose, but there is some duplication.

Example 4.62. Environment modification on entry to program unit

```
[restricted clause]  -- determines accessibility of nonlocal program units
[generic clause]  -- layer of local nomenclature (compile-time bound variables)
procedure procedure-name  -- can be used within and outside procedure
   [parameter specification]  -- layer of local nomenclature (run-time bound
                                -- variables
   [use clause]    -- abbreviations of nonlocal names
   [local declarations]  -- another layer of local nomenclature
begin
   statement sequence     -- statements are executed in the new environment
   [exception handlers]   -- obtained by modifying the old environment in
end;                      -- accordance with six potential modification mechanisms
```

The restricted clause and the use clause govern the mode of access to externally defined nonlocal names. They have program units as arguments, and introduce resources with implicit names and types into the name space. The program units mentioned in the restricted and use clauses must have previously compiled specifications, so that the compiler has access to these implicit names at the time that the given program unit is elaborated.

The fact that restricted clauses introduce implicit names means that the syntactic correctness of a program unit cannot be determined solely by the text of the program unit. This may complicate the task of reading and maintaining programs at the human interface. However, the compiler can always determine syntactic correctness, because all program units used in a given program unit must have previously compiled specifications. Moreover, the language support system will have a record of dependencies among program units, so that it will know exactly which compilation units must be recompiled if the specification of any given program is changed. Thus the programmer can rely on the support system to check interfaces among interdependent compilation units.

Whereas the restricted and use clauses are concerned with the interface to nonlocal names, the remaining nomenclature modification mechanisms are concerned with the creation of new local names. The generic clause introduces a translation-time layer of local names that disappears on instantiation, while the procedure name, parameter specification and local declarations determine the run-time local environment.

All locally created names require a complete type specification. Correct usage of local objects may be checked by both the user and the compiler by reference to local specifications.

It is interesting to observe the similarities and differences of parameter specifications and local declarations. Both use similar conventions for specifying the type and initial value of names. However, parameters are part of the interface of the procedure and may be used to transmit information between the environment of call and the environment of execution, while local declarations are temporary local resources needed to execute the procedure but totally hidden from the user.

Both parameters and local declarations can be initialized by assignment of an explicit value. However, in the absence of such explicit initialization, procedure parameters are initialized to actual parameters from the environment of call, while local declarations remain uninitialized and must have a value assigned by an assignment statement before they can be used.

Thus the principal differences between parameters and local declarations are in their degree of locality and their form of initialization.

The nomenclature modification mechanisms for procedures will be briefly compared with those of packages. The syntactic mechanisms for nomenclature modification within a package may be characterized as follows.

Example 4.63. Environment modification on entry to a package

```
[restricted clause]        -- determines accessibility of nonlocal program units
[generic clause]           -- layer of compile-time parameters
package package-name is    -- name is used outside but not within package
  [use clause]             -- abbreviations of nonlocal names
  [visible resource specifications] -- accessible outside (exported names)
end;                       -- imperfect analogy with procedure parameters
package body package-name is
  [local declarations]     -- local nomenclature (as for procedures)
  implementation of visible resources
  corresponds to statement part of procedure
[begin
  initialization actions]
end;
```

The restricted and use clauses determine the set of accessible nonlocal names, just as for procedures. The generic clause determines a layer of local environment but may be more important for packages than procedures, because, as indicated in the previous section, it provides a mechanism for parametrization and instantiation that would otherwise be totally absent.

Although there are great differences between procedure parameters and visible identifiers of a package, we may regard them as playing a similar role in providing a user interface. Visible identifiers of a package are not formal parameters but more like actual parameters. They represent "actual resources" that are shared by all users of the package rather than "formal resources" for which actual resources are substituted at the time of call.

As far as the package body is concerned, the visible resources of a package represent a layer of nomenclature which is part of the program unit interface, while the local declarations of the package body represent a layer of nomenclature which is completely hidden from the user. Thus from the point of view of nomenclature modification there are six potential mechanisms, each of which is analogous to a corresponding mechanism for procedures.

There is one additional important difference between the
environment determined by a package and that determined by a
procedure. In the case of procedures, the lifetime of objects
associated with parameters and local declarations is restricted
to the lifetime of execution of the procedure, and local objects
cannot endure between procedure calls. In the case of packages,
the lifetime of local objects is the lifetime of the package
declaration rather than the lifetime of calls of the package.
Thus both visible and hidden data structures are created at the
time of the package declaration and endure between calls of
visible procedures of the package. This allows us to represent
data bases and other computational structures which require a
local memory that endures bewteen activiations by packages.

4.12   Top-Down and Bottom-Up Program Development

The ability of Ada to separate the specification of a module
from its implementation provides language-level support for programming methodology. In particular, Ada supports both top-down
and bottom-up program development.

Bottom-up program development consists of first implementing
lower-level program units, and then implementing successively
higher-level program units in terms of previously developed
lower-level units.

Bottom-up programming is possible in any programming language whose program units have a well-defined user interface which
hides the implementation details. Subprograms provided this
facility in very early programming language, and bottom-up programming with the aid of subroutine libraries was commonplace
even in the 1950s.

Ada modules (packages and tasks) are an essentially different
mechanism for providing the user with modular computational
resources. They allow not only algorithms but also data objects
with associated operations to be independently developed and
used as components of larger programs. This fundamentally
increases the class of things we can specify as modular units,
and may fundamentally affect the way in which problems are organ-
ized into modular components.

Top-down program development starts from a high-level problem specification and "refines" it into successively lower-level
specifications until all specifications have been expressed at
the "lowest level" in the programming language. This approach
corresponds more directly to the tasks which must be performed
by the system analyst in reducing a problem posed by an end user
to computational form. However, the process of working with
specifications whose implementations do not yet exist is more
abstract than that of building up from already implemented specifications. The top-down approach is not open to engineers
constructing a building or a bridge, since it is impossible to
construct upper stories of a building before lower ones. The
"conceptual engineering" engaged in by programmers allows much

greater freedom in the order in which tasks are performed.

Support of top-down programming requires stronger linguistic mechanisms in a programming language than support of bottom-up programming. In particular, it requires the ability to treat specifications of program units as independent linguistic objects. Ada permits both subprogram and module specifications to be treated as separate linguistic objects which can be supplied to a program unit independently of the implementation. Separation between the specification and implementation of a subprogram or module is indicated by the keyword separate.

Example 4.64. Separate subunits of a compilation unit

```
function F(X: FLOAT) return FLOAT is separate; -- implementation is separately
                                                -- supplied
package body D is separate;        -- package body is separately supplied
```

Top-down programming will be illustrated by an example taken from the reference manual. The example consists of a procedure TOP containing a package D and a procedure Q with "separate" implementations.

Example 4.65. A top-down programming example

```
procedure TOP is
   type REAL is digits 10;
   R,S: REAL;
   package D is                       -- package specification
     PI: constant REAL := 3.14159_26536;
     function F(X: REAL) return REAL;
     procedure G(Y,Z: REAL);
   end D;
   package body D is separate;             -- start of D
   procedure Q(U: in out REAL) is separate; -- start of Q
begin                                  -- statement sequence of TOP
   ...
   Q(R);
   ...
   D.G(R,S);
   ...
end TOP;
```

The package body D and procedure Q are represented in TOP by stubs whose text is separately compiled. The texts corresponding to a stub are called subunits of the compilation unit in which the stub appears and are said to be enclosed by that compilation unit. The text of a subunit must have a restricted clause with a visibility list whose first element is the name of the enclosing compilation unit. Thus the subunit corresponding to procedure Q above might be specified as follows.

166

Example 4.66. Separate procedure subunit

```
restricted (TOP)
separate procedure Q(U: in out REAL) is
  use D;
begin
  ...
  U := F(U);
  ...
end Q;
```

    Note that restricted(TOP) causes the package D and the type
D to be visible in Q just as though Q appeared physically in
place of its stub. The use clause in procedure Q allows us to
refer to resources in D, such as F, without qualification.

    The subunit corresponding to the stub of the package body
might be specified as follows.

Example 4.67. Separate module subunit

```
restricted (TOP)
separate package body D is
  -- local declarations of D
  function F(X: REAL) return REAL is
  begin
    -- sequence of statements of F
  end F;
  procedure G(Y,Z: REAL) is separate;    -- stub of G, hierarchical top-down
end D;                                    -- design
```

    The package body above is a subunit of TOP and can therefore
make use of declarations of TOP, such as REAL. Note that package
bodies can also be separately compiled as stand-alone compilation
units. In that case they would have access only to the package
specification and not to other declarations in the environment of
the package specification.

    The procedure G in the package body was specified to be
separate, illustrating hierarchical top-down development. The
body of G might be specified as follows.

Example 4.68. Hierarchical top-down specification

```
restricted (TOP, INPUT_OUTPUT)
separate procedure G(Y,Z: REAL) is
begin
  -- sequence of statements of G
  -- including input-output statements
end;
```

    The separate procedure G is a subunit of the package D and,
by transitivity, a subunit of TOP. The restriction to TOP allows
access within G to local declarations of TOP such as REAL.

167

The above examples illustrate that both subprogram specifications and module specifications can be treated as separate linguistic objects in Ada. In order to do this it is necessary to clearly define exactly what is meant by a specification. Ada specifications do not completely specify the computational behavior of subprograms or modules. They are much weaker, specifying only the names and parameter types which the user must know in order to use the resources provided by a program unit.

The term "specification" as used above is a syntactic rather than semantic notion, and is (intentionally) inadequate as a basis for verifying the correctness of programs or defining what a program unit is supposed to do. It merely allows the top-down programmer to specify the syntactic interface with a promise that the semantic interface will be taken care of separately. It also allows the compiler to check syntactic interfaces. The use of weak syntactic specification as a programming language mechanism for defining relations among program units represents a compromise based on the realization that working with more complete forms of specifications is infeasible.

The systematic use of syntactic specifications as independent linguistic constructs represents a major innovation in language design which may well result in a major advance in supporting programming methodology at the programming-language level rather than in a separate program design package. The weakness of the notion of specification may in fact be one of the greatest sources of linguistic strength in allowing Ada to handle interfaces between interdependent language modules.

5

MULTITASKING

5.1 Introduction

There are two distinct reasons for the importance of concurrent programming facilities:

1. Concurrent execution can speed up execution by performing concurrently operations that would otherwise have to be done sequentially. Thus multiplication of two N×N matrices, which takes N^3 multiplications when done by a normal sequential matrix multiplication algorithm, can be performed concurrently in one multiplication time and log N addition times if N^3 processors are available.

2. A second, more fundamental reason for the importance of tasks is that applications such as airline reservation systems, banks, ships, navies and cities are naturally modelled by systems of concurrently executing tasks.

In the case of matrix multiplication concurrency is not inherent in the structure of the problem, and is introduced merely for the sake of efficiency. The real payoff of concurrent execution arises not from the fact that applications can be speeded up by artificially introducing concurrency, but from the fact that the real world functions by the execution of concurrent activities. Many applications are modelled more naturally by concurrent than by sequential activities, and should be specified in terms of concurrently executing tasks even if the program is to be executed on a machine with only a single processor. This avoids the need for programmers to specify the order of execution in cases where this is an "implementation detail".

The multitasking mechanisms of Ada are designed to be implemented on two radically different kinds of architectures:

a) Shared-memory architectures in which one or more physical processors share a common memory. In this architecture physical processors are generally a scarce resource, tasks must be scheduled to make optimal use of processors, and the efficiency of multitasking depends on task scheduling methods, processor switching time, and other implementation considerations.

    b) Distributed-processing architectures in which there is a large number of processors with local memory but no shared memory. In this case tasks may be dedicated to processors, and it may be assumed that there are enough processors to go around, but tasks can no longer rely on shared memory for purposes of communication but must rely on message passing.

In order to appreciate the implications of language mechanisms for multitasking, the reader should test them conceptually against both the shared-memory and distributed-processing models. The shared-memory model reflects current large computer architectures and initial implementations of Ada are exclusively on shared-memory architectures. However, the great reductions in processor costs which are currently occurring, the advent of microcomputers, and the nature of the applications for which Ada is likely to be used may well result in implementations of Ada for distributed-processing architectures quite early in its lifetime.

Concurrent execution can be very simply modelled if concurrently executing tasks are totally independent of each other. However, in most applications the set of concurrently executing tasks is working cooperatively on some larger task, and must perform both communication and synchronization at selected points of the computation. Ada permits two forms of communication among tasks which respectively reflect the shared-memory and message-passing models of computer architecture:

1. Communication by shared nonlocal variables;
2. Communication by message passing.

Communication by shared nonlocal variables may present problems both because careful synchronization is required to avoid access conflicts among tasks which share a variable, and because shared variables presuppose a shared-memory implementation which cannot easily be modelled by a distributed processing implementation.

However, in some instances shared variables may be both more natural and more efficient than message passing in modelling an application. Thus, shared memory is likely to remain an important resource at the hardware level, and shared variables are likely to remain an important mechanism for intermodule communication, even when distributed architectures become state-of-the-art.

In our discussion of concurrent processing we shall emphasize the language features for communication by message passing. However, before introducing these features we shall consider the case of totally independent tasks which do not require any communication or synchronization. This allows us to illustrate the basic mechanisms of initiation and execution of concurrent tasks in a context that is independent of complications associated with communication and synchronization.

5.2   Task Initiation and Execution

Tasks are declared by means of task declarations and initiated by the <u>initiate</u> statement. A task declaration consists of a specification part which specifies the resources provided by the task to its users and a task body which specifies a sequence of statements to be executed when the task is initiated.

When tasks perform totally independent computations their specification parts may be empty (degenerate). The procedure ARRIVE_AT_AIRPORT below contains three independent tasks, CLAIM_BAGGAGE, RENT_A_CAR and BOOK_HOTEL whose bodies and (degenerate) specification parts are declared in the procedure.

Example 5.1. Independent tasks with degenerate specification parts

```
procedure ARRIVE_AT_AIRPORT is
   task CLAIM_BAGGAGE ;              -- degenerate specification part
                                    -- of baggage claiming task
   task body CLAIM_BAGGAGE is       -- task body which specifies action
     -- code for claiming baggage   -- initiated by an initiate statement
   end CLAIM_BAGGAGE;               -- and executed concurrently with other actions
   task RENT_A_CAR;                  -- degenerate specification part
                                    -- of car renting task
   task body RENT_A_CAR is          -- body of car renting task
     -- code for renting a car
   end RENT_A_CAR;
   task BOOK_HOTEL;                  -- degenerate specification part

   task body BOOK_HOTEL is          -- body of hotel booking task
     -- code for booking hotel
   end BOOK_HOTEL;
begin                               -- statements of ARRIVE_AT_AIRPORT consist of
   initiate CLAIM_BAGGAGE, RENT_A_CAR, BOOK_HOTEL; -- initiate statement
end ARRIVE_AT_AIRPORT;   -- all tasks must complete before exit from program unit
```

Tasks may be "normally" terminated by executing the last statement of the task body. For example, the CLAIM_BAGGAGE task terminates after executing its last statement. However, a program unit containing local task declarations cannot be exited unless all locally declared tasks are inactive (terminated). Thus we cannot leave the procedure ARRIVE_AT_AIRPORT until all three tasks that are both declared and initiated in the procedure have completed execution.

The tasks CLAIM_BAGGAGE, RENT_A_CAR and BOOK_HOTEL are independent in the sense that they need not communicate with each other during execution. No synchronization or communication among them is needed once they have been initiated, and their specification parts may therefore be degenerate. However, tasks

171

are active modules which can affect their environment by modifying nonlocal variables and producing output even when they do not provide resources to other tasks. In this respect they differ from packages, which remain passively dormant unless their resources are accessed. It would make no sense to have a package with a degenerate specification part because there would be no way in which such a package could affect the rest of the program.

Every task T has an attribute T'ACTIVE which is TRUE when T has been initiated but not yet completed and is FALSE otherwise. An attempt to initiate an already active task (T'ACTIVE = TRUE) results in a task initiation error (raising the INITIATE_ERROR exception). Thus tasks are like packages in that there is at most a single instance at any given point of execution, and differ from procedures which may have multiple execution-time instances, both by being recursively called and by being concurrently executed by several tasks.

The parent of a task T is the task that is executing when the declaration of T is elaborated. The main program is considered to be a task for this purpose. If the procedure ARRIVE_AT_AIRPORT is called by the main program then the CLAIM_BAGGAGE task elaborated as a result of call will have the main program as its parent. A call of ARRIVE_AT_AIRPORT by some other task T will create a CLAIM_BAGGAGE task having T as its parent. Thus a task declared within a procedure may have different parent tasks for different calls of the procedure.

5.3   Task Synchronization and Communication

The specification part of a task may in general contain type, subprogram, exception and entry specifications, as illustrated in figure 5.1 below.

Type, subprogram and exception specifications may occur in the specification part of both tasks and packages. Entry specifications may occur only in task and not in package specifications. Variable and module specifications may occur only in package and not in task specifications.

Entry specifications are the principal mechanism for communication and synchronization among tasks. They were illustrated in Chapter 1 for a mailbox task with a SEND entry for sending messages from user tasks to the mailbox and a RECEIVE entry which allows user tasks to receive messages from the mailbox. The entry mechanism is illustrated below by a task called LINE_TO_CHAR with a SEND_LINE entry which allows other tasks to send lines of text to the task and a GET_CHAR entry which allows other tasks to receive characters from the task. The specification of LINE_TO_CHAR also contains a type specification for LINE so that all tasks which feed lines of text to the task have access to the type of associated lines.

```
+-----------------------------------------+
| task specification                      |
+-----------------------------------------+
| may include                             |
|    type specifications                  |
|    subprogram specifications            |
|    exception specifications             |
|    entry specifications                 |
| but may not include                     |
|    variable specifications              |
|    module specifications                |
+-----------------------------------------+

+-----------------------------------------+
| task body                               |
+-----------------------------------------+
|    contains hidden local                |
|    declarations which are               |
|    elaborated when the task             |
|    is initiated                         |
|    and a statement sequence             |
|    which is executed when               |
|    the task is initiated                |
|    and accept statements                |
|    which must be executed               |
|    in order to accept entry             |
|    calls from other tasks               |
+-----------------------------------------+
```

Figure 5.1 Task specification and task body.

Example 5.2. Type and entry specifications

```
task LINE_TO_CHAR is
    type LINE is array(1..80) of CHARACTER;
    entry SEND_LINE(L: in LINE);
    entry GET_CHAR(C: out CHARACTER);
end;
```

Entry specifications are syntactically like procedure specifications. They may have parameters with the same binding modes as procedure parameters, and may be called from other tasks by entry calls which are indistinguishable from procedure calls. However, whereas procedure calls serve to immediately invoke the called procedure, entry calls require synchronization with an accept statement in the task body before they can be executed.

The task body corresponding to the above task specification contains an accept statement for each entry declaration which allows calls of SEND_LINE and GET_CHAR from other tasks to be accepted by the given task.

173

Example 5.3. Task body with accept statements

```
task body LINE_TO_CHAR is
  BUFFER: LINE;                      -- buffer for 80-character line
begin
  loop                               -- infinite loop which accepts
    accept SEND_LINE(L: in LINE) do  -- a SEND_LINE entry call
      BUFFER := L;                   -- causing a line to be stored in BUFFER
    end SEND_LINE;
    for I in 1..80 loop              -- and then accepts
      accept GET_CHAR(C: out CHARACTER) do  -- 80 GET_CHAR entry calls
        C := BUFFER(I);              -- which read characters from buffer
      end GET_CHAR;
    end loop;                        -- when this is completed
  end loop;                          -- we are ready to accept another line
end LINE_TO_CHAR;
```

The task may be initiated by an initiate statement.

Example 5.4. Task initiation

```
initiate LINE_TO_CHAR;
```

We shall consider the execution of the LINE_TO_CHAR task,
emphasizing particularly the synchronization which must occur
between the LINE_TO_CHAR task and a calling task when an accept
statement is executed. The process of synchronization between
an entry call in a calling task and an accept statement in a
called task is referred to as rendezvous.

Execution of the initiate statement causes the initiated
task body to be executed concurrently with the task in which it
was initiated. In this case task initiation will result in
creation of a buffer for lines, followed by execution of an
infinite loop which alternately accepts a SEND_LINE entry call
from another task and then eighty GET_CHAR calls from one or
more other tasks.

When execution reaches the accept SEND_LINE statement, the
LINE_TO_CHAR task must perform a rendezvous with a SEND_LINE
entry call from another task before it can continue. During
the rendezvous the calling task is suspended while the sequence
of statements between do and end in the called task is executed.
When this sequence of statements has been executed the rendezvous is complete and the calling task may continue its computation in parallel with the called task.

In this case the single statement "BUFFER := L;" would be
executed during rendezvous. This statement transmits the line
of text L from the calling task to the buffer of the called task.
Statements executed during a rendezvous are generally concerned
with the transmission of information between a calling and a
called task.

As indicated in Chapter 1, the sequence of statements between the do and end following an accept statement is called a critical section because the calling task cannot execute while these statements are executed. In this case, it is clear that execution of the calling task while the line is being transmitted to the buffer might cause modification of the line while it was being transmitted, and should therefore not be permitted. Critical sections allow critical computations associated with an accept statement to be performed without interference from the calling task.

The general syntax of accept statements is as follows.

Example 5.5. Syntax of accept statements

accept entry-name [formal parameter list] do -- formal parameters are local
  sequence of statements (critical section) -- to the statement sequence
end [entry-name];

Execution of an accept statement requires synchronization between the task in which it occurs and a task containing an entry call for the entry name associated with the accept statement. If there is no waiting entry call the task must wait until an entry call occurs. If there is a waiting entry call, then a rendezvous with the task containing the entry call is performed, the critical section is executed while the calling task remains suspended, and both the calling and called tasks proceed merrily on their way.

Entry calls for a given entry name may occur faster than they can be handled by accept statements. In this case they are stored in a queue associated with the entry name and handled in order of arrival by accept statements of the called task. A task may in general have more than one accept statement for a given entry name in its task body, but contains only a single queue of waiting entry calls for each entry name.

A considerable time may elapse between the occurrence of an entry call and its execution. During this time the calling task is suspended. But the parameter values of the calling task may be modified by other executing tasks. The parameter values actually passed are those that obtain at the time of rendezvous during execution of the critical section of the accept statement. However, this interpretation depends upon the assumption that actual parameters which are variables are copied from their designated location to the called task only at the time of rendezvous. This assumption is reasonable in a shared-memory architecture. But in a distributed-processing architecture it is tempting to copy parameter values to be passed into an entry queue physically associated with the target task at the time of call, rather than waiting to copy parameter values till the time of rendezvous.

Entry call parameters should clearly not be modified between the time of call and the time of rendezvous. It might be

175

desirable to make this into a language requirement. However, checking of this requirement in general requires a run-time check and could be expensive. Programmers could ensure safety of their programs by making entry call parameters local to the calling task, but this might require an extra layer of encapsulation.

The rendezvous mechanism is the basic mechanism in Ada for synchronization among interdependent tasks. Synchronized communication is accomplished by passing of parameters during rendezvous. If our goal is to perform synchronization without communication, then parameterless entry calls can be used.

The following task for realizing semaphores is concerned primarily with synchronization rather than communication and uses parameterless entries for realizing synchronization.

Example 5.6. The semaphore task

```
task SEMAPHORE is              -- SEMAPHORE task has two entries
   entry P;                    -- P and V
   entry V;
end;
task body SEMAPHORE is         -- the task body
begin                          -- consists of
   loop                        -- an infinite loop
      accept P;                -- which alternately
      accept V;                -- accepts P and V entries
   end loop;
end;
```

A semaphore may be used to ensure mutually exclusive access to a critical resource such as a shared variable. If X is a shared variable accessible to a number of different tasks, then mutually exclusive access to X can be ensured by requiring all segments of code which access X to be preceded by an entry call of P and followed by an entry call of V.

Example 5.7. Use of semaphores for mutual exclusion

```
P;                 -- entry call of P preceding mutually exclusive access
   -- code which accesses
   -- the shared variable X
   -- in a mutually exclusive mode
V;                 -- entry call of V terminating mutually exclusive access
```

The semaphore task ensures that at most one code segment of this form can be executing at any given time, since a P entry call must be followed by a V entry call before a second P entry call can be executed. Thus, if each task accessing X places the accessing code between P and V entry calls, then mutually exclusive access to X is assured.

Semaphores are "low-level" synchronization primitives which are used in many languages for concurrent programming as a starting point for building higher-level primitives. In contrast, entry calls and accept statements are high-level primitives which allow low-level primitives such as semaphores to be easily defined, but provide a more direct "high-level" mechanism for synchronization and communication among interdependent tasks.

Entry calls and accept statements are essentially primitives for message passing. Occurrence of an entry call requires a signal to the called task that a message is ready to be passed, and completion of a rendezvous requires passing of a signal back to the calling task that passing of the message has been completed. Actual transmission of the message occurs during execution of the critical section of the accept statement.

The message passing protocol is defined independently of whether the underlying architecture is a shared-memory or distributed-processing architecture, but is designed to be implementable for both kinds of architecture.

The MAILBOX task of Chapter 1 is a classic example of message passing. We shall revisit the mailbox example, both in order to illustrate even more explicitly the connection between entry resources and message passing and in order to set up the mailbox task as a running example for illustrating select statements and generic tasks in later sections.

The mailbox example has a SEND entry which allows other tasks to send messages to the mailbox and a RECEIVE entry which allows other tasks to receive messages from the mailbox.

Example 5.8. Specification of mailbox task

```
task MAILBOX is
    entry SEND(INMAIL: in MESSAGE);        -- entry for sending mail to task
    entry RECEIVE(OUTMAIL: out MESSAGE); -- entry for receiving mail from task
end;
```

When the buffer has a capacity of only one message, the task body consists of a buffer which alternately accepts SEND entries which send messages from other tasks to the buffer and RECEIVE entries which cause some other task to receive the message stored in the buffer by the previously executed SEND entry.

Example 5.9. Mailbox with single-message buffer

```
task body MAILBOX is
  BUFFER: MESSAGE;                -- local buffer, can store single message
begin
  loop      -- infinite loop for alternately sending and receiving messages
    accept SEND(INMAIL: in MESSAGE) do  -- accept SEND call from other task
      BUFFER := INMAIL;                  -- store message from sending task
    end;
    accept RECEIVE(OUTMAIL: out MESSAGE) do  -- accept RECEIVE call
      OUTMAIL := BUFFER;                 -- transmit message to receiving task
    end;
  end loop;
end MAILBOX;
```

The SEND and RECEIVE entries of the MAILBOX task serve both
for synchronization between the calling and called tasks at the
time a message is sent or received, and for communication of
information (messages) between the calling and called task.
Just as for the LINE_TO_CHAR tasks, the accept statement has a
critical section which takes care of task communication while
the calling task remains suspended, and then allows both the
calling and called tasks to resume concurrent execution.

The mailbox task can handle only one message at a time. If
the rate at which messages are sent to the mailbox is greater
than the rate at which receiving tasks are ready to receive them,
SEND entries will be placed in a queue and each of the sending
tasks whose SEND entry has been received but not yet processed
will be suspended until it can be accepted by the mailbox task.

The above delays can be avoided if the buffer in the mailbox can store more than one message. However, this requires
considerable reorganization of the task body of the mailbox
task. In particular, we can no longer specify the order in
which SEND and RECEIVE entries are accepted by the mailbox task,
and must provide a language mechanism to specify that a SEND
entry should be immediately accepted whenever the buffer is not
full and a RECEIVE entry should be accepted whenever the buffer
is not empty. The language mechanism which allows us to do this
is called the select statement and is discussed in the next
section.

5.4 The Select Statement

An accept statement enables a task to wait for a predetermined event, indicated by an entry call. However, in many cases
we cannot predict the order in which entry calls will occur,
and wish to allow a task to base its next action on which entry
calls (if any) are waiting to be executed.

Choice among several entry calls is accomplished by a select
statement, which has the following syntax.

178

Example 5.10. Syntax of select statement

```
select                          -- select statement starts with keyword select
   [when condition =>]          -- followed by sequence of one or more
     select-alternative         -- "guarded" select alternatives
     [sequence of statements]   -- optionally followed by sequence of statements
{or [when condition =>]         -- which is executed when the action (rendezvous)
     select-alternative         -- associated with select alternative has been completed
     [sequence of statements]}
[else                           -- the sequence of select alternatives may be followed by
   sequence of statements]      -- a sequence of statements which is executed
end select;                     -- if no select statement can be immediately selected
```

A select alternative may be an accept statement (whose syntax was discussed in the previous section) or a delay statement with the following syntax. Select statements containing delay statements cannot have an else alternative.

Example 5.11. Syntax of delay statement

delay expression-specifying-delay-time;

A select statement is executed by first evaluating the conditions (called guards) associated with select alternatives to determine the set of currently admissible select alternatives (called open alternatives). If there is precisely one waiting entry call associated with an open accept statement it will be immediately accepted. If there is more than one waiting entry call associated with an open accept statement a "nondeterministic" choice will be made among waiting entry calls. If there are no waiting entry calls then the following cases must be considered.

1. If there are no open delay statements and no else clause the task will wait indefinitely for an entry call associated with an open accept statement and will execute the first one that arrives.
2. If there is an open delay statement the task will wait for an open entry call for the time interval determined by the delay statement, and will then execute the select alternative determined by the delay statement.
3. If there is no open delay statement but there is an else clause, the task will immediately execute the else clause if there is no waiting open entry call.
4. If there are no open alternatives and no else clause then the exception SELECT_ERROR will be raised.

The select statement has a rich range of features, but the central idea is to permit two levels of selection among select alternatives:

1. Selection of a subset of "open" select alternatives by evaluating guards on entry to the select statement.
2. Selection of a specific open alternative corresponding to an entry call which needs to be processed.

179

These two selection features may be illustrated by the buffered mailbox task. In this case the SEND entry can be executed when the buffer is not full and the RECEIVE entry can be executed when the buffer is not empty, so that we have a select statement with the following structure.

Example 5.12. Example of select statement

```
select
  when NOT_FULL =>
    accept SEND(..) do
      -- store message in buffer
    end;
      -- do bookkeeping to record that message was stored
or
  when NOT_EMPTY =>
    accept RECEIVE(..) do
      -- transmit message to receiving task
    end;
      -- do bookkeeping to record that message was transmitted
end select;
```

For a buffer size greater than one the buffer can be NOT_FULL and NOT_EMPTY simultaneously, so that both accept statements can be open, and the select statement can select the first SEND or RECEIVE entry call to arrive.

Since the buffer cannot be both full and empty simultaneously, at least one accept statement will always be open. If the buffer is empty only the SEND alternative is open and RECEIVE entry calls must wait in a queue because there are no messages for them to receive. If the buffer is full only the RECEIVE alternative is open, and SEND entries must wait in a queue because the buffer cannot accept any more messages until messages previously sent to the buffer are transmitted to receiving tasks.

The complete task body for the buffered mailbox task, given below, has the identifiers required for bookkeeping specified as local variables. In particular, SIZE is the buffer size, NEXTIN and NEXTOUT specify the indices of the next input (to be sent to the buffer) and the next output (to be transmitted from the buffer), and COUNT specifies the number of elements in the buffer. The condition NOT_FULL is represented by "COUNT < SIZE" and the condition NOT_EMPTY is represented by "COUNT > 0".

Example 5.13. Buffered mailboxes

```
task body MAILBOX is
   SIZE: constant INTEGER := 20;        -- buffer size
   BUFFER: array(1..SIZE) of MESSAGE;
   NEXTIN, NEXTOUT: INTEGER range 1..SIZE := 1;
   COUNT: INTEGER range 0..SIZE := 0;  -- number of items in buffer
begin
   loop
      select
         when COUNT < SIZE =>   -- guard which checks that buffer is not full
            accept SEND(INMAIL: in MESSAGE) do     -- before accepting message
               BUFFER(NEXTIN) := INMAIL;  -- critical section; must be executed
            end;                          -- before calling task resumes
            NEXTIN := NEXTIN mod SIZE + 1; -- statements outside critical section
            COUNT := COUNT+1;      -- may be executed concurrently with calling task
      or
         when COUNT > 0 =>        -- guard which checks that buffer is not empty
            accept RECEIVE(OUTMAIL: out MESSAGE) do  -- before transmitting message
               OUTMAIL := BUFFER(NEXTOUT);
            end;
            NEXTOUT := NEXTOUT mod SIZE + 1; -- bookkeeping operations which record
            COUNT := COUNT - 1;             -- that message was transmitted
      end select;
   end loop;
end MAILBOX;
```

The above task body may replace the task body of the previous section without any change in the task specification. Such
a change does not change the functional effect of a sequence of
SEND and RECEIVE calls, since entry calls are processed in a
first-in-first-out order both when they are waiting to be processed in an entry queue and when the messages associated with the
entry calls are sitting in the buffer of the mailbox. But the
change may affect the speed of processing messages by several
orders of magnitude.

This example illustrates the wisdom of defining tasks as
modules which allow separation between specification and implementation. In languages in which tasks are modelled by processes rather than modules, a mailbox would have been represented
by SEND and RECEIVE processes and the notion of a mailbox with a
private buffer which can be operated on only by SEND and RECEIVE
operations would have had to be defined by using a data abstraction mechanism (such as the package mechanism) on SEND and
RECEIVE processes. In Ada such abstraction may be obtained
effortlessly by using the module mechanism.

5.5 Generic Tasks

Tasks, like packages, may be specified as generic by means
of a generic clause. Generic tasks are useful both as a mechanism for introducing task parameters, including type and

181

procedure parameters, and as a mechanism for introducing multiple instances of a parameterless task.

The mailbox task is a good candidate for illustrating generic parameters. Suppose we wish to define mailboxes with different sizes and message types. This can be accomplished by defining the size and message type as parameters of a generic mailbox task.

Example 5.14. Generic mailbox task

```
generic(SIZE: INTEGER; type MESSAGE)
task MAILBOX is
  entry SEND(INMAIL: in MESSAGE);
  entry RECEIVE(OUTMAIL: out MESSAGE);
end;
```

The generic mailbox task may be instantiated and used as follows.

Example 5.15. Instantiation of generic mailboxes

```
procedure MAILBOXES is
  task M1 is new MAILBOX(50,INTEGER); -- mailbox of size 50, INTEGER messages
  task M2 is new MAILBOX(100,PERSON); -- 100 messages of type PERSON
begin
  initiate M1,M2;          -- initiate mailboxes
  M1.SEND(15);             -- send integer message to M1
  M2.SEND(JONES);          -- JONES is of the type PERSON
  M1.RECEIVE(K);           -- K is of the type INTEGER
end;
```

The parameters of a generic task may be initialized to default values.

Example 5.16. Initialized generic parameters

```
generic(SIZE: INTEGER := 20; type MESSAGE is INTEGER)
```

In this case instantiation to a default value can be implicit, while initialization to a non-default value must be explicit.

Example 5.17. Implicit initialization to default values

```
task M1 is new MAILBOX(50);           -- 50 messages of type INTEGER
task M2 is new MAILBOX(100,PERSON);   -- 100 messages of type PERSON
task M3 is new MAILBOX;               -- 20 messages of type INTEGER
task M4 is new MAILBOX(MESSAGE is PERSON); -- 20 messages of type PERSON
task M5 is new MAILBOX(SIZE := 50);   -- 50 messages of type INTEGER
```

Note that the first parameter SIZE can be initialized in positional notation (M1) or nonpositional notation (M5) while initialization of just the second parameter requires nonpositional initialization by explicit naming (M4).

Parameterless generic clauses are useful in creating multiple instances of a task even when there is no parametric variation among instances. Thus an application may well require several mailboxes of the same size and type.

Example 5.18. Parameterless generic mailboxes

```
generic task MAILBOX is
  entry SEND;
  entry RECEIVE ;
end;
task M1 is new MAILBOX;
task M2 is new MAILBOX;
```

Thus generic clauses for tasks, just as for packages, are useful both for parametrization and for multiple instantiation.

A parameterless generic task SEMAPHORE may be defined as follows.

Example 5.19. Generic semaphores

```
generic task SEMAPHORE is
  entry P;
  entry V;
end;
task body SEMAPHORE is
begin
  loop
    accept P;
    accept V;
  end loop;
end SEMAPHORE;
```

A nongeneric version of SEMAPHORE was considered in a previous section. The generic version of this task allows multiple semaphores to be created.

Example 5.20. Instantiation of semaphores

```
procedure SEMAPHORES is
   task S1 is new SEMAPHORE;
   task S2 is new SEMAPHORE;
begin
   initiate S1, S2;
   ...
   S1.P;    -- entry call to P entry of S1
     -- execute code in mutual exclusion
   S1.V;    -- must be executed before another task can execute S1.P
end;
```

Semaphores are a low-level primitive for realizing mutual exclusion which can be simply realized in terms of entry and accept statements. In the interests of efficiency, semaphores are predefined in the language so that an implementation can avoid the overhead of language-level context-switching and introduce other optimizations made possible by the underlying system and machine.

Because of the separation between specification and implementation, user programs are not affected by whether task bodies of tasks such as semaphores are implemented at the language level or are predefined and implemented by the system. This allows system designers to improve the efficiency of critical modules of a system by implementing them as part of the system software or system hardware. This change need not be decided on at the time of language design of system implementation, but can be introduced at any time during the lifetime of a program.

For example, if it is decided that mailboxes are a critical module then the system could be modified so that MAILBOX becomes a predefined generic task identifier whose task body is implemented by the system and whose entry calls can be efficiently handled without context-switching. All this can be accomplished without affecting user programs (except perhaps for removal of the language-defined task body of the MAILBOX task from the program).

5.6 Families of Tasks, Families of Entries and Task Priorities

Task families are useful in modelling systems having multiple concurrently operating subsystems with similar specifications. Consider, for example, a computer with sixteen concurrently executing line printers. The set of 16 printers may be modelled by a family of 16 printer tasks as follows.

Example 5.21. Specification of task families

```
task PRINTER(1..16) is          -- task family of 16 printers
   type LINE is STRING(1..80);   -- which share the type LINE
   entry PRINT(L: LINE);         -- and each have a PRINT entry
   entry STOP;                   -- and a STOP entry
end;
```

An **initiate** statement for a task family can initiate individual tasks of the family, or a contiguous subsequence of the tasks.

Example 5.22. Initiation of tasks in task families

```
initiate PRINTER(5);      -- initiate printer with index 5
initiate PRINTER(5..9);   -- initiate 5 printer tasks with indices 5..9
```

The task body of the PRINTER task is implemented below using the attribute PRINT'COUNT whose value is the number of waiting PRINT entry calls currently in the PRINT queue.

Example 5.23. Task body executed by each member of task family

```
task body PRINTER is               -- the task body of the PRINTER task
   BUFFER: LINE;
begin
   loop
      select
         accept PRINT(L: LINE) do   -- has a PRINT entry
            BUFFER := L;            -- which causes line to be stored
         end;                       -- and printed
            -- print line from buffer
      or
         when PRINT'COUNT = 0 =>
            accept STOP;            -- and a STOP entry
            exit;                   -- which causes exit from the task
      end select;         -- when there are no more waiting print entries
   end loop;
end PRINTER;
```

All tasks in a task family share a common specification and task body. However, initiation of a task in the family conceptually causes a separate copy of the task to be executed. If all 16 printer tasks have been initiated, there will be 16 concurrently executing printer tasks, each having a private copy of the BUFFER and of other local execution-time information. Entry calls for the task with index 5 could be specified as follows.

Example 5.24. Entry calls to a task in a family

```
PRINTER(5).PRINT(TEXTLINE);   -- print entry call for 5th printer
PRINTER(5).STOP;              -- stop entry call for 5th printer
```

Whereas entry calls require specification of a specific individual (index) of the task family, type specifications are shared among all members of a task family, so that object declarations require just the family name.

Example 5.25. Objects of a type declared in a family

```
X: PRINTER.LINE;          -- object X of type LINE
X: LINE;                  -- use statement allows omission of family name
```

More generally, types, constants and exceptions declared in the visible part of a task belong to the family as a whole, and may be accessed by mentioning just the family name, while entries and procedures belong to individual tasks and can be accessed only by identifying an individual (index) of the task family.

Families of entries in Ada permit several entry queues to be associated with an entry, and thereby facilitate priority scheduling of entries. For example, the REQUEST entry of the following task is a family of entries whose index specifies the level of urgency of a request and whose parameter specifies the data for the request.

Example 5.26. Task with a family of entries

```
task PRIORITIES is
   type LEVEL is(LOW,MEDIUM,URGENT);       -- priority level
   entry REQUEST(LOW..URGENT)(D: DATA);    -- family of entries
end;
```

A call of the REQUEST entry requires specification of an index which identifies an individual of the family of entries and an actual parameter value.

Example 5.27. Call of a member of a family of entries

```
REQUEST(URGENT)(X);
```

Each member of a family of entries is associated with a different entry queue. The task body can make use of this fact in scheduling entry calls of the REQUEST entry.

Example 5.28. Preferential scheduling among family members

```
task body PRIORITIES is
begin
  loop
    select
      accept REQUEST(URGENT)(D: DATA) do
        ...
      end;
    or
      when REQUEST(URGENT)'COUNT = 0 =>
        accept REQUEST(MEDIUM)(D: DATA) do
          ...
        end;
    or
      when REQUEST(URGENT)'COUNT = 0 and
           REQUEST(MEDIUM)'COUNT = 0 =>
        accept REQUEST(LOW)(D: DATA) do
          ...
        end;
    end select;
  end loop;
end PRIORITIES;
```

The task body ensures that requests of medium priority are taken only if there are no urgent requests, and request of low priority are taken only if there are no urgent or medium requests.

Every task has an associated priority which determines its scheduling when competing against other tasks. The set of permitted priority values is predefined by the following INTEGER subtype.

Example 5.29. System-defined PRIORITY subtype

```
subtype PRIORITY is INTEGER range SYSTEM'MIN_PRIORITY..SYSTEM'MAX_PRIORITY
```

The main program is started with an implementation-defined priority. When a task is initiated it normally takes the priority of its initiator. A task can set its own priority by a call to the predefined procedure SET_PRIORITY.

Example 5.30. Setting the priority of a task

```
SET_PRIORITY(P);        -- set priority of executing task to value P
```

The task scheduler handles tasks of higher priority before tasks with lower priority. Tasks with the same priority are handled on a first-in-first-served basis, which may include time slicing to ensure that there is no starvation among tasks with the same priority. However, "starvation" of tasks of low priority will occur if tasks of higher priority use up the complete computing capacity.

5.7 Task Termination

Normal termination of a task occurs when it reaches the end of its task body and when all locally declared tasks (if any) have terminated their execution.

Abnormal termination of a task T can be accomplished in two ways:

1. By raising of the exception T'FAILURE in some other executing task. This has the effect of raising the exception FAILURE at the current point of execution of T and propagating it using rules for exception propagation that are further described in the reference manual.
2. By execution of a statement "abort T;" which terminates the task T unconditionally.

Both termination mechanisms should be used with caution since they may give rise to tasking errors in other tasks with which the task T is currently communicating. The nature of such side effects is further discussed in the reference manual and rationale.

5.8 The Reader-Writer Problem

Now that the basic multitasking primitives have been described, we will consider examples which provide additional insights into how the multitasking primitives of Ada might be used. In particular, we shall consider a variety of solutions to the reader-writer problem.

The reader-writer problem is the problem of reading and writing in a protected data base so that writers are not changing information while readers are trying to read it. In particular, any number of readers are allowed to read if there is no writer, but every writer must have exclusive access in order to write.

A simple but inefficient solution is to allow only a single read or write operation at a time, as in the following example.

Example 5.31. Protected variables

```
task PROTECTED_VARIABLE is           -- task specification
   entry READ(V: out ELEM);          -- provides READ and WRITE entries
   entry WRITE(E: in ELEM);
end;
task body PROTECTED_VARIABLE is      -- task body
   VARIABLE: ELEM;                   -- with a local protected variable
begin                                -- and a statement sequence
   loop                              -- with a loop
      select                         -- which selects
         accept READ(V: out ELEM) do -- a READ entry
            V := VARIABLE;           -- which reads in the protected variable
         end;
      or
         accept WRITE(E: in ELEM) do -- or a WRITE entry
            VARIABLE := E;           -- which writes out the protected variable
         end;
      end select;
   end loop;                         -- and indefinitely repeats
end PROTECTED_VARIABLE;              -- selection of READ or WRITE entries
```

It is instructive to compare the PROTECTED_VARIABLE task with the single-message MAILBOX task. The MAILBOX task performs SEND and RECEIVE operations in strictly alternating order because receiving is considered to remove the message from the mailbox. The PROTECTED_VARIABLE task performs analogous WRITE and READ operations with a select statement because reading does not remove the value but merely transmits a copy of the value. Reading of the protected variable can thus be performed repeatedly. But this solution allows only one reader (or writer) at a time to access the variable V.

The next version of the reader-writer solution allows multiple readers to read V concurrently provided no writer is executing. This can be accomplished by making the READ entry of the task specification be a procedure rather than an entry.

Example 5.32. Specification of first reader-writer task

```
task READER_WRITER is
   procedure READ(V: out ELEM);
   entry WRITE(E: in ELEM);
end;
```

It should be noted that, because entry calls and procedure calls are syntactically identical, replacement of the previous reader-writer specification by the above specification will not require any change in user programs.

The READ procedure is a resource defined within the task body of READER_WRITER, which can be called by other tasks and executed without any need to perform a rendezvous. It is declared in the declarative part of the task body and is not part of the

189

concurrently executed statement sequence of the READER_WRITER
task.

Example 5.33. Task body of first reader-writer task

```
task body READER_WRITER is          -- body of READER_WRITER
  VARIABLE: ELEM;                    -- has a protected variable
  READERS: INTEGER := 0;             -- a counter to count number of readers
  entry START_READ;                  -- and two local entries for synchronization
  entry STOP_READ;                   -- within the READ procedure

  procedure READ(V: out ELEM) is     -- this procedure is in the declarative part
  begin              -- and is not part of the concurrently executing code
    START_READ;                      -- this entry call ensures no writing
    V := VARIABLE;                   -- while reading the protected variable
    STOP_READ;                       -- because START_READ increments READERS
  end;                               -- and writing requires READERS = 0

begin                                -- concurrently executing code starts here
  accept WRITE(E: in ELEM) do        -- first it is necessary to write
    VARIABLE := E;                   -- a value into the protected variable
  end;
  loop                               -- then there is a loop
    select                           -- with a select statement
      accept START_READ;             -- if START_READ is accepted
      READERS := READERS+1;          -- READERS is incremented
    or                               -- thus invalidating the guard on WRITE
      accept STOP_READ;              -- until STOP_READ
      READERS := READERS-1;          -- decrements READERS
    or                               -- and reduces it to zero
      when READERS = 0 =>            -- when READERS = 0
        accept WRITE(E: in ELEM) do  -- then WRITE can be accepted
          VARIABLE := E;             -- and a new value can be assigned
        end;                         -- but if there are sufficiently many readers
    end select;                      -- they can monopolize execution
  end loop;                          -- so that writers can never write
end READER_WRITER;
```

Procedures in a task specification can be called concurrently
from several other tasks and become part of the instruction
sequence of each of the calling tasks which execute it. Procedure specifications (such as READ) are included in a task body
(such as READER_WRITER) because they require access to local
objects of the task body (such as the protected variable), and
not because they are part of the concurrently executable code of
the task body.

Although the procedure READ can be executed concurrently from
several other tasks, each call must check that no writer is executing before actually reading the protected variable. This is
accomplished in the task body by means of two local entry calls
START_READ, STOP_READ which are used within the procedure both
for synchronization with the READER_WRITER task and for counting
the number of readers. Thus, in the task body we have the curious
situation that writing and counting the number of readers is

190

performed as part of the concurrently executing statement sequence of the READER_WRITER task, while reading, after appropriate synchronization, is specified within the READER_WRITER task but performed as part of the code of each of the calling tasks which wish to read the protected variable.

The above mechanism for allowing concurrent execution by several calling tasks of the code within a called task by making it into a procedure should be carefully studied. Our previous example allowed concurrent execution of different tasks. However, the reader-writer problem has the additional requirement that several readers concurrently execute the same code of a given task, and this is conveniently done by a READ procedure.

This implementation of the reader-writer problem is efficient in handling an arbitrary number of readers simultaneously, but may result in the indefinite lockout of writers if there is a continual rush of readers who increment the variable READERS without ever allowing it to reach zero. Such indefinite exclusion of an entry call is referred to as starvation.

A satisfactory solution of the reader-writer problem should guarantee that both readers and writers complete their task within a "reasonable" amount of time. One way of ensuring this is to schedule writers to execute immediately after all readers arriving prior to the writer have finished reading. When there is a queue of writers waiting to write, this strategy is modified so that all readers arriving before a write entry reaches the head of the queue are handled prior to handling of the write entry.

This solution may be implemented using the attribute WRITE'COUNT whose value is the number of entries currently in the WRITE queue.

Example 5.34. Second version of reader-writer task

```
loop
  select
    when WRITE'COUNT = 0 =>        -- when write queue is empty
      accept START_READ;           -- readers can be immediately accepted
      READERS := READERS+1;        -- but when write queue is non-empty
  or                               -- no more readers are accepted
      accept STOP_READ;            -- and readers are terminated by STOP_READ
      READERS := READERS-1;        -- until number of readers is zero
  or
    when READERS = 0 = >           -- when readers have all finished
      accept WRITE(E: in ELEM) do  -- a writer can be accepted
        VARIABLE := E;             -- to write in mutual exclusion
      end;
      loop                         -- when a writer finishes we loop
        select                     -- over a nested select statement
          accept START_READ;       -- which accepts all readers now waiting
          READERS := READERS+1;
        else                       -- the select statement has an else part
          exit;                    -- which exits when there are no more readers
        end select;
      end loop;          -- and returns control to the outer select statement
  end select;                      -- which allows started readers to terminate
end loop;                          -- and another writer to write
```

     This solution considerably reduces the chances that readers
will lock out writers. But this may still happen if readers arrive more rapidly than they can be initiated by the (inner)
START_READ entry. Since execution of a task is under system control and there can be real-time interruptions in execution at any
point in the code sequence, there is a possibility that, in certain
busy and nonreproducible operating conditions, writers could be
indefinitely locked out because of real-time interruptions of this
task which allow other tasks to generate read requests more
rapidly than the START_READ statement can accept them.

5.9 Separate Synchronization and Protection

     An alternative solution of the reader-writer problem, sugges-
ted by Tom Doeppner, separates protection and synchronization.
Protection is realized by a package whose body contains the
protected variable and whose specification part contains READ and
WRITE procedures for that variable. Synchronization is handled
by a task which can accept requests to read or write, and allows
concurrent reading by readers without starvation of writers. The
procedures READ and WRITE contain REQUEST entry calls to the task
preceding the read or write operation and FIN entry calls following the read or write operations.

     The specification and body of the PROTECT package has the
following form.

Example 5.35.   The PROTECT package

```
package PROTECT is                      -- package which realizes protection by means of
   procedure READ(V: out ELEM);         -- READ and WRITE procedures
   procedure WRITE(E: in ELEM);         -- which contain REQUEST and FIN entry calls
end;                                    -- to a synchronizing READER_WRITER task

package body PROTECT is                 -- the package body
   use READER_WRITER;                   -- uses the READER_WRITER task
   VARIABLE: ELEM;                      -- and contains the protected variable
   procedure READ(V: out ELEM) is       -- the READ procedure
   begin
      REQUEST(R);                       -- requests permission to read
      V := VARIABLE;                    -- before reading the protected variable
      FIN;                              -- and signals that reading is completed
   end;
   procedure WRITE(E: in ELEM) is       -- the WRITE procedure
   begin
      REQUEST(E);                       -- requests permission to write
      VARIABLE := V;                    -- before writing into the protected variable
      FIN;                              -- and signals that writing is completed
   end;
end PROTECT;
```

In this implementation of protected variables, both READ and WRITE are implemented as procedures. But from the point of view of the user, access to the READ and WRITE procedures of the package is identical to access to the READ and WRITE entry calls of the task. Thus user programs need not be modified even though the implementation was changed from tasks to packages.

The PROTECT package may be concurrently executed by a number of reading and writing tasks, and must be declared in an environment accessible to all tasks which wish to use it. The READER_WRITER task must in turn be declared in an environment accessible to the PROTECT package. Its specification part must contain the entries REQUEST and FIN, and an enumeration type with values R and W, used in REQUEST entry calls to indicate whether reading or writing is desired.

Example 5.36.   Specification of synchronizing reader-writer task

```
task READER_WRITER is
   type READ_OR_WRITE is (R,W);
   entry REQUEST(REQTYPE: in READ_OR_WRITE);
   entry FIN;
end;
```

The body of this task selects between a REQUEST and FIN entry call. For REQUEST entry calls the parameter value is saved (so it can later be used outside the critical section of the accept statement). For a WRITE call, readers are counted down to zero within the critical section, the critical section is exited, allowing the WRITE procedure to do the writing, and the FIN for WRITE is executed.

193

Example 5.37. Body of synchronizing reader-writer task

```
task body READER_WRITER is
  T: READ_OR_WRITE;          -- distinguishes between READ and WRITE requests
  READERS: INTEGER := 0;     -- counter for number of current readers
  begin;
    loop
      select
        accept REQUEST(REQTYPE: in READ_OR_WRITE) do    -- REQUEST entry
          T := REQTYPE;                 -- stores the request type
          if REQTYPE = W then           -- if it is a write request
            while READERS>0 loop        -- readers are counted down to 0
              accept FIN;               -- by accepting FIN calls
                READERS := READERS-1;   -- from currently active readers
            end loop;
          end if;
        end;            -- on exit from critical section calling task may resume
        if T = W then accept FIN;    -- if WRITE request wait for FIN of WRITE
        else READERS := READERS+1; --- if READ request, increment READERS
        end if;
      or
        accept FIN;                      -- note that FIN needs no critical section
          READERS := READERS-1; -- READERS is decremented concurrently with
      end select;                  -- calling task
    end loop;
end READER_WRITER;
```

With the above mechanism read and write requests are queued
in a single queue (the REQUEST queue) and handled in a first-come-
first-served order. Read requests may be executed concurrently.
Even the incrementing of the counter READERS can be executed concurrently with the reading task. However, writers require readers
to be counted down in the critical section of the accept statement
so that writing cannot start till all reading has been completed.
The writer must then execute FIN outside the critical section
before any other request can be accepted.

The new version of the PROTECT and READER_WRITER tasks is
quite different in structure from the previous ones. It illustrates how two different entry calls can be made to share the same
queue by introducing a "bookkeeping" entry call (REQUEST) whose
parameter is used to distinguish between the entry calls in which
we are locally interested (R, W). It illustrates a critical section of an accept statement which contains nested accept statements. It shows that critical sections are useful not only for
transmitting parameter information but also for holding up the
calling task (writing task) until certain computations (completion of reading tasks) have been performed.

Thus the above development of several versions of the reader-
writer problem is useful not only for the light it throws on the
reader-writer problem but also because the various solutions
illustrate ways of using multitasking primitives.

Before leaving this topic, let us consider the relation
between the final version of the READER_WRITER task and the

PROTECT package. If the task is used just to protect the variable V it can be declared to be local to the package body of PROTECT. This would entail replacement of the use statement in the task body either by the entire task or by the task specification and a separately compiled task body.

Example 5.38. PROTECT package with local reader-writer task

```
package body PROTECT is         -- version of PROTECT package
  task READER_WRITER is         -- with local READER_WRITER task
    type READ_OR_WRITE is (R,W);
    entry REQUEST(REQTYPE: in READ_OR_WRITE);
    entry FIN;
  end;
  task body READER_WRITER is separate; -- but separately compiled task body
  VARIABLE: ELEM;                 -- the protected variable
  procedure READ(..).... end READ;  -- and the READ and WRITE procedures
  procedure WRITE(..).... end WRITE;  -- are as before
end PROTECT;
```

This PROTECT package could be used to protect several variables by making both the variable and its type generic parameters of the package.

Example 5.39. Generic PROTECT package

```
generic (type is ELEM; VARIABLE: ELEM)  -- generic PROTECT package
package PROTECT is
  procedure READ(V: out ELEM);
  procedure WRITE(E: in ELEM);
end;
```

This generic package may be instantiated as follows.

Example 5.40. Instantiation of generic PROTECT package

```
package PROTECT_X is new PROTECT(INTEGER,X);  -- protected INTEGER variable X
package PROTECT_Y is new PROTECT(FLOAT,Y);   -- protected FLOAT variable Y
package PROTECT_VECT is new PROTECT(VECTOR,Z); -- protected VECTOR variable Z
```

Each of these instances of the PROTECT package will have a different local task for performing synchronizations. The internal task names will be different for each instance, so that concurrent execution of tasks for each instance will not give rise to an initiate error.

Now that we have considered what we can do by having the READER_WRITER task local to the package body, let us consider the case for a nonlocal READER_WRITER task available to a variety of other program units.

Having a nonlocal READER_WRITER task would allow us to explicitly declare several (nongeneric) protection packages PROTECT_X and

PROTECT_Y with different local variables. These tasks would
differ from the generic instances in the following ways:

1. Protected variables would all be of the same type (ELEM)
    since there is no provision for type parameters.
2. All instances would share the same READER_WRITER task,
    and be serviced by a single REQUEST queue. Writing
    any one of the protected variables would require termina-
    tion of read requests for all protected variables.

This solution penalizes concurrent reading for all protected
variables when any one of them is writing, and is therefore not
recommended. However, this disadvantage can be avoided by making
the READER_WRITER task into a parameterless generic task and
instantiating it in individual protection packages.

Example 5.41. Generic READER WRITER task

```
generic task READER_WRITER is          -- generic READER_WRITER task
  type READ_OR_WRITE is (R,W);
  entry REQUEST(REQTYPE: in READ_OR_WRITE);
  entry FIN;
end;
```

A package body for PROTECT_X could now be written as follows.

Example 5.42. PROTECT package which instantiates generic READER WRITER task

```
package body PROTECT_X is           -- package body
  task RWX is new READER_WRITER;    -- with local instance of generic
  X: ELEM;                          -- READER_WRITER task
  procedure READX(..).... end;
  procedure READY(..).... end;
end PROTECT;
```

The READER_WRITER task in fact has nothing to do with protection or even reading and writing. From an abstract point of
view, it is simply a scheduling device which allows two kinds of
entry calls with different constraints on concurrent execution to
share a common queue. There might well be other entirely different applications which require the same synchronization discipline
as protected variables. They could use the synchronization mechanism provided by a generic READER_WRITER task, instantiating the
task for each application so that each application has its own
request queue with two classes of entry calls, one permitting
concurrent execution and the other requiring mutual exclusion.

The above discussion indicates that multitasking introduces
an entirely new dimension into the design of programs which requires exploring a much richer range of possibilities than in the
sequential processing case. We have explored this range of possibilities in some depth for the reader-writer problem in order
to illustrate the flavor of such thinking.

196

5.10 Efficiency of Multitasking

Efficiency of language features is not, strictly speaking, a topic that should be discussed in an introductory manual. The discussion of multitasking efficiency is included in this chapter because of the insight it provides into the nature of multitasking primitives, rather than to convince readers that the primitives are efficient. By showing how the executable code of a task can be distributed among the tasks which use it, we hope to provide the reader with a better understanding of the dynamics of concurrently executing tasks.

The efficiency of multitasking can be considered at three levels.

1. The user level. Can the user express concurrent processing computations in a manner that directly models the requirements of the computation without introducing extraneous constructs and computations due to the nature of the language primitives?

2. The scheduling level. Can computations be performed so that there is no "unnecessary" waiting over and above that imposed by the hardware and the requirements of the application? In particular, can thrashing, deadly embraces and other potential scheduling problems be easily recognized and avoided?

3. The implementation level. Can multitasking primitives be efficiently implemented in (a) shared-memory architectures and (b) distributed-processing architectures? In particular, can we avoid delays due to context switching among tasks in time-critical computations, and perform optimizations which allow called tasks to be executed "in line" by the tasks which call them so as to avoid context switching altogether?

Definite assertions about multitasking efficiency must await experience with both language usage and language implementation. However, certain insights already developed are of interest not only because they tell us something about efficiency but also because they help us to gain a better understanding of the language constructs.

Entry calls and accept statements provide a high-level mechanism that appears to be "natural" for specifying communication and synchronization at the user level. Like other high-level mechanisms, there will be cases when lower-level primitives are more appropriate, and semaphores (the go to statements of multitasking) are provided for this purpose.

At the scheduling level, it is convenient to distinguish between the "fast production" case where entry calls are produced more rapidly than accept statements can handle them and the "fast consumption" case where accept statements of the called task are ready to gobble up an entry call the moment it appears.

From the point of view of the caller, the fast consumption

case is clearly preferable to the fast production case. However, the fast production case can give rise to considerable delays in calling processes.

One solution is to introduce third-party processes (server processes) such as mailboxes between the producer and the consumer which can store the messages produced by the fast producer in a buffer until they are needed by the consumer.

Third-party processes reduce the waiting time of fast production processes, but interpose an extra task between the producer and the consumer. The extra context switching time for tasks may be unacceptable in certain time-critical computations.

The overhead for interposing a third-party task depends upon the underlying architecture. Three cases should be considered:

1. A distributed-processing architecture where the third-party task (mailbox task) has its own processor and local memory.
2. A shared-memory multiprocessing architecture in which there are many concurrently executing processors and the third-party task is executing on a dedicated processor.
3. A shared-memory uniprocessing architecture in which there is only a single processor, and task switching involves storing the state information of the executing task and installing the state information of the next task to be executed.

Since the uniprocessing case is the most common on current computers, we will consider mechanisms for improving its efficiency. In particular, we will consider how entry calls to certain kinds of third-party tasks may be replaced by procedure calls which avoid the overhead of synchronization and which, in the uniprocessing case, also avoid the overhead of switching statements.

Consider a third-party task T whose executable code consists of a loop containing a select statement, all of whose alternatives are guarded entry calls of the following form.

Example 5.43. Restriction on select statement for optimization

```
task body T is
  -- local declarations
begin
  loop
    select
      when guard1 => accept entry1(..)do..end; statements
    or when guard2 => accept entry2(..)do..end; statements
      ...
    or when guardn => accept entryn(..)do..end; statements
    end select;
  end loop;
end;
```

The task T can be eliminated and its code can be distributed among its callers provided each entry call is executed in mutual exclusion, and guarded entry calls whose guards are invalid are required to wait for later execution. In particular, each entry call to the select alternative

   when guard => accept entry(..)do..end; statements

can be replaced by the following code sequence in the calling program:

Example 5.44. Code for optimized entry calls

```
loop
  P(T_LOCK);       -- semaphore for mutual exclusion of entry calls
  if guard then    -- if guard is TRUE we can "execute" simulated entry
    -- perform code in critical section of accept statement
    -- perform statements following critical section of accept statement
    V(T_LOCK);      -- release T_LOCK on completion of simulated entry call
    exit;           -- exit loop after completing simulated entry call
  end if;
    V(T_LOCK);      -- unlock to allow other entries to execute
    -- wait for signal (probably completion of some other entry call)
end loop;
```

   This process of replacement will be illustrated for the MAILBOX task. The MAILBOX task has precisely the required form, with two select alternatives SEND and RECEIVE. The code which must replace each entry call is illustrated first for SEND entries and then for RECEIVE entries.

   In the case of SEND entries we first perform a P operation on a mutual exclusion semaphore for mailboxes, say M_LOCK. Then we test the guard for SEND entries. If the buffer is not full, and sending is permitted, we perform both the instructions in the critical section and the instructions following the critical section and perform a V operation on M_LOCK so that some other entry call can be performed. A signal which allows waiting guards to be reevaluated should also be sent. If the buffer is full, a V operation to release M_LOCK is immediately performed, and the task must wait for a signal from a completed RECEIVE call so that this entry can be reevaluated.

Example 5.45. Optimized SEND entry

```
loop
  P(M_LOCK);              -- mutual exclusion semaphore for mailbox entries
  if COUNT<SIZE then   -- if buffer is not full
    BUFFER(NEXTIN) := INMAIL;   -- read message into buffer
    NEXTIN := NEXTIN mod SIZE + 1;  -- and update NEXTIN
    COUNT := COUNT+1             -- and COUNT
    V(M_LOCK);                   -- then release semaphore
      -- signal completion of SEND entry
    exit;                -- exit loop after completing simulated SEND entry
  end if;                -- if buffer is full
    V(M_LOCK);           -- release mutual exclusion semaphore immediately
    -- wait for completion signal from RECEIVE entry
end loop;
```

Similarly, each RECEIVE entry could be replaced by the following code.

Example 5.46. Optimized RECEIVE entry

```
loop
  P(M_LOCK);
  if COUNT>0 then
    OUTMAIL := BUFFER(NEXTOUT);
    NEXTOUT := NEXTOUT mod SIZE + 1;
    COUNT := COUNT-1;
    V(M_LOCK);
    -- signal completion of RECEIVE entry
    exit;
  end if;
    V(M_LOCK);
    -- wait for completion signal from SEND entry
end loop;
```

Replacement of the executable code of a task in the manner indicated above represents a compiler optimization which is worthwhile provided the following conditions are met:

1. Guards are generally true when an entry call occurs and are false only a small proportion of the time. In particular, the queue of unexecutable entry calls waiting for a signal is not too large.
2. If a guard for a given entry call is false then a call of some other entry will make it true. In particular, re-evaluation of guards of blocked entry calls on completion of an unblocked entry call will unblock one or more entry calls.
3. The executable statements following the critical section are not too time-consuming.

The mailbox task has the first property provided the buffer is sufficiently large to handle the message traffic. It has the second property because completion of a RECEIVE entry when the SEND entry is full will cause unblocking of at least one SEND entry, and vice versa.

200

Thus the above optimization procedure would be worthwhile for the programmer-defined mailbox task given in section 5.4. However, if the mailbox task were treated as a predefined task, then the system could perform even more refined optimizations, based on explicit knowledge of the fact that execution of a RECEIVE entry when the buffer is full always frees up precisely one space in the message buffer for a SEND entry call.

Although the above optimization can, in certain cases, considerably speed up execution of concurrently executing programs, it can also result in less efficient execution when guards are often false or when there are substantial computations outside the critical sections of accept statements which are executed concurrently with calling tasks in the unoptimized case but non-concurrently in the optimized case.

Considerable additional study is required before the above optimization feature can be included in a production compiler. However, the objective of this section is not to propose this optimization to production compiler writers but rather to offer some provocative ideas concerning tradeoffs between concurrent and sequential computations to language users.

Appendix: SYNTAX SUMMARY

This syntax summary presents the complete syntax of Ada. The section numbers of syntax definitions are taken from the reference manual. Sections 2, 3, 4 and 5 deal respectively with literals, types, expressions and statements. Sections 6, 7, 8 and 9 deal with subprograms, packages, visibility rules and tasks. Sections 10-14 deal with program structure, exceptions, generic program units, representation specifications and input-output.

The definition style will be briefly explained by commenting on the first definition:

    identifier ::= letter {[underscore] letter-or-digit}

This definition contains the token "::=" which may be read as "is defined as", square brackets which denote optional occurrence of the enclosed construct, and curly brackets which denote an arbitrary (possibly zero) number of occurrences of the enclosed construct. Thus this definition may be read as:

An "identifier" is defined as a "letter" followed by an arbitrary number of "letters or digits" each of which may be optionally preceded by an "underscore".

We shall illustrate the use of this syntax summary to check that tasks with degenerate specification parts (example 5.1, p. 171 of the present book) are legal syntactic constructs.

Since tasks are modules, the first step is to check the syntax of module specifications in section 7.1 of the appendix (section numbers correspond to sections of the reference manual in which the constructs are introduced):

    module_specification ::=
      [generic_clause]
      module_nature identifier [(discrete_range)] [is
        declarative_part
      [private
        declarative_part]
      end [identifier]];

If we eliminate the optional generic clause, discrete range, private part and terminating identifier, and substitute task for "module_nature", we are left with

    task identifier [is
      declarative_part
    end];

When the declarative part is empty, the syntactic components "is declarative_part end" can be omitted, resulting in the syntax "task identifier;" given in example 5.1.

The above check that a general syntactic definition fits a particular example is typical of the way in which a programmer might use the syntax definition to check that a program is syntactically correct.

2.3

```
identifier ::=
    letter {|underscore| letter_or_digit}

letter_or_digit ::= letter | digit

letter ::= upper_case_letter | lower_case_letter
```

2.4

```
number ::= integer_number | approximate_number

integer_number ::= integer | based_integer

integer ::= digit {|underscore| digit}

based_integer ::=
    base # extended_digit {|underscore| extended_digit}

base ::= integer

extended_digit ::= digit | letter

approximate_number ::=
      integer.integer |E exponent|
    | integer E exponent

exponent ::= |+| integer | - integer
```

2.5

```
character_string ::= " {character} "
```

2.7

```
pragma ::=
    pragma identifier |(argument {, argument})|;

argument ::= identifier | character_string | number
```

3.1

```
declaration ::=
      object_declaration      | type_declaration
    | subtype_declaration     | private_type_declaration
    | subprogram_declaration  | module_declaration
    | entry_declaration       | exception_declaration
    | renaming_declaration
```

3.2

```
object_declaration ::=
    identifier_list : |constant| type |:= expression|;

identifier_list ::= identifier {, identifier}
```

3.3

```
type ::= type_definition | type_mark |constraint|

type_definition ::=
      enumeration_type_definition | integer_type_definition
    | real_type_definition        | array_type_definition
    | record_type_definition      | access_type_definition
    | derived_type_definition

type_mark ::= type_name | subtype_name

constraint ::=
      range_constraint  | accuracy_constraint
    | index_constraint  | discriminant_constraint

type_declaration ::=
    type identifier |is type_definition|;

subtype_declaration ::=
    subtype identifier is type_mark |constraint|;
```

3.4

```
derived_type_definition ::= new type_mark |constraint|
```

3.5

```
range_constraint ::= range range

range ::= simple_expression .. simple_expression
```

3.5.1

```
enumeration_type_definition ::=
    (enumeration_literal {, enumeration_literal})

enumeration_literal ::= identifier | character_literal
```

3.5.4

```
integer_type_definition ::= range_constraint
```

3.5.5

```
real_type_definition ::= accuracy_constraint

accuracy_constraint ::=
      digits simple_expression |range_constraint|
    | delta simple_expression |range_constraint|
```

*Reproduced with permission from the Ada reference manual.

3.6

array_type_definition ::=
  array (index {, index}) **of** type_mark {constraint}

index ::= discrete_range | type_mark

discrete_range ::= {type_mark **range**} range

index_constraint ::= (discrete_range {, discrete_range})

3.6.2

aggregate ::=
  (component_association {, component_association})

component_association ::=
  {choice {| choice} => } expression

choice ::= simple_expression | discrete_range | **others**

3.7

record_type_definition ::=
  record
    component_list
  end record

component_list ::=
  {object_declaration} {variant_part} | **null**;

variant_part ::=
  case discriminant **of**
    {**when** choice {| choice} =>
      component_list}
  end case;

discriminant ::= *constant_component*_name

3.7.3

discriminant_constraint ::= aggregate

3.8

access_type_definition ::= **access** type

4.1

name ::=
    identifier | indexed_component
  | selected_component | predefined_attribute

indexed_component ::= name(expression {, expression})

selected_component ::= name . identifier

predefined_attribute ::= name ' identifier

4.2

literal ::=
  number | enumeration_literal | character_string | **null**

4.3

variable ::= name {(discrete_range)} | name.**all**

4.4

expression ::=
    relation {**and** relation}
  | relation {**or** relation}
  | relation {**xor** relation}

relation ::=
    simple_expression {relational_operator simple_expression}
  | simple_expression {**not**} **in** range
  | simple_expression {**not**} **in** type_mark {constraint}

simple_expression ::=
  {unary_operator} term {adding_operator term}

term ::= factor {multiplying_operator factor}

factor ::= primary {** primary}

primary ::=
    literal | aggregate | variable | allocator
  | subprogram_call | qualified_expression | (expression)

4.5

logical_operator	::=	**and** | **or** | **xor**
relational_operator	::=	= | /= | < | <= | > | >=
adding_operator	::=	+ | - | &
unary_operator	::=	+ | - | **not**
multiplying_operator	::=	* | / | **mod**
exponentiating_operator	::=	**

4.6

qualified_expression ::=
  type_mark(expression) | type_mark aggregate

4.7

allocator ::= **new** qualified_expression

5

sequence_of_statements ::= {statement}

statement ::=
    simple_statement | compound_statement
    | <<identifier>> statement

simple_statement ::=
    assignment_statement | subprogram_call_statement
    | exit_statement | return_statement
    | goto_statement | assert_statement
    | initiate_statement | delay_statement
    | raise_statement | abort_statement
    | code_statement | **null**;

compound_statement ::=
    if_statement | case_statement
    | loop_statement | accept_statement
    | select_statement | block

5.1

assignment_statement ::=   variable := expression;

5.2

subprogram_call_statement ::= subprogram_call;

subprogram_call ::=
    *subprogram*_name
    [(parameter_association {, parameter_association})]

parameter_association ::=
    [formal_parameter :=] actual_parameter
    | [formal_parameter =:] actual_parameter
    | [formal_parameter :=:] actual_parameter

formal_parameter ::= identifier

actual_parameter ::= expression

5.3

return_statement ::= **return** [expression];

5.4

if_statement ::=
    if condition **then**
        sequence_of_statements
    {**elsif** condition **then**
        sequence_of_statements}
    [**else**
        sequence_of_statements]
    end if;

condition ::=
    expression {**and then** expression}
    | expression {**or else** expression}

5.5

case_statement ::=
    case expression **of**
        {**when** choice {| choice} => sequence_of_statements}
    end case;

5.6

loop_statement ::= [iteration_specification] basic_loop

basic_loop ::=
    loop
        sequence_of_statements
    end loop [identifier];

iteration_specification ::=
    for loop_parameter **in** [**reverse**] discrete_range
    | **while** condition

loop_parameter ::= identifier

5.7

exit_statement ::= **exit** [identifier] [**when** condition];

5.8

goto_statement ::= **goto** identifier;

5.9

assert_statement ::= **assert** condition;

6.1

declarative_part ::= [use_clause]
{declaration} {representation_specification} {body}

body ::= [visibility_restriction] unit_body | body_stub

unit_body ::=
    subprogram_body | module_specification | module_body

6.2

subprogram_declaration ::=
    subprogram_specification;
    | subprogram_nature designator **is** generic_instantiation;

subprogram_specification ::= [generic_clause]
    subprogram_nature designator [formal_part]
    [**return** type_mark [constraint]]

subprogram_nature ::= **function** | **procedure**

designator ::= identifier | character_string

formal_part ::=
    (parameter_declaration {; parameter_declaration})

parameter_declaration ::=
    identifier_list : mode type_mark [constraint] [:= expression]

mode ::= [**in**] | **out** | **in out**

206

6.4

subprogram_body ::=
    subprogram_specification **is**
        declarative_part
    begin
        sequence_of_statements
    | **exception**
        |exception_handler||
    end |designator|;

6.7

block ::=
    | **declare**
        declarative_part|
    begin
        sequence_of_statements
    | **exception**
        |exception_handler||
    end |identifier|;

7.1

module_declaration ::=
    |visibility_restriction| module_specification
    | module_nature identifier |(discrete_range)|
        is generic_instantiation;

module_specification ::=
    | generic_clause|
        module_nature identifier |(discrete_range)| |**is**
        declarative_part
    | **private**
        declarative_part|
        end |identifier||;

module_nature ::= **package** | **task**

module_body ::=
    module_nature **body** identifier **is**
        declarative_part
    | **begin**
        sequence_of_statements|
    | **exception**
        |exception_handler||
    end |identifier|;

7.4

private_type_declaration ::=
    |restricted| **type** identifier **is private**;

8.3

visibility_restriction ::= **restricted** |visibility_list|

visibility_list ::= (*unit*_name |, *unit*_name|)

8.4

use_clause ::= **use** *module*_name |, *module*_name|;

8.5

renaming_declaration ::=
        identifier : type_mark   **renames** name;
    | identifier : **exception**   **renames** name;
    | subprogram_nature designator **renames** |name.|designator;
    | module_nature identifier **renames** name;

9.3

initiate_statement ::=
    initiate task_designator |, task_designator|;

task_designator ::= *task*_name |(discrete_range)|

9.5

entry_declaration ::=
    entry identifier |(discrete_range)| |formal_part|;

accept_statement ::=
    accept entry_name |formal part| |**do**
        sequence_of_statements
    end |identifier||;

9.6

delay_statement ::= **delay** simple_expression;

9.7

select_statement ::=
    select
        |**when** condition =>|
            select_alternative
    | **or** |**when** condition =>|
            select_alternative|
    | **else**
        sequence_of_statements|
    end select;

select_alternative ::=
        accept_statement |sequence_of_statements|
    | delay_statement |sequence_of_statements|

9.10

abort_statement ::= **abort** task_designator |,task_designator|;

10.1

compilation ::= {compilation_unit}

compilation_unit ::=
    {visibility_restriction}{**separate**} unit_body

10.2

body_stub ::=
        subprogram_specification **is separate**;
    | module_nature **body** identifier **is separate**;

11.1

exception_declaration ::= identifier_list : **exception**;

11.2

exception_handler ::=
    when exception_choice {| exception_choice} =>
        sequence_of_statements

exception_choice ::= *exception*_name | **others**

11.3

raise_statement ::= **raise** {*exception*_name};

12.1

generic_clause ::=
    generic {(generic_parameter {; generic_parameter})}

generic_parameter ::=
        parameter_declaration
    | subprogram_specification {**is** {name.}designator}
    | {**restricted**} **type** identifier

12.2

generic_instantiation ::=
    new name {(generic_association {, generic_association})}

generic_association ::=
        parameter_association
    | {formal_parameter **is**} {name.}designator
    | {formal_parameter **is**} type_mark

13

representation_specification ::=
        packing_specification | length_specification
    | record_type_representation | address_specification
    | enumeration_type_representation

13.1

packing_specification ::= **for** *type*_name **use packing**;

13.2

length_specification ::= **for** name **use** *static*_expression;

13.3

enumeration_type_representation ::=
    for *type*_name **use** aggregate;

13.4

record_type_representation ::=
    for *type*_name **use**
        record {alignment_clause;}
            {*component*_name location;}
        end record;

location ::= **at** *static*_expression **range** range

alignment_clause ::= **at mod** *static*_expression

13.5

address_specification ::=
    for name **use at** *static*_expression;

13.8

code_statement ::= qualified_expression;

INDEX